LATIN AMERICAN TRAVEL

Face to Face
with the Mexicans

Fanny Chambers Gooch

Edited and with an Introduction by
C. HARVEY GARDINER

Southern Illinois University Press

CARBONDALE AND EDWARDSVILLE

Feffer and Simons, Inc.

LONDON AND AMSTERDAM

Copyright © 1966 by Southern Illinois University Press
Library of Congress Catalog Card Number 65–27285
Printed in the United States of America
Designed by Anda Salins

Contents

Introduction

A period of consolidation of authority by Porfirio Díaz, the decade of the 1880's brought many things to Mexico, and many persons who either contributed to the changing order of Mexican life or registered their awareness of it.

New forces and changing directions beset Mexico on every side. Political instability yielded to stability, lawlessness to security. Anti-United States sentiment, which had pivoted on frontier troubles, claims and nonrecognition in the previous decade, was replaced by an expanding pro-United States outlook. The diplomatic channels between the two governments were regularized, extradition and boundary treaties effected, and calm characterized the frontier. Numerous concessions were lavished on railroad promoters from north of the Rio Grande. The new mining code of 1884, stripping the Mexican government of its age-old hold on subsoil riches, lured even more investment capital from the United States. And Mexico was rapidly expanding her identification with various hallmarks of modern economic life: banking, transportation, heavy industry, stable currency, sound international credit ratings, etc.

The 1880's vibrated with challenge in Mexico, and many travelers, like the investors, glimpsed opportunity on the peaceful Mexican scene. Attesting the deluge of attention accorded Mexico in this period is the increased volume of writing about it, scores of travel titles emerging as by-products of experiences during the early years of Porfirio Díaz' hold on the Mexican presidency.

Citizens of the neighboring republic to the north wrote the majority of these travelers' accounts but many German, French, Spanish, Dutch, and Latin American authors also penned personal assessments of Mexico, as did the ubiquitous Briton.

Colombian presbyter-journalist Federico C. Aguilar's experience (August 1881–November 1883) led him to stress political stability and economic prosperity in *Último año de residencia en México* and to ignore the social aspects which resembled those of his own background. Experienced travel-writer Maturin M. Ballou's *Aztec Land*, based on a stay of two months in Mexico, was a shallow smattering of everything which proved more exasperating than satisfying. Clément Bertie-Marriott, as he wrote *Un parisien au Mexique* concerning experiences of 1884–85, penned in lively journalese a sympathetic and exuberant account steeped in comparisons within the comprehension of Parisians. The optimistic appraisal of William Henry Bishop stemmed from somewhat more than one month south of the border. His *Old Mexico and Her Lost Provinces*, according railroads, mines, and haciendas heavy attention, smacked of the channeled mentality of a propagandist-promoter. When Mrs. Mary Elizabeth Blake and Mrs. Margaret F. Sullivan spent six or seven weeks in Mexico with the first Raymond Excursion, they adjudged that meager experience sufficient for writing *Mexico: Picturesque—Political—Progressive*. Padded with historical incident and dripping an ecstatic naïveté, it tried to depict Mexico of the middle 1880's. Even though Thomas Unett Brocklehurst, a wealthy Briton and a seasoned traveler, strengthened his *Mexico Today* by leaning on his journal, he still wrote against the personal backdrop of no knowledge of Spanish and a pattern of movement in Mexico which so featured foreigners as to insulate him from the natives. French merchant Émile Chabrand, summarizing twenty years of reactions to land and people, wrote with optimisim of the economic future of Mexico as he discussed both its Indian and non-Indian elements in *De Barcelonnete au Mexique*. . . . Howard Conkling, armed with letters of introduction and a philosophy of Manifest Destiny, hailed the investment prospects offered by Mex-

ico. His *Mexico and the Mexicans* . . . derived from a visit
of several weeks, early in 1883. Cora Hayward Crawford,
ignorant of Spanish and insulated by the tour party in
which she traveled, conceived *The Land of the Montezumas*
on the basis of one month south of the Rio Grande. John
Watson Foster, despite seven years in Mexico, recalled
only his official acts when he penned *Diplomatic Memoirs*.
Albert Zabriskie Gray, desirous of furthering Protestant
missions in Mexico and focusing most of *Mexico As It Is* on
religion, embellished his book with that peculiar authority and prejudice which a stay of several weeks often
evokes. Solomon Bulkley Griffin's *Mexico of To-day* represented the topical writing of an experienced traveler-
reporter. More interpretive than narrative, the book
offered estimates of both the land and the people. Jules J.
Leclercq, an able author, exhibited sympathy and sophis-
tication in his *Voyage au Mexique* . . . , a work which
mingled the chronological and the topical, the personal
and the general, first impressions and careful reflections,
the urban and the rural. Meanwhile Mrs. Alice Dixon
LePlongeon, wife of a doctor of medicine with a penchant
for Mayan studies, gave her readers an episodic treatment
of peoples and places off the beaten track in *Here and There
in Yucatan: Miscellanies*. Businessman-author Thomas W.
Price, in Mexico for his health, consumed most of his eight
weeks there among fellow Americans. His *Brief Notes Taken
on a Trip to the City of Mexico* . . . featured a running com-
mentary on Roman Catholicism and Methodism, plus
reiterated appeals for a more vigorous Protestant mission-
ary effort. Francis Hopkinson Smith, an artist, took his
easel to Mexico for several weeks. His book, *A White Um-
brella in Mexico*, presented episodically that which ap-
pealed to a painter and idler. Sensitive and ranging, it
generously included the daily activities of plain Mexicans.

Dozens of other accounts of Mexico of the period
were published by foreign observers but generally they
were more of the same: overwhelmingly the short-term
observation and superficial appraisal of Mexican life;

commonly the word of the linguistically ignorant and the culturally arrogant. Unprejudiced outsiders were unusual, and sympathetic inquirers and balanced reporters were met even less frequently. The final proof that most traveler-writers went to Mexico as narrowly selfish individuals was the mirroring of that narrowness and selfishness in their writing.

Consequently it is all the more pleasing to find an author of the 1880's who epitomizes breadth and magnanimity—to find a work based on long-term residence, unchanneled and ranging curiosity, and linguistic competence.

Face to Face with the Mexicans: the Domestic Life, Educational, Social, and Business Ways, Statesmanship and Literature, Legendary and General History of the Mexican People, as seen and studied by an American woman during seven years of intercourse with them, written by Fanny Chambers Gooch and based on her experiences between 1880 and 1887, was initially published in the latter year.

The aim of the book was the promotion in the United States of better understanding and appreciation of "our near-at-hand, faraway neighbors, the Mexicans." Reflecting upon experiences in Saltillo, her first place of residence in Mexico, Fanny Gooch insisted, "one of the happiest discoveries I made during those days of a bewildering struggle with a new civilization, was that, despite the representation of many of my own countrymen, fidelity, tenderness, and untiring devotion were as truly Mexican characteristics as American." But all was not a gigantic oneness; and as Mrs. Gooch fought losing skirmishes with a cook who would not pluck fowls, a manservant who refused to clean floors and a porter whose ways were impervious to change, she sensed historical, climatic, and other reasons for cultural variation. "At last," she confided, "I became convinced of the perfect and complete fitness of things, and of their self-vindication."

At times paradox pervaded the writing. Her detailing of advantages and opportunities constituted a frank invitation to the American to introduce himself and his ways into Mexico. However, speaking of the Mexicans, she declared, "may you . . . continue to live out your lives, undismayed and undisturbed by any progressive, distracting or contaminating influence!" And as she declared "the United States has great need for a wider market for her manufactured goods," Fanny Gooch also proclaimed, "May no ruthless innovator remodel your simple adobes! no insatiate gringo invade and despoil your sacred domain!" At times the materialist and the romantic warred in her nature. Generally specifics validated such generalizations as "A vein of sentiment and poetry . . . runs through every detail of their lives. . . ." and "Mexico is an earthly paradise for children" and "a new era is dawning in Mexico."

Penned by a promoter of better cultural relations between Mexicans and Americans, *Face to Face with the Mexicans* is rich in many areas in which other travel accounts exhibit poverty. It is rich in organization, a sound thematic approach to multiple aspects of Mexican life characterizing the work. To present its ideas it entwines narration, reflection, anecdote, and conversation in lively fashion. A certain well-roundedness in reference to vocabulary, themes and all else enables the book to escape being dated or obviously feminine and delicate. The writing, on the contrary, exhibits a robust appeal.

A Mexican writer, Josefina Trottner Wologviansky, dissecting Fanny Gooch's book from the vantage point of the 1960's—as she wrote "Diálogo con los mexicanos (visión histórica de Fanny Chambers Gooch)"—holds it in high esteem. Gooch's observations, she insists, are usually accurate and penetrating, often humorous or passionate. Although Fanny Gooch's writing lacks elegance, it bristles with clarity and colorful adjectives. For Trottner Wologviansky, the American woman's style exhibited three fine characteristics: simplicity of language, fluency of narration, and facility in description. For many reasons, including validity and style, the Mexican insists that *Face to Face with the Mexicans* should again be available to readers—in both Spanish and English this time.

Because Fanny Gooch was curious about language as a key to the nature of nationality—and because she studied and learned that language, she employed Spanish expressions in a flavorful and meaningful fashion. Yet the reader who knows only English is never left with an obscure meaning.

Any nineteenth-century female traveler-writer on Mexico must automatically face comparison with Madame Calderón de la Barca, and her book must be compared with *Life in Mexico*. In this dual comparison Mrs. Gooch and her book fare very well.

Both women, despite their Protestant Anglo-Saxon backgrounds, were religiously tolerant and culturally sympathetic. Both developed expanding commands of the Spanish language during long stays in Mexico. Whereas Madame Calderón de la Barca moved almost exclusively in the highest social circles, Mrs. Gooch blended her awareness of Mexican society from contacts at the highest level—with Porfirio Díaz, Vicente Riva Palacio and others, from numerous contacts with the emerging middle class, and from many sought-for and sustained contacts with the poorer classes, including the Indians. Whereas Madame Calderón de la Barca derived her awareness of Mexico almost entirely from the capital city and environs, Fanny Gooch's understanding of Mexico combined immersion in provincial life with that of the unique metropolitan district. Thematically the range of materials in *Life in Mexico* cannot match that in *Face to Face with the Mexicans*. Finally, Madame Calderón de la Barca's work, a chronological file of letters to relatives, was an accidental book. Mrs. Gooch, on the other hand, went to Mexico imbued with the idea of writing a volume intended for a large audience and the planning and execution of the resultant book stamp it anything but an accident.

A small portion of the information in *Face to Face with*

the Mexicans is derived rather than firsthand. However, it rather naturally follows that any sensitive writer who is culturally sympathetic, as Fanny Gooch was, must delve somewhat into the historical literature related to the nation under consideration. Having done so, some of that background material inescapably shines through occasionally, even in the phrasing of firsthand experiences of the author. Fanny's background reading on Mexico ranged from Bernal Díaz del Castillo through Humboldt, Alamán, Madame Calderón de la Barca, Prescott, G. W. Kendall, and Brantz Mayer to Vicente Riva Palacio and H. H. Bancroft.

Because it would be exceedingly difficult to cite a single work that is richer on diverse components of nineteenth-century Mexican social life, Fanny Gooch's *Face to Face with the Mexicans* deserves special mention for its coverage of the following themes, among others: architectural details on Mexican housing; mistress-servant relationships; minute consideration of holiday activities—as those of All Saints' Day, the Feast of the Virgin of Guadalupe, Christmas, etc.; full accounts concerning courtship, marriage, and baptism; and the detailed presentation of songs, riddles, recipes, vendors' cries, and popular stories. Balance and fulness result from a telling that is minute and exact as well as nationwide and intangible.

More than two hundred illustrations, of uneven quality, support this searching inquiry into the nature of Mexico and the Mexican. Some were executed by the New York artist Isabel V. Waldo, whom Mrs. Gooch met in Mexico, others by Ramón Castañeda, a student of the Academy of San Carlos in Mexico City. Numerous illustrations depict those characteristic shrugs and movements of the hands which constitute a language of their own in Mexico.

Fanny's short simple sentences often couched long-term, complicated truths. "The older guests," she wrote of a wedding party, "remain at the table drinking *pulque* and recall their youth, until this cheerful beverage reconciles them to the epoch in which they live." A totally different prospect led her to say, "Face a stampede of buffaloes—jump into the raging sea, or risk the relentless cyclone—but always keep clear of a Mexican mob." Her own countrymen in mind, she wrote, "if you go to Mexico, do not hope to effect radical changes, or constitute yourself judge and reformer, but rather be prepared, instead of teaching, to be taught." The indestructibility of the bases of Mexican nationality she recognized again when she exclaimed, "No foreign power need ever expect with ruthless hand to break down Mexican customs, laws, peculiarities and institutions."

The author of *Face to Face with the Mexicans* was born the eighth of the thirteen children of William and Feriba Magee Chambers of Hillsboro, Mississippi, the date of birth disputedly ranging from 1842 to 1851. After a few years in Mississippi, young Fanny went to live with her brother Lem in Weatherford, Texas, whence she moved with him to Waco. There he operated a grocery store and she gained the formal schooling and early maturity which derived in part from her intelligence and precocity and in part from the lack of parental restraints commonly applied to young ladies in that area and era. From an early age she insisted that woman's place was bigger than the home.

A short, stout person with a clear voice, she early developed the talkative nature and range of ideas that made those in her presence listeners most of the time. Later her writing—correspondence and books—also exhibited her verbosity. For a time Fanny studied in France. Her early addiction to travel, in addition to reinforcing her loquacity, readied her for years in Mexico.

The first of Fanny's three marriages, all of which are shrouded in uncertainty because of the paucity of records, was to G. W. Gooch, a Virginian. It was with him that she made her initial trip to Mexico. Precise chronology seldom troubled the writer who eventually reduced several Mexican trips to one composite account of Mexican life on a thematic basis so it follows that she did not record the moment of her entry into Mexico.

In Saltillo, where the Gooches settled and Fanny managed a household, she spent virtually all of her first long stay in Mexico. There, in her adobe house, in the market place, and in the Sunday classes she conducted for Mexicans in order to perfect her own Spanish, Fanny quickly developed the friendships which contributed to her rich awareness of Mexican life. Bold, optimistic, and expansive by nature, she knew no restrictions in her approach to Mexico. Nor did she allow her senses to be dulled by repetition of experience.

The date of her return to Texas is likewise unknown, but her communicative nature so led her to talk and even write, for newspapers, about her impressions of Mexico that the plea of friends became insistent that she do a book on the subject. Apparently it was at this time—most probably early in 1883—that the almost crusading zeal which forever after insisted that she help her countrymen to understand Mexico came upon her.

Intent upon describing "certain phases of Mexican life and character, necessary to be understood in order to fully appreciate the people," Mrs. Gooch returned to Mexico to widen her knowledge of both the land and its people. To past experiences at Saltillo, she now added new ones at Aguas Calientes, Lagos, León, Mexico City, Morelia, Orizaba, Puebla, Querétaro, Silao, Toluca, Zacatecas, and other places.

Prior contacts and letters of introduction she reinforced with her warm, friendly disposition. At times her romantic nature and imaginative vein approached simpering sentimentality. But, as she avoided the pedantic, she also escaped the maudlin. Her social nature, however, was only one key to her penetration of Mexican society.

Before going abroad, she had studied Spanish. Many of her activities in Saltillo had been planned intellectual ventures on Fanny Gooch's part. In time, in Mexico City, she came to know many of the leading intellectuals of the day, among them novelist-historian Vicente Riva Palacio and poets Guillermo Prieto, Ignacio Manuel Altamirano and Juan de Dios Peza. Mrs. Gooch worked hard to master the idiomatic Spanish which enlarged her understanding of various Mexican elements. Because her book was intended to challenge the mind of her fellow American, she permitted herself to be challenged by the Mexican mind, as well as by the landscape, etiquette, dress, diet, and dozens of other components of life below the Rio Grande.

The book that resulted from her off-and-on experience across seven years was itself a product of four years of dedicated labor. Writing from Washington, D. C., to her friend Julia Pease, daughter of an ex-governor of Texas, Mrs. Gooch indicated early in 1888 that her New York publisher, Fords, Howard, & Hulbert, had released *Face to Face with the Mexicans* to the public on 24 December 1887. By that time Fanny's first marriage had ended and her financial condition was far from enviable. In correspondence now in the Austin-Travis County Collection at the Austin (Texas) Public Library, Fanny informed Julia, "I have invested my *little all* in this great enterprise. I am now instructing lady agents as well as taking orders myself and obtaining testimonials from distinguished men whose names as subscribers will be of national importance."

This badgering and buttonholing of prominent people was reflected in the addenda to the preface of the London edition which soon emerged from the house of Sampson Low, Marston, Searle, & Rivington. Reference was made there to "the generous and spontaneous indorsements given it by distinguished Mexicans and Americans—including Judges of the United States Supreme Court, nearly one hundred United States Senators and Congressmen, the House Committee on Foreign Affairs, and all the Foreign Ministers from Mexico and the Central and South American Republics. . . ."

Lest this activity in Washington be considered simply

the zealous promotion of an author drunk on the wine of publication, it is noteworthy that the sense of mission that had prompted the book still motivated Fanny. The purpose of her visit to Washington, where she remained for months, was, so she informed Julia Pease, "to place the work in the hands of our leading lawmakers and let the great aim and object for which I had labored receive a decisive impetus here. . . ."

Unknown is the relationship between the publication of *Face to Face with the Mexicans* and the emergence of the Pan-American outlook which encouraged Secretary of State Blaine to play host to the opening meeting of the modern Pan-American movement but it is evident that many men of influence in Washington at that time were increasingly aware of Latin America because of Fanny Chambers Gooch.

On another front, namely Texas, the fledgling author also strove to advance Mexican-American relations. Governor Ross was urged by Fanny to invite the Mexican cadets of Chapultepec to participate in a drill competition. Receiving no reply, she next urged Julia Pease to organize a group of women to call upon the governor. Meanwhile Fanny dreamed of issuing invitations to President Díaz, the Mexican Press Association, and other notables.

Fighting for one cause on many fronts, Fanny Chambers Gooch was a precursor of things to come—and like that of other forerunners, the impact of her labors is difficult to assess, and overly easy to underestimate.

Face to Face with the Mexicans was reviewed favorably in both the United States and England. William Dean Howells, writing the "Editor's Study" in *Harper's*, accorded it pages of approbation. The book, Howells said, "has a value that only a quick, intelligent, sympathetic woman could give her study of a foreign people's life." Accepting the purpose behind the book, Howells added, "she unlocks the door everywhere to our intimate acquaintance with neighbors whom we cannot afford to ignore." *The Spectator* said, "Many books have been written about Mexico, and in none are there more interesting details to be found about the people and their ways than in this one. . . ." *The Athenaeum* declared, "The city of Mexico has been often and well described in recent works of English and American travellers; but the inner aspect of the daily life of all classes . . . has never been so faithfully portrayed as in the present pages."

Despite its value, promotion, and reception, *Face to Face with the Mexicans* chalked up a mediocre publishing record. To give maximum appeal to their edition of 1887, the only American edition, Fords, Howard, & Hulbert had offered the book in a variety of bindings, with and without gilt edges, the price ranging from $4.25 to $7.50. The English edition of 1890 was based on sheets shipped from New York. No record exists of later editions, in Europe or America.

Late in 1889 Fanny was once more in Austin, the wife of cotton factor D. T. Iglehart. As she planned a cotillion at which she expected Julia Pease among her guests, she diligently searched for unique and charming decorations to go along with the supply of favors which she had acquired from Baltimore. Many years of social activity inspired the appellation "a social genius" which Mrs. V. O. King bestowed upon Fanny in *The Texas Women's Hall of Fame*. That same writer was impressed by Mrs. Iglehart's "commanding presence," "personal magnetism," "infinite tact," "grace and sympathy," and "wit and repartee."

Fanny continued to write, and most of what she penned related to Mexico. In 1900 she returned to Mexico, after an absence of more than twelve years. Her *Tradition of Guadalupe and Christmas in Old Mexico* combined old and new experiences. Some of the text and virtually every illustration came from *Face to Face with the Mexicans*. That portion which dealt with Mexico of 1900 teemed with adulation of Díaz. As she considered the betterment of Mexican life—the almost incredible signs of thrift, progress, and prosperity, she concluded, "To one great cause alone can these marvelous changes and improvements be attributed: TO THE SOLDIER-PRESIDENT—GENERAL PRESIDENTE PORFIRIO DÍAZ."

In the 1880's many hopeful Mexican prospects could be and were entertained by Fanny and many others. She then had had reason to hope for progressive elements of democracy in Mexico and little of Díaz' capacity for ignoring the peasant and the urban masses was a matter of record, but in 1900 a multifaceted tyranny embracing social stratification, judicial favoritism, economic privilege, and political dictatorship was the order of the day. These and other things that she did not see in the 1880's because they were then in their infancy under Díaz, Fanny did not see in 1900 because she fell into that well-known tourist trap which equates the capital with the country and that on the basis of a fleeting glimpse.

A decade later, after appearing at least partially in a San Antonio weekly, her last book, *The Boy Captive of the Texas-Mier Expedition* was published. On the death of her second husband, Fanny married Dr. Richard H. L. Bibb, whom she later divorced. Bibb received considerable publicity when he killed a man named Grey. Defense of Fanny's honor had inspired his action, it was claimed, and Bibb was acquitted of the charge of murder.

Like most of the years of her life, and all three of her marriages, Fanny's last days and death are cloaked in uncertainty. Despite her place in Texas letters at the turn of the century, her political and social contacts, and her inclusion in biographical dictionaries—albeit sketchily, the date of her death is unknown. Rumor places it about 1913.

Known, however, is the fact that in the 1880's her abilities and desires combined to produce the finest statement of the social aspects of the early years of the Díaz era. Generations later the most ardent advocate of the Good Neighbor Policy of the 1930's was but subscribing to Fanny's half-century old "sentiment of neighborly goodwill." And today, as in the 1930's and the 1880's, *Face to*

Face with the Mexicans remains a noteworthy contribution toward the understanding of the Mexican by his northern neighbor.

In the present abridged edition, which is based on that of 1887, the editor's role, beyond this introductory essay, has included the following: deletion of the original preface, musical scores, illustrations and textual comment thereon, and those materials which were basically historical or thematically repetitive. In the restyling of the chapters, some headings have been altered to accommodate consolidations. Spelling and accent marks have prompted some corrections. Modern rules of capitalization have also been applied. However, the words of the abridged text are, at all times, those of Fanny Chambers Gooch.

The kind assistance of the following persons is gratefully acknowledged.: Nettie Lee Benson, Librarian of the Latin American Collection and Llerena Friend, Librarian of the Barker Texas History Library, both within the University of Texas Library; Helen S. Swanson of the Austin-Travis County Collection of the Austin Public Library; and Willie B. Rutland, Curator of the Elisabet Ney Museum of Austin, Texas.

C. HARVEY GARDINER

"The Oaks"
Murphysboro, Illinois
February 1, 1966

FACE TO FACE WITH THE MEXICANS

A New Home and New Friends

Saltillo! Saltillo! Saltillo!

Saltillo was once the capital of Texas when that great state formed an unwilling member of the Mexican federation. It has a population of about twenty thousand, and is situated on the Buena Vista tableland in the Sierra Madre Mountains, at an elevation of about five thousand five hundred feet above sea level.

It was founded on the 25th of July, 1575, by one Francisco Urdiñola, who brought with him sixty Tlaxcalan families who were bitter foes of the Aztecs and firm allies of the conquerors.

The city is the seat of important manufactures, both woolen and cotton. Here are made rebozos (a long narrow shawl worn by women over their heads), and also those gorgeous and durable serapes (blankets), of finest wool and most brilliant colors, which have gained so wide a celebrity that the term "Mexican blanket" is a synonym for a genuine and almost everlasting fabric.

It has the usual places for recreation, a bull ring, plaza, and alameda; a cathedral worthy of inspection, also numerous churches, with a full quota of schools and colleges.

We were a party of Americans on business, health, and pleasure bent. As the hotel accommodations were meager and uncomfortable, and it not being the custom of the country for families to live in hotels, we concluded to go to housekeeping, as our stay was indefinite, and might extend through a few weeks or months.

We found this picturesque old city teeming with interest; many quaint old *adobe* bridges span the arroyos (dry streams), and the drives through the orchards in the Indian *pueblos* adjoining are full of exuberant life and

3

color. The noblest view is from the brow of the San Lo-
renzo, where are situated the fine medicinal springs and
baths which tourists as well as natives enjoy. The drives
in whatever direction are full of thrilling historic associations, the city having been the coveted ground of the con-
testing forces in untold battles and desperate encounters.

But no street or highway interested me so much as
Calle Real, one of the principal and most delightful thor-
oughfares of the city. By a circuitous route and steep ascent
it led to the American fort, and, circling to the right over
the smooth tablelands, on to La Angostura (the Narrows),
where lies the famous battlefield of Buena Vista.

Since the founding of the city, Calle Real has figured
conspicuously in its history. The patriot Hidalgo and his
chosen brave followers must doubtless have passed down
this street to meet their fate—betrayed by friends.

The history of this grand captain's career was fresh
in my mind, and, as I looked upon this long, narrow, and
winding street, I pictured the fearless leader of the great
cause of the Mexican people, with head erect and eye as
bright as, when a victor, he heard the wild plaudits from
the thousand dark brothers of his race who had flocked to
his standard.

Then the scene would change, and the forms of my
own martial countrymen, who had so often passed up and
down this street, nearly two score years ago, would take
the place of the dauntless Hidalgo. I lost sight of the present, and saw American soldiers, with stars and stripes
floating proudly, move rapidly in solid columns of infantry, and heard the tread of the bronzed cavalrymen,
and the rattle of sabers and the clear-ringing words of
command in my own language. I saw the angry gleam os
dark eyes and heard mutterings in the strange tongue af
the Americans marched up the steep hill to take possession
of the fort that commanded the city.

Another change: the shade of Hidalgo has vanished;
the stars and stripes no longer float under the unclouded
sky. In imagination I see the flag of the French Empire and

the eagles of Austria streaming over the city, and the gorgeous uniforms of the soldiery of two mighty empires mingling with the rude, dark forms that look on them with wondering eyes of mute protest and reluctant admiration. Wild carousal is heard on every side, and wine flows like water. The harsh accents of the Austrian and the volatile utterances of the Frenchman fill the air.

The panorama moves on. Gone are the foreigners. Their chief lies dead in the stately burial place of the Habsburgs. Miramón and Mejía rest in San Fernando, and the banner of the Republic, with its emblematic red, green, and white bars and fierce eagle, waves proudly over the people freed from a foreign foe and hated alien rule.

War and revolution have yielded in turn to the softening influences of well-earned peace and tranquillity. The passions of those perilous times are long since dead; our quondam enemy is now our friend, and an American woman is at liberty to peacefully erect her household gods among them.

Both courage and resolution were necessary in transplanting ourselves to this *terra incognita*; but the climate, the hospitality of the people, the beautiful scenery, the novelty of the surroundings, which every day afforded delight, would of themselves reconcile one to exchanging the old, the tried, and the true for the experiences of an unknown world.

The house selected for our Bohemian abode, we were assured, was almost one hundred years old, and had an air of solemn dignity and grandeur about its waning splendor. It was of startling dimensions, capable of quartering a regiment of soldiers with all their equipments. It was one story in height, with a handsome orchard and garden in the rear, extensive corrals for horses, the whole extending from street to street through a large square of ground.

The distinguishing features of Mexican and Spanish architecture were evident throughout the patio (courtyard), with fountain in the center, flat roof, barred win-

dows, and parapet walls. These latter rise often to the
height of six feet above the main structure, and, in times
of war and revolution, have proved admirable defenses to
the besieged. Intrenching themselves behind these walls,
passageways are made from one house to the other, until
the entire block of buildings is one connected fortification.
The strife may continue for weeks uninterruptedly, the
fusillade not ceasing long enough to remove the dead from
the streets.

The size and unwieldiness of the front doors were
amazing—noble defenses in time of revolution, it is true,
but when with my whole strength I could not move one
on its antiquated, squeaking hinges, almost a half yard in
length, the question of how to pass from house to street
became a serious one. The happy discovery was made at
last that, instead of two, there were four doors all in one,
the two smaller ones within the greater serving for our
usual ingress and egress. The huge double doors, spacious
enough to admit a locomotive with its train of cars, were
never opened except on state occasions or for the admittance of a carriage, buggy, or something out of the ordinary, such as a dozen or so wood-laden donkeys. Not only
funerals and bridal parties, but every imaginable household necessity for pleasure or convenience, must pass
through the front doors.

In the zaguán (front hall), high up in the cedar
beams, darkened by age to the color of mahogany, was
this inscription or dedication in large, clear letters: "*Ave
María Santísima.*" In other houses these dedications varied according to taste. One read "Siempre viva en esta
casa Nuestra Señora de Guadalupe" (May the Virgin
Guadalupe always watch over this house). Still another
inscription in the house of a friend read: "Aquí viva con
V. José y María," "May Joseph and Mary dwell with you
here."

We were astounded at the size and length of the keys,
and the number of them; they were about ten inches long,
and a blow from one would have sufficed to fell a man. As

there were, perhaps, thirty of them, my key basket, so far from being the dainty trifle an American woman dangles from one finger in her daily rounds, would have been a load for a burro, as they call their little donkeys. The enormous double doors connecting the rooms were as massive as if each room were intended for a separate fortification. The opening and closing of these heavy doors as they scraped across the floors gave forth a dull, grating sound which added to the loneliness of our castle.

Our venerable mansion was constructed of adobe, the sun-dried brick peculiar to the country, and of which almost the entire city is built. The walls were from two to four feet in thickness, and the ceilings thirty feet in height. Surrounding the beautiful courtyard were many large and handsome rooms, frescoed in brilliant style, each different from the other. Besides these there were many smaller apartments, lofts, nooks, and crannies, more than I at first thought I should ever have the courage to explore.

The drawing room was the first thing to attract my attention, as it was about a hundred feet long and fifty wide. Its dado was highly embellished by a skillful blending of roses and buds in delicate shades, while the frieze was the chaste production of a native artist. The ceiling, as before mentioned, was thirty feet in height, and another source of surprise to me was the discovery that the foundation of all this elaborate workmanship was of the frailest material. These wonderful artisans, in making ceilings that are apparently faultless, use only cheesecloth. After stretching it as tightly as possible, and adding a coat of heavy sizing, the beautiful and gorgeous frescoes are laid on, and the eye of an expert cannot detect the difference between a cloth ceiling and the more substantial plaster with which we are familiar in the United States.

The floor of this room presented another subject of inquiry as to its materials and the method employed in making it so hard, smooth, and red. Mortar, much the same as is used for plastering, but of a consistency which hardens rapidly, is the basis of operations. On this a coating of fine gravel, very little coarser than sand, is applied. Then comes the final red polish which completes a floor of unusual coolness and comfort, and admirably adapted to the country. The material used to give the red finish is *tipichil*, an Indian word, in some places known as *almagra*, an abundant earthy deposit to be found principally in the arroyos. For ages this substance has been an important article for ornamentation, even the wild tribes of Indians using it to paint their faces and bodies. When the floor is hardened, a force of men is employed, who, by rubbing it with stones, produce a beautiful glazed polish. If time were of any value, these floors would cost fabulous sums, as it takes weeks to complete one of them. It required months almost for me to comprehend the manner of cleaning them.

The floors of the other rooms were of imported brick and tiles, the former not less than a foot square and perhaps half as thick, while the latter were octagonal and of fine finish, though, like the mansion itself, they bore the evidences of age and decay.

We enjoyed the unusual luxury of glass windows, and it was enough to puff us up with inordinate pride to look out and see our neighbors' houses provided with only plain, heavy wooden shutters. When it rained or was cold, however, our ill-fitting windows proved an inadequate protection, and it became necessary to close the ponderous wooden shutters, thus leaving the rooms in total darkness.

Our windows were also furnished on the outside with iron rods, similar to those used for jails in the United States, and quite as effective, while those of many of our neighbors had only heavy wooden bars, so close together as scarcely to permit the hand to pass between them. These, I was told by a Mexican lady, were called "jealous husbands' windows."

In the middle of many of the shutters of some of these houses were tiny doors, whose presence, when closed, would never be suspected. They were just large enough for a face to peer through, and when passing along the street on cold or windy days, hundreds of soft, languishing, dreamy eyes might be seen gazing out of these little windows.

In Mexican architecture the window is second in importance only to the roof itself. For, the next thing to being protected from the rain, is the necessity for the family to be able to see into the street. The walls are of such thickness that one window will easily accommodate two of their quaint little home manufactured chairs, and as there is no front stoop, each afternoon finds the señoritas seated in these chairs, taking in the full enjoyment of the usual street scenes.

The roof being flat, was constructed in a unique manner, having first heavy wooden beams laid across the top of each room, and then planks coated with pitch placed on these, after which twelve inches of mother earth were added; then a coating of gravel, and lastly one of cement, the whole making a roof impervious to rain or heat, and proving the admirable adaptability of Mexican architecture to the climate and the people.

The houses in general are provided with roofs of adobe, and some of the plainer ones in which I became a visitor, when the rainy season was at its height, gave me an amusing insight into the freaks and tricks of the "doby," as they are familiarly termed. When there were no frescoes on the cheesecloth canvas, it would be taken down periodically, washed and then replaced as smoothly as a plaster ceiling. But woe betide the "doby" roof, when the rainy season makes its advent. The treacherous mud covering succumbs to the pressure of the driving water, and often the entire room or house is submerged in the twinkling of an eye. Besides the main leaks, numerous little bubblelike projections, like pockets, each filled with water, sagged down the canvas in various places. To my great amusement I found that my ingenious native friends had always on hand the essentials for stopping the leak, such as an old broom handle or strip of wood, which by the aid of a bent pin and a string, manipulated by dexterous fingers, soon repaired all damages.

First, all the little sacks of water are conducted by

means of the broom handle into the larger one, where the bent pin has been previously attached to the canvas and also to one end of the string. To the other end the strip of wood is fastened, and under this a bucket placed. Twenty minutes from the time of the first onslaught of the torrent through the roof all is serene and calm as a May morning.

Orders were given at once to the *mozo* to sow the roof with grass seed, so as to prevent another catastrophe. No greater protection is found for an ordinary earthen roof than that afforded by a solid greensward. The roots form a compact network, so that it must be an unusually heavy storm that can penetrate it.

The method of conducting the water from the roof is in keeping with everything else. Great heavy gargoyles or stone spouts, weatherbeaten and moss-covered, tipped with tin, full ten feet in length, six in a line on either side of the court, answered the purpose in our mansion. During a heavy rainstorm it was interesting to watch the steady streams of water foaming and surging into the court. I saw a dog knocked senseless to the ground by one of these streams, and it was several minutes before he recovered his breathing and yelping faculties.

The ends of these spouts, in many instances artistically ornamented, protrude over the street. In more modern houses conduits, a few inches wide, are cut into the sides of the wall and cemented, taking the place of the stone spouts. They are quite as effective, but the quaintness and antique appearance of the houses is greatly diminished by them.

In the carriage house there still remained a silent old relic of Mexican grandeur and aristocratic distinction, with wheels like an American road wagon and hubs like a water bucket. In the garden were fruit trees and the family pila (bath). The latter was built of adobe, three feet high and twelve feet square, without cover, the water being supplied by means of earthen pipes from the mountain springs. A fountain and exquisite flowers adorned the patio, a climbing rose of unusual luxuriance at once attracting special notice. It was evergreen, and of extraordinary size, extending in graceful festoons fully one hundred feet on either side. We were told that at the time of the occupation of Saltillo by Taylor's army this same vine was an attractive feature of the court.

Imagine the dismay and apprehension of several American women at thus finding themselves surrounded by so many evidences of ancient refinement and culture, and yet by none of the modern necessaries of housekeeping. In this old city of twenty thousand inhabitants there was not a store where such indispensables as bedsteads or furniture of any kind, pillows or mattresses, could be purchased; while coffee or spice mills, cookstoves or washtubs, were absolutely out of the question. How we managed will be related in the succeeding chapters. It was not by any means a question of money or price that prevented one from being comfortable at the outset.

We ladies were constantly portraying to each other, in a humorous way, how frightened we should be if circumstances should ever require any one of us to remain alone in this old castle over night; of how the ghosts and hobgoblins that were perhaps concealed in some unexplored crannies might come forth in all their blood-curdling hideousness. These idle fancies and banterings of the hour were vividly recalled one night, when I unfortunately found myself the only one to entertain the phantom visitors.

Every other member of the household had gone for a day's jaunt into the country, and was detained from home over night by a terrific rain and thunder storm. The servants, supposing they would return, went to their homes, as is customary, which I did not discover until after they had left.

In the dead hours of the night I was aroused from deepest sleep by a terrific noise. Quaking with fear in the dim light, and gripping the pistol which was on a chair at the head of my bed, I proceeded, like Rosalind, with a "swashing and martial outside," to reconnoiter. A brief investigation revealed the fact that the fancied ghost or hobgoblin was nothing more alarming than a "harmless necessary cat," which had crept in surreptitiously through the bars, on feline mischief bent. By a misstep of her cat-ship there was a general crash of crockery, and the sudden clatter, breaking with startling effect on the stillness of the night, made me imagine that the hobgoblins had really trooped forth from their hiding places.

I had flattered myself that the diligent study I had given the grammar, previous to my going to Mexico, would prove an "Open, Sesame!" to the language, but I soon found myself sadly mistaken when I heard it spoken idiomatically and with the rapid utterance of the natives. But by eagerly seizing every opportunity, however humble, of airing my incipient knowledge, and by aid of grammar and dictionary, my inseparable companions, I found myself in a few weeks equal to the exigencies of the case, and rattled off my newly acquired accomplishment with a reckless disregard of consequences.

Speculation and curiosity were ever on the alert to make discoveries in this old house, and at every turn a thousand echoes seemed answering my timorous step.

Generations had here lived their lives of sorrow and joy, and the lightest vibration seemed the ghost of some long-past sigh or laugh, to which these walls had re-sounded; and to me these vast old rooms were peopled again by my own vivid imaginings. To walk twice or thrice around the courtyard and through this interminable array of rooms, seemed as fatiguing as half a day's tramp.

In one of these perambulations I opened the door of a room into which I had never ventured before. An ancient-looking cupboard stood in one corner, filled with odd remnants of dainty china, vases, bottles, plates, glass, a dilapidated but highly decorated old soup tureen, and some pieces of broken crockery almost half an inch in thickness. Many faded letters were thrown loosely about on shelves and in crevices. A descendant of Mother Eve could do no less than look at the dates. Some were a hundred years old, written in Spain, and the chirography was exceedingly beautiful. One was written in the city of Mexico, by a husband to his wife. He wrote most tenderly to the pretty, young *esposa*, begging her to be patient until his return, which was to be in the near future.

Hanging upon the wall near the door was a well-executed oil portrait, representing a lovely Spanish face. The graceful pose of the figure attracted my attention, and the luminous, speaking eyes held me spellbound—the same eyes which have so long made Spanish and Mexican women famous in song and story. The patrician nose, the classic brow, the shapely, rosy-lipped mouth, and the perfect hand and arm, completed a picture of unusual beauty. A richly gemmed crown rested upon the dark hair, and in the lower corner of the picture, inside the massive, gilded frame, were the words: "Ana su digna esposa"—"Hannah, your worthy wife."

Carefully removing all dust and cobwebs, I carried my prize to the drawing room; and hung it over the mantelpiece. I am sure I never passed it without glancing at that perfect face, so sweet and womanly in its expression, and experiencing feelings of mingled reverence and pleasure.

Much diligent inquiry on my part elicited the information that the portrait was of Doña Ana, wife of the Emperor Augustín de Iturbide, the first and only crowned head to occupy a throne in North America since its settlement by Europeans.

The first Sunday morning after taking possession of our house, I was sitting in the sunshiny court alone, every one, even the *mozo*, being absent. The bells from perhaps half a dozen churches answered each other across the bright air, reminding me with some painfulness of the church bells in my American home, the thought of which had filled my mind with longings all the morning, as I saw the gayly dressed populace hurrying past on their way to mass. Suddenly there was a gentle tap on the ponderous outer door. Responding, I found myself confronted by a tall youth of perhaps sixteen, fair, rosy-cheeked, black-haired, dark-eyed, and beautiful. He lifted his hat politely and said in good English, "Good morning, Madame!"

The sound of my dear native tongue in a land of strangers and from the lips of one of them brought my heart into my mouth with delight and surprise. My visitor introduced himself as Jesús, taking care to spell his name plainly for me, and I fear my face betrayed my horror at the sight of an ordinary mortal endowed with that holy name. He informed me with considerable hesitation that he was a student in the college, and wished to call frequently to have an opportunity of conversing in English.

Having obtained permission to call whenever it pleased him, he asked if he might bring a friend. Accordingly, Antero P—— was introduced—another promising youth, equally determined to improve his English. They soon brought others, and among my most pleasing recollections are the occasions when the college boys—sometimes a dozen—gathered about me on Sunday mornings, with bright, dark faces, flashing eyes, and determined expression, as they wrestled with the difficulties of our language. Their great deference and thoughtfulness for me added to the pleasure I derived from their visits—for the advantage was mutual. I learned the Spanish while they conquered the English.

I could not but pity the other members of our party who so languished with home sickness that they quite failed to reap the pleasure I did from this study of the natives.

Every day I found some new object of interest, and after the house had been explored I spent hours gazing from the windows upon some of the strangest scenes I had ever beheld. Some were extremely pathetic and others mirth provoking.

The young children of the lower classes, especially the girls from five to ten years, were objects of peculiar interest to me. Dozens of these were to be seen in the early morning hours going upon some family errand apparent-

ly, judging from the haste and the pottery vessels they carried. Their tangled hair, peeping out from under the
rebozo, their unwashed faces and jetty eyes, their long
dresses sweeping the ground—and looking like the ground
itself—their little naked, pigeon-toed feet going at an even
but rapid jog-trot, all formed a laughable and ridiculous
picture.

Often their hands were thrust through the bars,
begging money in the name of some saint for a sick person.

"Tlaco, señorita, para comprar la medicina para un
enfermo," ("A cent and a quarter, lady, to buy medicine
for a sick person"). If I asked what was the matter, the
reply, "Tiene mal de estómago" ("Sick at the stomach"),
came with such unfailing regularity, I was forced to the
conclusion that "mal de estómago" must be an epidemic
among them.

The school children came in for a profitable share of
my most agreeable observations, as they presented themselves before me in all their freshness and originality.

It is not the custom for the daughters of the higher
classes to appear on the street unattended. I rightly concluded, therefore, that these happy little friends of mine,
who created such a fund of amusement for me, were the
public-school children who belonged to the lower classes.

They passed in the mornings about eight o'clock, and
returned at five in the evening. The girls wore rebozos
differing from their mothers' only in size; and a surprising
unanimity of style seemed to prevail.

Their hair was drawn tightly back, plaited behind,
the ends doubled under, and almost universally tied with
a piece of red tape. Their white hose, a world too short,
had an antique look to eyes accustomed so long to the brilliantly arrayed legs of the children of the United States.
Evidently extra full lengths had not reached that country,
as the above-mentioned hose terminated below the knee,
where they were secured (when secured at all) with a rag,
string, or a piece of red tape of the same kind that adorned
their braided locks. Those who wore shoes had them laced

up the front, sharp pointed at the toes, and frequently of gay-colored material. As their dresses sometimes lacked several inches of reaching the knees, the intervening space of brown skin exposed to view was sometimes quite startling, especially so, if—as was often the case—their pantalets were omitted. Frequently, when these were worn, they were very narrow and reached the ankle, the dress retaining its place far above the knee. A row of big brass safety pins down the front of their dresses performed the office of buttons.

The boys were simply miniature copies of their fathers, wearing sashes, snug little jackets, blouses, and in some cases even the sandal.

The advent of one of these lighthearted groups was always a happy diversion to me. Often they came laughing and chattering in a gentle monotone down the street, throwing paper balls at one another, playing "tag"—it has a finer and more sonorous name in their majestic tongue, for it rolled off euphoniously into "ahora tu me coges" ("now you've caught me")—performing many other pretty, childish antics just after some peculiarly heart-rending spectacle of poverty and suffering had wrung my heart. They soon learned to divine my sympathetic interest in them, and occasionally some of them would stop before my window, and exchange with me amusing remarks. They were very bright, and laughed incredulously, exchanging winks and nods with each other, when I tried to make them believe that I was a Mexican. I asked if they could not see from my dark hair and eyes that I was one; but they refused to be convinced, saying: "You may look like a Mexican, but you can't talk like one." In the course of time, all shyness vanished, and often, when in other parts of the house, the young voices gleefully calling "Señorita! Señorita!" would bring me to the drawing room, and there would be my barred windows, full of little dark mischievous faces, their brown hands stretched out to me through the iron bars, through which their dancing eyes peeped. When my housekeeping was in better running order—comparatively speaking, of course—I sometimes gave them trifling dainties. Cakes they accepted gladly, but when in my patriotic zeal I tried to familiarize them with that bulwark of our Southern civilization—the soda biscuit—they rejected it uncompromisingly, spitting and sputtering after a taste of it, and saying: "No nos gusta," ("We don't like it"), "Good for Americans—no good for Mexicans."

A pretty child in a nurse's arms stopped before the window, and laid her tiny brown hand on me caressingly. Nurse told her to sing a pretty song for the señora, when she began:

> No me mates! no me mates! no me mates!
> Con pistola ni puñal;
> Matame con un besito
> De tus labios de coral.

> Don't kill me! don't kill me! don't kill me!
> With a pistol nor a dagger;
> But kill me with a little kiss
> Of your pretty coral lips.

I asked her to come again, and as they moved along the pretty creature waved her hand at me, saying: "¡Mañana! en la mañanita" ("Tomorrow morning very early"), which aroused my fears, justly enough, for I never saw her again, it being their universal custom to postpone everything for the morrow—a time which I felt would never come.

The mansion and its associations were so well known that every servant whom we employed could contribute some item of interest concerning its history. An old citizen related to me that at the time of Gen. Taylor's entrance into the city there were in it nine most beautiful and interesting señoritas, daughters of the original founder, Don A——. Naturally, every little detail and event concerning them was eagerly absorbed, and nothing gave me more thorough gratification than the discovery that my very first and best friends made after arriving were the descendants of one of these nine señoritas. Don Benito G——, an accomplished gentleman of Castilian descent, who has occupied the highest positions in the state, wooed and won his lovely bride when she was in her early teens, and for many years they remained under the paternal roof. Here their three beautiful children first saw the light, and their infantile days were spent in these grand old rooms, amid the flowers of the court and surrounded by an atmosphere of beauty and refinement.

At the time of our acquaintance these favored children of a distinguished family were in the bloom of early manhood and womanhood, José María, the oldest, aged twenty-six; Benito, twenty-two; and Liberata, a lovely, dark-eyed girl of sixteen. She was a charming representative of her Andalusian ancestors; the graces of her person added to the beauty of her disposition. In imagination her exquisite flower-sweet face rises before me, her soft luminous eyes, shaded by lashes of wondrous length and beauty, sweeping a cheek that glowed like a luscious peach.

These friends began at once, without ceremony or ostentation, to show me the gentlest attentions, and from the unlimited treasure house of their warm Mexican hearts they bestowed upon me a generous devotion that brightened my life and made me love and respect their land and their people for their sakes. In every circumstance they proved to be animated by the noblest impulses of our common nature, and one of the happiest discoveries I made during those days of a bewildering struggle with a new civilization, was that, despite the representation of many of my own countrymen, fidelity, tenderness, and untiring devotion were as truly Mexican characteristics as American. It is doubtful in my mind if the people of any country lavish upon strangers the same warmth of manner or exhibit the same readiness to serve them, as do our near-at-hand, faraway neighbors, the Mexicans.

At daylight one morning, soon after we were installed in the house of his ancestors, Don Benito, Jr., accompanied by several young friends, favored us with a delightful serenade, in which the beautiful Spanish songs were rendered with charming effect. He was an excellent sportsman, and always remembered us after his shooting excursions, while I received daily reminders of affectionate regard from Liberata, the gentle sister.

Don José María was a young man of varied accomplishments and acquirements, among which the knowledge of English was duly appreciated in our growing friendship. He had liberal and progressive ideas; was well versed in American literature, was a regular subscriber to the *Popular Science Monthly*, *North American Review*, *Scribner's*, *Harper's Magazine* and *Bazaar*, besides others of our best periodicals—and took a lively interest in our politics.

To all these magazines we had free access through his kindness, and welcome as waters in a thirsty land were these delightful home journals, where mails were had but once or twice a week in this literary Sahara.

After the death of his mother, when Liberata was only an infant, desiring to relieve his grief-stricken father, this admirable elder brother took almost entire charge of the little creature, filling the place of mother, sister, and brother. It was to me an exquisitely pathetic story, this recital of the young brother's effort to train and care for the motherless baby girl, even superintending the buying and making of her wardrobe, which must have been the most bewildering feature of his bewildering undertaking.

Among other things he was anxious to have her become familiar with American methods of housekeeping and cookery. I could but laugh, though a tear quickly followed, when she described how her brother translated the cooking receipts in *Harper's Bazaar*, and then requested her to have American dishes concocted from them; what moments of despair she had over the unfamiliar compounds, and what horrible "messes" sometimes resulted from the imperfectly understood translations.

In due time I had gathered about me many kind and congenial friends, who vied with each other in contributing to my happiness. One of these, Doña Pomposita R——, without knowing my language, began to instruct me in her own. Winks, blinks, and shrugs did the most of it: but come what would, she never gave up until everything was clear. We sat in the patio on the afternoon of her first visit, and among other things was her determination that we should converse about Don Quixote, she being familiar with his story in the original and I in my own tongue. Many of the humorous adventures of the Don were called up by her in the most amusing manner. In rapid succession she mentioned the men with their "pack staves," the "wine bags," and was finally overcome with laughter as she said that our grand old house reminded her of the isle of Barataria, where Sancho Panza was governor.

She then sang in a low, sweet tone many operatic airs, among them, "Then You'll Remember Me," and others equally familiar, possessing an added charm in the sweet Spanish. Near nightfall she arose to go home, saying Pancho—meaning her husband—would soon be there, and she wished him never to enter their home and find her absent. Placing her arm affectionately about my waist, in her sweet Spanish she said to me: "In my country it is very sad for you, and you are far from your home and people, but do not forget I am your friend and sister; what I can do for you shall be done as for a sister." Her husband, Don Pancho, shared fully in her professions of friendship, and on one occasion, when a hundred miles away from the city, sent us a regalo (gift) of a donkey-load of grapes.

In striking personal contrast were my two most intimate friends among Mexican women. Pomposita, like Liberata, had the petite figure, the dainty feet and hands peculiar to the women of that country; but unlike her, she possessed the high cheekbones, the straight black hair, the brown skin indicating her Indian origin, of which she was justly proud.

But there was no contrast in the exhibition of their devoted kindness and friendship. Both were equally ready to assist me in adapting myself to the strange order of things and to aid in my initiation into the mysteries of their peculiar household economies. In case of sickness it seemed worth while to suffer to be the object of such exquisite tenderness, and experience the unspeakable sweetness of their sisterly ministrations.

The time came when an overwhelming affliction fell upon me. My sister Emma, the loveliest and most devoted of women, was suddenly called from this bright world in the summer bloom of her loving life, leaving four young and tender children, leaving all her relations and friends grief-stricken and myself in the depths of such anguish as only God and the good angels know. When we came into this world, it was in a large family of brothers who loved and petted the two wee girls with all the devotion of noble-hearted men. Now that she was taken, it seemed to me there was a void that no space nor object of the affections could fill, and the better part of my life was gone.

In these darkened and burdened days of grief I can only tell how true, loving, and tender were the hands that ministered to me. The other members of our party were absent on a journey, and these strangers nobly filled their places. In the long and painful illness that followed, Pomposita, Liberata, and other friends never left me for a moment, day or night, and in deference to my sorrow all were robed in somber black. Every possible delicacy that could tempt a wayward appetite was brought; notes and messages came daily to my door, and numberless inquiries, all expressive of sympathy and a desire to serve me, from the male relatives of my friends. These affectionate and tender attentions could not have been exceeded by those endeared to me by ties of blood.

Pomposita, though so young, as a matron took precedence, constituting herself my special nurse, in full accord with the Gospel injunction to love her neighbor as herself. In the fevered, silent watches of the night, how gently her soft little brown hand would pass across my brow as she murmured her sweet words of endearment, and how lovingly her arms encircled me as she held me to her warm and noble heart. She constantly reminded me of her first visit and her assurance that she would be my sister.

In every way they all sought to win me from my grief. Indeed, it seemed that the ministering angels themselves had deputed their high mission to my devoted, faithful, and gratefully remembered Mexican friends.

"Muy amable—muy simpática"*

The dearth of household furniture and conveniences already mentioned, put ingenuity and will force to their utmost tension, and I felt as if transported to antediluvian days. I have a candid conviction that Mother Noah never had cooking utensils more crude, or a larder more scant, than were mine. It may be, however, that the "old man" was "good to help around the house."

This was before the time of railways in Mexico, the "Nacional Mexicano" having only penetrated a few leagues west of the Rio Grande. With the primitive modes of transportation which served in lieu of the railway it was not advisable to attempt bringing household goods so far over a trackless country. The inconveniences that followed were not peculiar to ourselves, but common to all strangers, who like us could neither anticipate nor realize the scarcity of every household appurtenance.

The natives who enjoyed the luxury of furniture—and there was a large number who had everything in elegance—had also the romantic recollection, that great old two-wheeled carts, towering almost above the housetops, had brought it from the capital, nearly a thousand miles, or it was manufactured by the carpenters of the town.

In the division of the apartments of the house, one half was allotted to us, while our friends distributed themselves among the remaining rooms, on the opposite side of the courtyard, the drawing room being used in common. Mr. and Mrs. R—— employed a cook and had their own *cuisine*, the other flitted about from fonda to fonda (restaurant) in search of sustenance. In the evening of each day

*In this and the two succeeding chapters, and wherever the common people are mentioned, the Spanish used is idiomatic, peculiar to the class it represents.

we would meet and compare notes on the varied and amusing experiences of the day. However, I am not relating the adventures of our friends, but will generously leave that happy task to them.

Progress in furnishing our quarters in this great massive structure was slow indeed. How I longed for the delightful furnishings of my own home, which remained just as I had left it.

Fortunately for us, a druggist had two spare, pine single bedsteads, which he kindly sold to us for the sum of forty dollars. At an American factory they would have been worth about four dollars each. One was painted a bright red, the other an uncompromising orange. They were cot-like and had flat wire springs, while Mexican blankets constituted the entire bedding, mattresses and all. Pillows were improvised from bundles of wearing apparel. Fancy how they looked, the only furniture in a gorgeously frescoed room twenty-five by thirty-five feet, and of proportionate height!

A friend lent us six haircloth chairs, and a table which had many years before been the operating table of his brother, a surgeon. It was long, green, and sagged in the middle. A carpenter was employed to make the remaining necessary articles of furniture. He labored on the customary mañana system, and while his calculations as to time ranged all the way from eight to fifteen days, I found he actually meant from six weeks to three months. He showed samples of his workmanship, rocking chairs with and without arms, made of pine, stained or painted or varnished, and upright chairs with cane seats. I ventured to ask when he could complete for us a dozen chairs, four rockers, and some tables. Utterly amazed, he looked at me with a smile of incredulity, as if to say, "What can you do with so much furniture?" He disapproved of my wish to have oblong and round tables, so I yielded acquiescence to the customary triangular ones which grace the corners of every parlor of respectability.

It now becomes necessary to introduce what proved

to me the most peculiar and interesting feature of home life in Mexico. This is not an article of furniture, a fresco, a pounded earthen floor, or a burro or barred casement, but the indispensable, all-pervading, and incomparable manservant, known as the mozo. According to the prevailing idea, he is far more important than any of the things enumerated in my household ménage, for from first to last he played a conspicuous rôle.

Forewarned—forearmed! The respectability of the household depending on his presence, one was engaged, the strongest character in his line—the never-to-be-forgotten Pancho.

It was perhaps not a just sentence to pronounce upon this individual, but circumstances seemed to warrant the comparison I involuntarily made between our watchful Pancho and a sleepless bloodhound. At night he curled himself up on a simple petate with no pillow and only a blanket, and was as ready to respond to our beck and call as in the day.

In this house were two kitchens, representative of that part of the country. In the center of one was a miniature circus ring about three feet in circumference, consisting simply of a raised circle of clay about one foot high. This constituted the range. Little fires were built within this ring, one under each of the pottery vessels used in the operations. After this uncomfortable fashion the cooking was done, the smoke circling about at its own sweet will and at length finding vent through a small door at one side, the only opening in the room.

The sole piece of furniture was a worm-eaten table supported on two legs, the inner side braced against the wall. Its decayed condition indicated that it was at least a hundred years old.

The second kitchen contained another style of range equally primitive in its design. Along the wall was built a solid breastwork of adobe, about two feet high, two feet deep, and extending the entire length of the room. An opening was left in the roof over this structure for the escape of smoke, but the grimy walls proved that it failed to answer its purpose. Upon this ledge, projection, or whatever it may be termed, the cook places her various pottery vessels with fires made of charcoal or small bits of wood under each, and there the stewing, boiling, frying, and crying go on all day. This cook, unlike the one in kitchen No. 1, stands up in the performance of her duties.

When I inspected these kitchens, it may be imagined that the sight was rather depressing, coupled with the certainty that I could effect no improvement. But we had the luxury of one tiny fireplace, to which in my despair I fled for refuge. In this little treasure our scheme of housekeeping was inaugurated with results both brave and gay.

Among the latter experiences I may class my first coffee roasting, not realizing till then that the essential feature of a mill was lacking, and that I was at least five hundred miles from any possible purchase of one.

Pancho, however, was equal to the emergency, and, going off, soon returned with a *metate*. It was a decidedly primitive affair, and, like the mills of the gods, it ground slowly, but like them, it also ground to powder.

The metate is cut from a porous, volcanic rock, and is about eighteen inches long by a foot in width and eight inches in thickness. The upper surface, which is generally a little concave, is roughened with indentures; upon this the article is placed and beaten with another stone called a mano, resembling a rolling pin. Almost every article of food is passed between these stones—meat, vegetables, corn, coffee, spices, chocolate—even the salt, after being washed and sun-dried, is crushed upon it. Such a luxury as "table salt" was not to be had. Previous to use these stones are hardened by being placed in the fire. The rough points become as firm as steel, and one metate will last through a generation.

This necessity of everyday life was a revelation to me. The color of an elephant, it was quite as unwieldly and graceless, but its importance in the homely details of the ménage was undeniable. It had but two competitors to

divide the honors with—the maguey plant and the donkey. They were all three necessary to each other and to the
commonwealth at large.

Equipped with an inconceivable amount of pottery
of every shape and kind, maguey brushes, fans of plaited
palm—the national bellows—wooden forks, spoons, and
many other nameless primitive articles, my collection of
household gods was complete.

The first meal cooked in that dainty little fireplace
was more delicious than any that could be furnished at
Delmonico's. In his quaint efforts to assist, Pancho per-
ambulated around with an air as all-important as though
he were chef of that famous café. But the climax of all was
reached in Pancho's estimation when I put a pure white
linen cloth on my green, historic table and arranged for
the meal. He said over and over: "¡Muy bonita cena!"
("Very pretty supper"). But I discovered it was the attractions of my silver knives and forks and other natty table
ware from home that constituted the novelty. In his experience fingers were made before knives and forks.

I found my majordomo knew everything and everybody; the name of every street, the price of every article
to be bought or sold. My curiosity, I presume, only stimu-
lated his imagination, and the more pleased I appeared at
his recitals the more marvelous were his tales.

He gave the lineage of every family of the "gente decente," for generations, his unique style adding pith and
point to his narrations. He told me the story of Hidalgo
and Morelos and Iturbide, the coming of the Americans,
the French Intervention, and all the late revolutions, until
my head rang with the boom of cannon and the beat of
drum. But invariably these poetic narratives were rudely
interrupted by some over-practical intrusion. In the same
breath in which he completed the recital of the Emperor
Iturbide, he suggested that wood was better and cheaper
than charcoal for cooking.

With my approbation he went to the plaza, returning in a little while with a man who brought ten donkeys,

all laden with wood packed on like saddlebags. I asked the wood vender to drive his vicious-looking dog out, when he complied by saying: "¡Hist! ¡hist! Sal!" Of course I then thought the dog's name was *Sal*, but soon found the word meant "get out!" As the dog howled on being railed at, the man of importance again yelled at him, "¡Callate! ¡callate el ocico, cuele!" ("Shut up—shut your mouth, and get out!")

Constant surprises were developed before my eyes every hour in the day. The yolks of the first eggs I bought were white—indeed, this was often the case—which for a moment dazed me, as I had never expected to find my old friend, the hen, so different in her habits from her sisters in the States. But the qualities of the egg were identical with those familiar to me; however, yielding to prejudice, I rejoiced that eggs were not numbered among my favorite edibles.

The difficulties of all strangers not familiar with the language and idioms of the country were a part of my daily experience. Pancho was by that time master of the situation, and although evidently often amused, his thoughtfulness in relieving me of all embarrassment never failed. Though grave, he had a sense of humor. This was made evident, on one occasion, when I had been using a hot flatiron. Having finished, I told Pancho to put it in the cocinera, meaning the kitchen. I heard a low chattering and smothered laughter between him and the cook. Pancho then returned to my room, and half quizzically, half serio-comically said: "Please come to the kitchen." I went, when he placed himself in front of the cook, with his left hand on her shoulder, waved his right arm around the room and said: "Señora, look; this is the cocinera"— (cook)—"and this," again waving the right hand around the room, "is the cocina! Do you want me to put the plancha caliente (hot iron) in the cook, or in the kitchen?" Then with the forefinger of his right hand moving hastily before his nose, and a waggish smile on his face, the pantomime closed with, "No usamos así" ("We don't use them this way").

Another ridiculous mistake I made when I wanted Pancho to buy me some cake, and told him to get four gâteaux, forgetting that bizcocho and not gâteau was the Spanish for cake. Folding his arms, he quietly answered without a smile, if he might presume to ask the Señora what she wanted with cuatro gatos—(four cats!) As the house was already overrun with these animals that had flocked in from all quarters, Pancho naturally wondered why I wanted to add to my feline tenants.

Itinerant venders of every imaginable commodity were constantly passing, and nothing pleased me better than to hold conversations with them, which they too evidently enjoyed.

Soon after the episode of the flatiron, I heard the long drawn intonation of a vender and paid little heed to him, supposing he was running off a list of his stock in trade, such as pins, needles, tape, thread and other things too numerous to mention. Wanting none of these, I replied:

"Tenemos bastante adentro" ("We have plenty in the house").

A roar of laughter near by, and a familiar voice interpreted the man's question humorously enough; he was only asking if I wanted a chichi (wet nurse).

The common people of all ages were always bringing me regalitos (tokens of good will), and these were of every conceivable variety. A little girl whom I had often fed through the window came into the house with her rebozo drawn closely about her, saying she had a regalito for me. I supposed it to be fruit or flowers, and so motioned to her to put it on the table in the dining room.

In a moment she was at my side, saying:

"No quedarse allí" ("It will not stay there"), and going out I found a young chicken running around.

To pay fifty cents for every donkey load of wood, as I had done, seemed preposterous; and, as Pancho knew everything, I asked him to suggest some more economical system of purchase. He recommended watching for the *carretas* at five o'clock in the morning. Promptly at the hour indicated, I was before the barred window, when I heard the awful screech, thump, bump, and rumble of the lumbering carretas. About a dozen in a line, they advanced slowly—their great old wooden wheels wabbling from side to side—drawn by oxen with rawhide trappings; their sturdy drivers sandal-footed and clothed in cotton cloth, with an iron-tipped goad in hand, punching and pushing the beasts at every step. Here was the wood—the entire tree, roots and all—ghosts of the forest hauled twenty-five miles, rolling down the street on an antiquated vehicle. In response to Pancho's handclap, the manager of the caravan demanded fifteen dollars a load, the dollars being the only part of the transaction that belonged to our age. But the wood was duly bought.

Pancho had so far held the reins as to all household purchases, but in accordance with my ideas of independence and careful management, I announced that I was going to market. He kindly told me it was not customary for ladies to go to market—"*the mozo did that*"—throwing in so many other arguments, also of a traditional nature, that I was somewhat awed by them, though not deterred. Having been accustomed to superintend personally all domestic duties, to be bolted and barred up in a house, without recreation and outdoor exercise, induced an insupportable sense of oppression.

Walking leisurely along the street, absorbed in thought, with Pancho near at hand carrying a basket, I was attracted by the sound of voices and the tramp of feet. Glancing backward, I saw a motley procession of idlers of the lower classes following, which increased at every corner, reminding me of good old circus days, though without the blare of brass instruments, the small boys bringing up the rear. The very unusual occurrence of a lady going to market had excited their curiosity.

The market was a large, pavilion-like building, occupying the center of a spacious plaza. Little tables and bits of straw matting were distributed on all sides; and upon these the tradespeople, chiefly women, displayed their wares, fruits, vegetables, nuts, and other commodities.

On seeing me, every vender began shouting the prices and names of articles, entreating the *señora extranjera* to buy. But the strange medley, together with their earnestness, took my breath away, and I could only stand and watch the crowd. In the fantastic scene before me, it would be impossible to tell which of the many unaccustomed features took precedence of the others in point of novelty.

Notwithstanding the crowd, there was no disorder, no loud laughter or unseemly conduct. The courteous meetings between acquaintances, the quiet handshakings, the tender inquiry as to the health of each other, the many forms of polite greeting, were strangely at variance with their dilapidated and tattered condition, their soiled garments, half-faded blankets, and time-stained sombreros.

Whole families seemed to have their abiding places in the market. Babies! babies! everywhere; under the tables, on mats, hanging on their mothers' backs, cuddled up in heaps among the beets, turnips, and lettuces, peeping over pumpkins larger than they; rollicking, crying, crowing, and laughing, their dancing black eyes the only clean, clear spots about them—with and without clothes—until my head and the air were vocalizing the old-time ditty of "One little, two little, three little Injuns." But instead of stopping at "ten," they bade fair to run up into the thousands.

Parrots were there by the dozen. On seeing me, some began screaming and calling in idiomatic Spanish: "Look at the señora extranjera! look! look! Señorita, tell me your name!" The rest joined in chorus, and soon an interested crowd surrounded me. They kept close at my heels, inspecting every article I bought, even commenting on my dress, the women lightly stroking it and asking me a thousand questions as to where I came from, how I liked their country, and if I was not afraid of the Mexicans, and invariably closing by saying, "She is far from her home. It is sad for her here."

Here and there the amusing spectacle presented itself of men intently engaged in the occupation among us assigned to women, that of knitting and crocheting baby hoods and stockings of bright wool, and of the funniest shapes I ever beheld!

Vegetables, fruits, and nuts of all kinds were counted out carefully in little heaps, and could only be bought in that way, by retail, wholesale rates being universally rejected. I could buy as many of these piles as I wanted, but each one was counted separately, and paid for in the same way. I offered to buy out the entire outfit of a woman who had a bushel basket in reserve, even agreeing to pay her for the basket; but she only shook her head, and wagged the forefinger, saying, "No, señora, no puedo"—("No, madame, I cannot"). A woman held in her hand a corn husk, which she waved continuously up and down. On examination, I found it was butter rolled up snugly, which she assured me was "fresca sin sal"—"fresh, without salt." A new revelation, but in the course of time I learned to appreciate this primitive method, and that in this climate salt was a hindrance to its preservation for any length of time. At last I became convinced of the perfect and complete fitness of things, and of their self-vindication.

In making the tortilla, the corn is first soaked for several hours in a solution of lime-water, which removes the husk. Then a woman gets down upon her knees and beats it for hours on the metate. Small pieces of the dough are worked between the hands, tossed and patted and flattened out, until no thicker than a knife blade, after which they are thrown upon the steaming hot comal, a flat, iron affair something like a griddle. They are never allowed to brown, and are without salt or seasoning of any kind; but after one becomes inducted into their merits, they prove not only palatable, but they make all other cornbread tasteless in comparison, the slight flavor of the lime adding to the natural sweetness of the corn.

There were tamales rolled up in corn husks, steaming hot and sold in numbers to suit the hungry purchasers. I found that this remarkable specimen of food was made, like the tortillas, from macerated corn. Small portions of the dough were taken in hand and wrapped around meat which had been beaten to a jelly and highly seasoned with pepper and other condiments. The whole was then folded snugly in a corn husk and thrown into a vessel of boiling lard.

When I witnessed this operation, the woman whose enterprise it was, began singing in a cheery voice and making crosses before the fire, saying, "If I don't sing, the tamales will never be cooked."

In my market experiences nothing imparted a greater zest than watching the multitude of homeless poor taking their meals all around the border of the market. All the compounds they ate were complete mysteries; but before going home I had secured many of the various receipts from the venders. I found plain atole much the same in appearance as gruel of Indian meal, but much better in taste, having the slight flavor of the lime with which the corn is soaked, and the advantage of being ground on the metate, which preserves a substance lost in grinding in a mill.

Tortillas, likewise, lose their flavor if made of ordinary meal. Atole de leche (milk), by adding chocolate takes the name of champurrado; if the bark of the cacao is added, it becomes atole de cáscara; if red chile—chile atole. If, instead of any of these agua miel, sweet water of the maguey, is added, it is called atole de agua miel; if piloncillo, the native brown sugar, again the name is modified to atole de piñole.

The meal is strained through a haircloth sieve, water being continually poured on it, until it becomes as thin as milk. It is then boiled and stirred rapidly until well cooked, when it is ready for the market. As served to the wretched-looking objects who so eagerly consume it, one felt no desire to partake, but in the houses, there is nothing more delicious and wholesome than atole de leche.

All the stews, fries, and great variety of other edibles

were patronized and dispatched with the greatest eagerness. Barbacoa is one of the principal articles of food known
to the Mexican market—and is good enough for the table
of a king. The dexterous native takes a well-dressed mutton, properly quartered, using also head and bones. A hole
is made in the ground, and a fire built in it. Stone slabs are
thrown in, and the hole is covered. When thoroughly hot,
a lining is made of maguey leaves, the meat put in, and
covered with maguey, the top of the hole is also covered,
and the process of cooking goes on all night.

The next morning it is put in a hot vessel, ready to eat
—a delicious, brown, crisp, barbecued mutton.

As the process is difficult and tedious, it is not generally prepared in the families, and even the wealthiest
patronize the market for this delicacy, ready cooked.

From Pancho's manner I am sure he felt as if his vocation were gone, by the way I had overleaped the bounds
of custom in finding out things for myself. Nevertheless,
he managed now and then to give some of the venders an
account of our house, its location, and my singular management. But though looking mystified, he never left me
for a moment, no matter how long I talked, or asked ex-
planations.

We went into the stores, Pancho keeping between
me and the crowd. The shopkeepers were as much surprised and as curious as the people in the streets, to see me
marketing. But when the crowd of idlers closed up around
me, they were polite and solicitous to know if the "procession" annoyed me.

The arrangement of the merchandise and the method
of trafficking elicited an involuntary smile from me at
every turn; so, if the merchants, clerks, and the "procession" found fun at my expense, I was no less amused at
theirs.

Dozens of mozos bought from them, in my presence,
a tablespoonful of lard, which the agile clerk placed on a
bit of brown paper for transportation; three or four lumps
of sugar, a tlaco's worth of salt, the same of pepper, were

all taken from immense piles of these articles, near at hand, wrapped and ready for the purchaser.

Dainty china teacups hung closely together by their handles on the edge of every shelf, and up and down the walls in unbroken lines; but not a saucer was in sight, nor could a dish be had at any price.

Anticipating that I would take a tlaco, medio, and real's worth, like the *mozos*, the clerk took in his nimble fingers a few of the little packages; but my extraordinary announcement despoiled him of his ordinary sales.

Every eye was upon me when I had the temerity to ask for twenty pounds of sugar, ten pounds of coffee, and a gallon of vinegar. Sugar and coffee were abundant, but the vinegar was in bottles. He handed me one with a flourish, saying, "Vinagre de Francia. We have no other." I began to feel that faraway France had become my ally, having, like me, made an invasion on the "costumbres"; the only difference being that the vinegar bottles were jolted on the backs of meek burros, or in carts, a thousand miles, and I had arrived, safe and sound, by diligence.

I asked: "Have you ham?"—"No hay" (pronounced *eye*), ("There is none").

"Pickles?"—"No hay."

"Powdered sugar?"—"No hay."

"Crackers?"—"Tampoco" ("Neither").

"Salt?"—"Sí hay" ("Yes, there is some").

"Coffee?"—"Sí hay."

"Frijoles?" (beans)—"También" ("Also").

"Candles?"—"Sí hay."

"Potatoes?"—"Ya no hay, se acabaron" ("They are finished—all gone").

Going to market, a matter-of-fact affair in the United States, resolved itself into a novel adventure.

The heterogeneous assemblage of goods, and the natural and artificial products of the country, astonished me equally with the strange venders. There was so much that was at once humorous, pitiable, and grotesque, all of which was heightened when I reached home, and observed quite a number of the "procession" in the rear. Once over the threshold, Pancho slammed the door in their faces, saying, " ¡Son pobres todos, y sin vergüenzas!" ("They are all poor and without shame").

Every day the strange enigma unfolded itself before me, with accrued interest. My lot had been cast among these people, when in total ignorance of their habits and customs. My aim and purpose, above all things, was to establish a home among them on the basis of the one left behind. The sequel will show how well I succeeded. But while endeavoring to cope with the servants, and comprehend their peculiarities, I found nothing more amusing.

Our Mexican friends made daily visits to the house, and were always ready to enjoy with me the latest humorous episode furnished by the servants. I was often assured by these friends that the oddities of their mozos and other servants had not occurred to them, as so striking, until my experiences, together with my enjoyment, had presented them in a new light; and that for them I had held the mirror up to nature. This was only possible by keeping up an establishment, and making one's self part and parcel of the incidents as they occurred. It may seem that I was constantly involved in annoyances and disagreements with the servants; but such was not the case. Inconveniences more than can be named, were mine in the Sisyphean task of establishing an American home in Mexico, but if the reader can picture a perpetual treat in noting the strict adherence of the mozos to inbred characteristics, surely that privilege was mine.

As time goes on, and I no longer come in actual daily contact with them, in gay retrospect I see moving about me the phantom parade of blue-rebozoed women and white-garbed mozos.

Variety of scene and character was never wanting. If the interior workings of the household failed to interest me, I had only to turn and gaze through my barred window upon the curious street scenes.

On Saturdays, beggars were always out in full force,

and on these days my time was mainly occupied in conversing with them, thereby obtaining many threads in the weft I was hoping to weave. A very old man, stooped and bent with age, applied to me for alms, when I asked his age. "Eleven years," he replied. "Oh!" I said, "that is a mistake. Why do you think you are only eleven?"—"Because I was a little boy when the Americans came." From that date—as I understood it—life was over to him and mere existence remained; added years had accumulated, but he was still a boy. I soon found that this class dated every notable event from either the cholera, the advent of the French, or the coming of the Americans.

An American Negro was a welcome sight on one of these occasions, and his, good old-time familiar darky dialect, together with the sight of his kinky head, was refreshing. He stopped in front of my window, saying: "Well, now, mis', what is you a doin' heah? 'Marican white ladies neber likes dis country; dey isn't yo' kin o' people." He gave me his history in exaggerated Negro style; how he had been in the war with his young master; had been taken prisoner, made to serve as cook on a Yankee gunboat, had escaped, married a Mexican; and, after so many vicissitudes, had not forgotten his early training in his manner of addressing me.

Foremost among the objects that claimed my sympathy were the poor, overladen, beaten donkeys; they seemed ubiquitous, and the picture my window framed never lacked a meek-eyed burro, until I could not separate them from their surroundings. They were typical figures, and at last I came to regard any scene from which they were absent as incomplete.

They passed in a never-ending procession, bearing every imaginable commodity. I soon noticed that if the leader or "bellwether" of the gang stopped, the rest did the same. If goaded to desperation by the merciless driver, the only resistance they offered was to quietly but doggedly lie down.

Often dozens of them passed, with green corn on the

stalks, suspended gracefully about them, and in such quantities that nothing was visible but the donkeys' heads and ears, the corn spread out in fan-shape, reminding me of a lady's train, or a peacock in full plumage. The burros moved evenly and silently along, without an undulation to disturb the beauty and symmetry of the cornstalk procession.

Pancho's knowledge of burros was as profound as of other subjects. As fifty of them were passing one morning, he happened to see me gazing on the strange scene, when the oracle broke silence by saying: "Allí va el ferrocarril Mexicano" ("There goes the Mexican railroad"), adding parenthetically, "También se llaman licenciados" ("They are also called lawyers"); "tienen cabezas muy duras" ("they have very hard heads").

At last I was convinced that burros are possessed of an uncommon amount of good sense as well as much patience and meekness. Their shrewdness was intensely amusing to me when I saw how keenly they watched the arriero—driver—unburden one of their compañeros, and how quickly they jumped into the place to be also relieved of their terrible loads.

A man with a crate of eggs hanging from his head went trotting by, advertising his business by screaming, "¡Huevos! ¡huevos!" in deafening tones. Pancho, at his post of duty in the zaguan, called the vender with the long tangled hair and swarthy skin. After peeping cautiously around, he entered, when I went at once to make the bargain for myself, and to turn over another leaf in the book of my experiences. I wanted to buy two dozen, and handing him fifty cents, told Pancho to count the eggs. The man turned the half-dollar over and over—looking at me and then at the half-dollar; and at last handed the money back to me, saying: "No se venden así" ("They are not sold in this way")—"solamente por reales" ("only by reals"). I said: "You sell six for a real, (twelve and one-half cents), it is the same at twenty-five cents a dozen." The words had hardly passed my lips, when he turned and

looked me directly in the eye, with an expression which
meant, "Well, now, look here, madame, you'll not take
advantage of me in that way; I know the customary manner of doing business in this country, and there will be no
change in selling eggs." Pancho put in a plea for him, adding: 'Es costumbre del país" ("It is the custom of the
country"), which reconciled me.

The vender began counting slowly the fingers of his
right hand with his left—"uno, dos, tres, cuatro, cinco"—
then holding up the index finger of the left hand—seis—
and extending the six fingers, palms to the front, waved
them back and forth before his determined face, as in low
guttural tones that made me shiver, he said: "¡No, señ-o-
ri-ta, so-la-men-te á se-is por un re-al!" ("I will only sell
them at six for a real"), by dozens—never! Lifting his hat
politely, he took his departure saying, "¡Hasta luego!"
("I'll come again"). But I thought he need not trouble
himself.

Seeing everything and everybody so conservative,
running in the groove of centuries, reminded me that I was
losing sight of my own "costumbres." The little fireplace
in which the cooking had been done became distasteful,
and I longed for a cooking stove. A Mexican gentleman
whom I did not know, on hearing of my desire, kindly
offered to lend us one that he had bought about twenty
years before, but had been unable to have it used to any
extent, owing to the prejudices of the servants.

With the utmost delight, I saw the cargador (porter)
enter the big door with this time-worn rickety desire of
my heart. But when he slipped it from his head, the rattle
of its dilapidated parts made me quake with anxiety.

Both Pancho and the cargador exclaimed in one
voice,

"¡Caramba!" ("Goodness gracious alive!"), gazing
with puzzled expressions on the wreck.

The cargador was the first to break the silence that
followed this ebullition of astonishment.

"¡Qué atroz!" ("How atrocious!") he exclaimed.

"¡Qué barbaridad!" ("How barbarous!") echoed Pancho.

"¡Por supuesto que sí!" ("Well, I should say so!"), quoth the cargador.

"¡Pos cómo no!" ("Well, I'd like to know why it isn't!"), said the disgusted Pancho.

"She will never get a cook to use it, never!" The cook came into the patio to inspect the stove, and she too spoke in a low voice to the men, but folding her arms and emphatically raising her tone on the last word "el higado," which explained itself later.

As there was not a flue in the building, the stove was placed in the little fireplace. It had only two feet, which stood diagonally opposite each other, causing the stove to nod and bend in a grim, diabolic way. Being duly settled on its own responsibility by the aid of bricks, Pancho opened one of the doors, when instantly it lay full length on the floor. He walked away, looking back in disgust on the wreck. I ventured to touch the door on the opposite side, when, as if by magic, it, also, took a position on the floor as vis-à-vis; the servants exclaiming: "¡Muy mal hecho!" ("A very bad make, or job!"), "¡tan viejo!" ("so very old!").

"¡Pos cómo no!" ("Well, I should say so!") they all chimed in, the cook glancing at me suspiciously, and folding her arms as she added: "No, señora, I cannot use the estufa."

"Why not?" I asked.

"Porque me hace daño en el higado."

"Because it will give me disease of the liver; Mexican servants dislike stoves, and if you keep this one, no cook will stay here," she replied.

A blacksmith was called to renovate the treasure, but he also worked on the mañana system, taking weeks to do his best, and still leaving the stove dilapidated. The cook took her departure, and on Pancho's solicitation dozens came, but a glance at the stove was enough.

Politeness ruled their lives, and native courtesy was

stronger than love of truth. Without saying a word about the stove, they would say, "I would like to work for you—you are muy amable—muy simpática—amiable and agreeable; but,"—her voice running up to a piping treble—she would add, "tengo mi familia"—I have my family—or, "I am now occupied," meaning employed, by Don or Doña Such-a-one.

Pancho always looked on with keen interest during such conversations, his face saying, without a word: "I told you so; these cooks will never adopt your costumbres Americanos."

The stove was always falling, or some part dropping off.

At last one day I went in and saw it careened to one side—both feet off—and both doors down, suggesting that some canny hand had dismantled it. The wreck presented a picture painfully realistic; but before I had time to inquire as to the perpetrator, the stove addressed me:

"I was once an American citizen, bred and born. My pedigree is equal to any of your boasted latter-day ancestry. A residence of twenty years in Mexico has changed my habitudes and customs. You need not try to mend and fix me up—to erect your American household gods on my inanimate form. I am a naturalized Mexican, with all that is implied. I have had my freedom the greater portion of the time since they bought me from a broken-down gringo; for neither the señora nor the cooks would use me. I'll do you no good; if you mend and fix me up in one place, I'll break down in another. Content yourself with our braseros (ranges) and pottery. Accept our usages, and you will be happy in our country.

"You need not wonder at my rust-eaten and battered condition. I have lain undisturbed in the corral for nearly twenty years. During the rainy season, when the big drops pelted me unmercifully, snakes, lizards, centipedes, and tarantulas came habitually to take refuge inside my iron doors. So many different natures coming in close contact, there were frequently serious collisions. These warlike engagements have crippled and maimed me, more than the weather, or any service I have rendered. You will not find a cook who will even know how to make me hot for your use. Take me back to the corral! Take me back!"

III

"No es costumbre"

We were overshadowed by the dome of a magnificent cathedral, the exterior of which was embellished with life-sized statues of saints. The interior presented a costly display of tinted walls, jeweled and bedecked images, and gilded altars. Its mammoth tower had loomed grimly under the suns and stars of a hundred years, and the solidity of its perfect masonry has so far defied the encroachments of time.

The city of our adoption boasted an Alameda, where the air was redolent of the odor of the rose and violet, and made musical with the tinkling of fountains; and where could be seen the "beauty and chivalry" of a civilization three centuries old, taking the evening air.

Plazas beautified with flowers, shrubs, and trees, upon which neither money nor pains had been spared, lent a further charm. Stores were at hand wherein could be purchased fabrics of costly texture, as well as rare jewels—in fact, a fair share of the elegant superfluities of life; and yet in the midst of so much civilization, so much art, so much luxury of a certain kind, so much wealth, I found to my dismay, upon investigation, that I was at least fifty miles from an available broom!

Imagine the dilemma, you famously neat house-keepers of the United States! A house with floors of pounded dirt, tile, brick, and cement, and no broom to be had for money, though, I am pleased to add, one was finally obtained for love. My generous little Mexican neighbor and friend, Pomposita, taking pity on my despair, gave me one—which enabled me to return the half-worn borrowed broom of another friend.

Owing to the exorbitant demands of the customhouse, such humble though necessary articles were not then im-

ported; and the untutored sons of La República manufactured them on haciendas, from materials crude beyond
imagination.

Once or twice a year long strings of burros may be
seen, wending their way solemnly through the streets,
girt about with a burden of the most wonderful brooms.

These brooms were of two varieties; one had handles
as knotty and unwieldy as the thorny mesquite, while the
other was still more primitive in design, and looked like
old field Virginia sedge grass tied up in bundles. They
were retailed by men who carried them through the streets
on their backs.

For the rude character of their brooms, however, the
manufacturers are not to blame, but the sterility of the
country, and the failure of nature to provide suitable
vegetable growths.

Every housekeeper takes advantage of the advent of
the escobero (broommaker), to lay in a stock of brooms
sufficient to last until his next visit. It was two months before an opportunity of buying a broom, even from a
"wandering Bavarian," was afforded me, and during
that time I came to regard Doña Pomposita's gift as the
apple of my eye.

"¡Mer-ca-ran las es-co-bas !" One morning a new sound
assailed my ears, as it came up the street, gathering force
and volume the nearer it approached. I heard it over and
over without divining its meaning. But at last a man entered our portal and in a tone that made my hair stand
on end and with a vim that almost shook the house, he
screamed—"¡Es-co-bas, señ-o-ra !"—drawling each word
out as long as a broom handle, then rolling it into a low
hum, which finally died into a whispered—"Will you buy
some brooms ?" Had he known my disposition and special
fondness for broom handles—without reference to my
household need—he would have brought them to me directly, dispensing with his earsplitting medley—to a
woman for three months without a broom!

On ascertaining that the escobero would not visit the

city again for some time, I bought his entire stock, and laid them up with prudent foresight, against the possibility of another broom famine.

With a genuine American spirit, I concluded to have a general house cleaning, and, equipped with these wonderful brooms, with Pancho's assistance the work began. The first place demanding attention was the immense parlor, with its floor of solid cement. Pancho began to sweep, but the more he swept, the worse it looked—ringed, streaked, and striped with dust. I thought he was not using his best efforts, so with a will, I took the broom and made several vigorous strokes, but to my amazement, it looked worse than ever. In my despair a friend came in, who comprehended the situation at a glance, and explained that floors of that kind could not be cleaned with a broom; that amoli—the root of the ixtli (eastly)—soaproot—applied with a wet cloth, was the medium of renovation.

The amoli was first macerated and soaked for some time in water. A portion of the liquid was taken in one vessel and clear water in another. The cleansing was done in small squares, the rubbing all in one direction. The effect was magical—my dingy floor being restored to its original rich Indian red.

Now and then, while on his knees, rubbing away with might and main, Pancho would throw his eyes up at me with a peculiar expression of despair, while he muttered in undertone: "No es costumbre de los mozos lavar los suelos" ("It is not customary for mozos to wash floors").

Insatiable curiosity is the birthright of the poor of Mexico, and on this remarkable day they gathered about the windows until not another one could find room—talking to Pancho, who looked as if already under sentence for an infraction of the criminal code. They made strange motions with their fingers, exclaiming at the same time: "¡Es una vergüenza el mozo hacer tales cosas!" ("It is a shame for a mozo to do such things!") Others replied by saying: "¡Es un insulto!" ("It is an insult!"), while others took up the argument of the case by saying: "Por supuesto que sí" ("Why, of course it is"). But all this did not cause Pancho to give me a rude look or an impertinent word.

The floor now looked red and shiny, the windows were clear and glistening, and the six haircloth chairs stood grimly along the wall, in deference to the custom. My little friend took her departure, and Pancho moved lamely about, as if stiffened by his arduous labor.

In all my housekeeping experiences nothing ever occurred which for novelty was comparable to the events of that morning. I felt sure that when Mother Noah descended from Mount Ararat, and assumed the responsibilities of housekeeping—or more properly tentkeeping—on the damp plain, however embarrassing the limitation of her equipments may have been, she was at least spared the provocation of a scornful and wondering audience, greeting her efforts on every side with that now unendurable remark, "No es costumbre."

I afterward learned the cause of the commotion, when it transpired that such services as floor cleaning are performed, not by the mozo, but by a servant hired for the occasion, outside the household.

In a few moments my lavandera—washerwoman— entered, accompanied by her two pretty, shy little girls. Having complimented the fresh appearance of the house —Pancho now and then explaining what he had done— she informed me that the following day would be the día de santo—saint's day—of one of her bright-eyed chiquitas, and "hay costumbre" ("there is a custom") of receiving tokens on these days from interested friends. Acting upon this hint, I went to my bedroom, followed by Juana and the niñas, who displayed great surprise at every step. My red and yellow covered beds they tapped and talked to as if they had been animate things, calling them, "¡camas bonitas, coloradas y amarillas!" ("pretty beds, red and yellow!")

I turned the bright blankets over, that they might see the springs, and the sight utterly overcame them. Their astonishment at the revelation of such mysterious and luxurious appendages made them regard me with mingled awe, astonishment, and suspicion. The mother struck the springs with her fists, and as the sound rang out and vibrated, the children retreated hastily, shaking with alarm.

Wishing to conform to the customs, and remembering Juana's hint, I unlocked my "Saratoga." The chiquitas stood aside, fearing, I suppose, that from the trunk some frightful apparition might spring forth. When the lid went back they exclaimed: "¡Válgame Dios!" ("Help me, God"), and crossed themselves hastily, as if to be prepared for the worst. I invited them to come near, at the same time opening a compartment filled with bright flowers and ribbons.

This was a magnet they could not resist, and overcoming their fears, they came and stood close to the trunk, now and then touching the pretty things I exhibited to their wondering eyes. I gave each of them a gay ribbon, and while they were talking delightedly and caressing the pretty trifles, by some mischance the fastening of the upper tray lost its hold. Down it came with a crash—being still heavily packed—and away went the children, screaming and crying, one taking one direction, the other another.

We went in pursuit of them, and when found, one was crouching down in the courtyard under a rosebush, while the other stood in terror behind the heavy parlor door. Both were shaking, their teeth chattering, while they muttered something about "¡el diablo! ¡el diablo!"

By this time I understood the line which people of this class in Mexico unflinchingly draw between their own humble station and mine, yet I felt moved to treat the frightened children with the same hospitality which in my own land would have proved soothing under similar circumstances. Acting upon this inspiration, I went quickly and brought a basin of water to wash their tear-stained faces. To my utter surprise, they exclaimed in the same breath: "¡No lo permito!" ("I cannot permit it!") "No es costumbre."

The mother approached me with an expression of

deep concern and seriousness in her eyes, and with her forefinger raised in gentle admonition. Looking me earnestly in the face, she began moving her finger slowly from side to side directly before my eyes, saying: "Oiga, señorita, sepa V. que en esta tierra, cuando nosotros los Mexicanos" (referring of course to her own class) "tenemos el catarro" (emphasizing the last word on G sharp), "nunca nos lavamos las caras" ("Listen to me, my good lady, in this country, when we have the catarrh (meaning a bad cold), we never put water on our faces").

"Why not?" I asked.

"Porque no estamos acostumbradas, y por el clima, sale más mala la enfermedad" ("Because we are not accustomed to it, and on account of the climate, the sickness is made worse").

Thus ended the dialogue. But the children did not hold me responsible for their fright, and bade me a kindly adiós, promising to return again, a promise fulfilled every week, but on no account would they ever venture near *that* trunk again.

Pancho was determined to give to us and our belongings, as far as possible, the exterior appearance of the "costumbres." On entering my room after a little absence, one day, I found him straining every nerve and panting for breath. He had made a low bench, and was trying to place my Saratoga on it, but his strength was not equal to the task. The explanation came voluntarily that, on account of the animalitos, it was customary for families to keep trunks on benches or tables. I soon found the animalitos had reference to the various bugs and scorpions which infest the houses, and all trunks were really kept as Pancho said.

As time passed, Pancho constituted himself our instructor and guide in every matter possible, including both diet and health. He warned us against the evil effects of walking out in the sun after ten o'clock in the morning, and especially enjoined upon us not to drink water or wash our faces on returning, as catarrh and headache would be sure to follow. Supposing this only the superstition of an ignorant servant, I took a special delight in taking just such walks, and violating these rules, but every time I paid the forfeit in a cold and headache, according to prediction. I was now satisfied that Pancho was not only wise as a serpent and harmless as a dove, blest with a keen eye of discrimination, but also a first-class health officer, and in the movement of his forefinger lay tomes of reason and good sense. But I had soon to discover that he would have no infringement of his privileges; and, come what would, he was determined to have his *pilón* in the market.

The servants who came and went often warned me that under no consideration must I go to market, but this was one of my home customs, and I could see no reason for its discontinuance. The system of giving the pilón (fee) to the servants, by merchants and market people, as I already knew, would be a stumbling block in my way. I had discussed in Pancho's presence my determination to go regularly, when I fancied I saw a strange light come into his eyes, which soon explained itself. He came humbly before me, in a short time, hat in hand, his face bearing the sorrowful, woebegone look of one in the depths of an overwhelming calamity, saying, that a cart had run over his grandmother, and he would have to leave. He had been so kind and considerate in every way—never tiring of any task he had to perform—and so faithful, that I would prove my sympathy and good will to him by an extra sum —outside his wages—which might be a blessing, and aid in restoring his aged grandmother. He walked off, as if distressed beyond measure, at the same time assuring me that he would send his comadrita (little godmother of his children) and her husband, who would serve me well.

They came, but it was unfortunate for Pancho. The woman was an inveterate talker, and soon informed me that she was not the comadrita of his children; nor had a cart run over his grandmother; in fact, he had none, as she had died before Pancho was born. This was a new phase of the subject, but I was not long in solving the enigma. He had been goaded long enough by my American methods; he had become the butt of ridicule from his friends, and now he would assert himself.

However well he was treated in our house, to be called upon to surrender the most precious boon of all his "costumbres"—the market fees—never! But to wound my feelings in leaving was far fom his wishes, so he shrewdly planned and carried out the tragic story of the mishap to his grandmother.

The comadrita introduced herself with chastened dignity as Jesusita López; but with head loftily erect, and an air of much consequence, informed me that the name of her marido—(husband)—was Don Juan Bautista (John the Baptist), servidores de V.—("your obedient servants").

She smiled at every word, a way she had of assuring me of her delight in being allowed to serve me, but at the same time, glanced ominously at the cooking stove. The smile lengthened into a broad grin when Don Juan Bautista came in sight; in her eyes he was "kingdoms, principalities, and powers." Together they examined the stove—talking in undertone—stooping low and scrutinizing every compartment. At last Don Juan Bautista arose, and turning to me said, "Jesusita cannot cook on this máquina Americana" (American machine).

"Why?" I asked. He straightened himself up to the highest point, half on tip toe, at the same time nodding his head, and pointing his forefinger at Jesusita, emphatically replied:

"Because it will give her disease of the liver—como siempre—as always, with the servants here."

On going to the kitchen a little later, I was surprised to see the gentle Jesusita seated in the middle of the floor, by a charcoal fire, with all my pottery vessels in a heap beside her. Meats, vegetables, and water were all at hand, and she was busily engaged in preparations for dinner.

I told her to come and see how well she could cook on that American machine, but she only answered, "No es costumbre;" besides, "Don Juan Bautista said it would give her the enfermedad, or sickness, before mentioned—and no man knew more than he"—which meant I should use my own machine.

I called upon Don Juan Bautista to go with me to market, when he at once entered into a lengthy discourse about ladies going to such places; that the gente decente (people of pedigree) never did such things; that "the people in the streets and markets would talk much and say many things." But of this I had already had a foretaste.

I was about to lead the way through the big door, when Jesusita came forward and laid her soft hand upon me, saying: "Señora, *do* not go; Juan knows better than you about such business. In this country ladies like you send the mozo." But I was proof against her persuasive eloquence. To surrender my entire nationality and individuality was not possible for a good American.

The pair talked aside in low undertone, which I watched with feigned indifference and half-closed eyes. Jesusita glanced commiseratively at me, as if she had used her best efforts to no purpose; but Don Juan Bautista threw his most determined and unrelenting expression upon me, as if to say: "Well, she has had enough warning; now the responsibility rests on her own shoulders!"

He looked back at Jesusita as he stepped from the door, nodding his head—"Well, I will go; but she will wish she had not gone!"

In the market Juan Bautista never left me for a moment, inspecting closely everything I bought—now and then throwing in a word when he thought I was paying too much. He counted every cent as fast as I paid it out, and noted every article placed in the basket. I had nearly completed my purchases, and was talking to a woman about the prospect for butter—regretting the difficulty of getting it—when she leaned across the table, waggling that tireless forefinger at me, saying, "En este tiempo ya no hay, no es costumbre" ("At this time of the year there is none"), Juan Bautista chiming in (with the interminable waggle of his forefinger also), "¡No! ¡no hay! ("No, indeed, there is none").

The last purchase was made, and I was about closing my purse, when glancing up, I saw Juan Bautista's great merciless eyes fixed upon me, while he said in a firm voice: "But, mi pilón, señora!" This is the custom of the country. If you stay at home, I get my pilón from the merchants and market people; if you come—I must have it anyhow. A wrangle was impossible, and handing him dos reales (twenty-five cents), I went home a far wiser woman.

Jesusita looked proudly upon the towering form of Juan Bautista as he entered the portal—basket in one hand, dos reales in the other. Not a word was spoken between them, but looks told volumes. *She* knew what Juan could do, and *he* had proved to her his ability to cope with the stranger from any part of the world. To myself I confessed that in Don Juan Bautista I had found a foeman worthy of my steel.

I asked him to light the fire in the stove and I would make another effort to instruct Jesusita in its management. He went about it, while I withdrew for a few moments to my room. Very soon I noticed that the house was full of smoke. Supposing it to be on fire, I ran to the kitchen, which was in a dense fog, but no fire visible. Nor was Jesusita or Don Juan Bautista to be found. The cause of the smoke was soon discovered. He had built the fire in the oven, and closed the doors!

I clapped my hands for them, according to custom; but they came not. I then found them sitting in the shady court; Jesusita's right arm lay confidingly on Juan Bautista's big left shoulder, as she looked up entreatingly at the harsh countenance of the arbiter of her fate.

I gleaned from their conversation that she wished to remain, but her marido was evidently bent on going. On my approach they rose politely, and Juan Bautista delivered the valedictory, assuring me in pleasant terms of their good will; and it was not the pilón business—*that* had been settled—but the certainty that Jesusita's health would be injured by using the cooking stove decided him.

He said they would go to their *"pobre casa"*—I knew they had none; then gathering up their goods and chattels, with the unvarying politeness of the country, "Hasta otra vista" ("Until I see you again"), ¡Vaya V. con Dios!" ("May God be with you!"), they stepped lightly over the threshold—looked up and down the street, uncertain which way to go—then out they went into the great busy world. Thus disappeared forever from my sight Pancho's comadrita.

In every new servant we employed new characteristics were developed. All agreed in their leading costumbres, yet differed in the manner of carrying them into effect, while their quaintness and individuality afforded me constant entertainment. Some came humbly, giving only one name, while others used much formality, never failing to give the prefix Don or Doña.

Their names were as puzzling as their hereditary customs. I found that while the Southern Negro had been shrewd in appropriating the names of such great men as George Washington, Henry Clay, and Thomas Jefferson, the Mexican servants had likewise availed themselves of the names of their own great men. I hired Miguel Hidalgo twice, Porfirio Díaz once, Manuel Gonzales three times, as also numerous others. But when a little, old, wizened, solemn-looking man, with a face as sanctimonious as an Aztec deity, wanted employment, and gave his name as "Pio Quinto" (Pius V.), assuring me he would guard well my front door, he quite took my breath away.

Among the many who came immediately under my observation was a newly married pair who had walked a hundred miles, seeking employment. They had neither beds nor bedding; nor, in fact, anything save the soiled, tattered clothing they wore.

The wife's name was Juanita, and knowing that Juan

meant John, I then supposed that the addition of the *ita*, signifying little, made it Little John; but a further knowledge of names and idioms revealed the fact that Juana was Jane, and Juanita little Jane. But I began by calling her Little John, and so continued as long as she was in my employ. The diminutive was peculiarly appropriate. I see her now—this patient, docile, helpful child-woman. Her wealth of shining black hair hung in a long plait; her eyes, soft, yet glowing with a strange, peculiar, half-human, half-animal fire.

When the rebozo fell from her shoulders, a dainty figure was revealed—the contour exquisitely rounded. Her hand and arm would have delighted an artist for a model. Her step on the stone floor was light and free—noiseless as that of a kitten. Her voice was plaintive, sweet, and low, accompanied by a manner so gentle, so humble—expressing without saying, "May I do something for you?" If I were sick, Little John would take her place on the floor by the bedside, hold my hands, stroking them tenderly, bathe my brow and feet, murmuring in pathetic tones, "¡Mi pobre señora!" ("My poor lady or madame"), which finally died away on half-parted lips, with "¡Pobrecita!" ("Poor little thing!")

I was curious about her family ties, and asked her of her people, a hundred miles away. "Have you a father and mother?" said I one day. The little form swayed back and forth. She made a low wail—the most pitiful heart-cry —a smothered pent-up sob, laden with all the griefs of Little John's orphaned life. With tearful eyes and bowed head, clasping my hands, she wailed out again and again, "¡Muertos!" ("Dead!") "¡No tengo más que mi marido!" ("I have only my husband"). The poor little creature's story was told.

In consideration of my many difficulties in this line, I was glad to give them employment, when, according to custom, they solicited a portion of their wages in advance. Having received it, the wife, ignoring her own great needs, bought material for clothing for her husband. She borrowed my scissors; and I, curious to see how she would manage the cutting, went to her room to note the process.

As thought Pancho about "fingers having been made before knives and forks," so thought this young pobre about seats, as she sat, tailor fashion, on the dirt floor.

Such measuring and calculating as she had, in order to get two shirts out of three yards and a half! I laughed until I cried over her dilemma, as well as over the solicitude of her spouse about the result. He was evidently deeply interested.

She was only fourteen years of age, which gave an additional interest and a touching pathos to her anxious devotion. I thought to myself: "Woman-like, you will give your last farthing, take sleep from your eyes, even die, for the man you love!"

She finally cut out the shirts, the material being heavy brown domestic, and with the same untiring earnestness drew threads, made tiny tucks in the bosom, and when they were completed, brought them to me for inspection. More exquisite stitching or more perfectly made garments I never saw; but, as might be imagined, they would have been a close fit on a mere boy. This, however, was no impediment to the enthusiastic zeal of this interesting pair, and the shirts were duly worn by his lordship.

All the money which they earned jointly, with commendable unselfishness on her part, went for his adornment, she continuing, with the aid of a calico dress which I gave her, the possessor of one suit and a half. With the same ever predominating feminine instinct, shoes were purchased for the husband; and very soon he was strutting about the premises as if monarch of all he surveyed.

In every possible way he made pretexts for errands that he might show off his clothes. His peacock strut was inimitably funny, and caused me unending amusement, though the smile was often checked by the thought of the poor little wife's unselfishness. The heart of woman is, after all, everywhere the same, and too frequently her devotion must be its own and sole reward.

One of his edicts was, that his wife should not dress fowls. The custom of skinning instead of plucking fowls exists in Mexico. But I was leaving nothing untried to have everything done according to my notions. One day, when he was detained away for several hours, I ordered a pair of chickens for dinner, and directed poor Little Johnny how to prepare them. Without remonstrance she went willingly at the task; but before the chickens were ready for cooking, señor, the husband, returned.

I was watching with bated breath, feeling sure there would be a tempest. He did not intend I should witness the dénouement, but I was determined to see the fun.

Without speaking audibly, he passed by where she was standing, wrenched from her hands the partly dressed fowls, and in a moment more disappeared in the corral.

I took another route to find my chickens, and instinct led me to the spot. On going to the carriage house, I found them with strong cords tied around their necks, suspended from the old vehicle. By hanging the poor dead chickens, he retaliated for my presumption in directing his wife to prepare them without his consent and in his absence.

My curiosity next led me to see whether he had hanged his wife, or was erecting a gallows for me. Searching about the garden and outhouses, I found the couple in an unfrequented walk. She was wringing her hands and crying, while he stood bolt upright, bestowing upon her every severe expression and word of chastisement at his command. His jetty, straight hair stood up all over his head, his eyes glittered with rage, his brown lips were white, and his teeth champed viciously! All this was accompanied by the popping of his fists together, in the most effective manner. Every time this tragic part of the performance was executed, she would jump, and give a fresh howl of agony over the disobedience she had so innocently practiced, saying: "Perdóname, no lo vuelvo a hacer" ("Oh, forgive me, I won't do it again").

The end of all this was that they took up their pallets of maguey and walked, leaving me to a pious meditation on the frailties and foibles of human nature in general, and on the peculiarities of Mexican servants in particular; and also to the disagreeable necessity of cutting the chickens down, and preparing my dinner singlehanded.

The meek little wife, guarded by her grim liege, looked back at me askant, slyly kissed her hand, and smiled. This was the last I saw of Juanita.

The mozo, of all the various servants, was daily becoming more and more a vexatious problem. Indispensable, but to the last degree puzzling, I was anxious to know at what point in my experience the tolerated or "customary" labors of this individual would be introduced. The time had now come when, as I feared, his entire vocabulary would narrow down to this one familiar sentence, "No es costumbre," and he would assume the immovable and useless position of a mere figurehead. My imagination was wrought to an exalted state of anticipation, and I knew not what a day would bring forth. Every day carried me nearer to the time of Mother Noah, and to a world of chance. Wood, when not in small pieces and sold from the backs of burros, brought root, branch, and top, on ancient carts with wooden wheels, larger than the Aztec calendar; dogs called "Sal" regardless of sex; the yellow of the egg white; corn husks sold by the hundred; vinegar from France; and the tomato, our delicious vegetable, here assuming the masculine prefix he-tomato (spelled jitomate); all these things formed a grotesque panorama of curious contradictions all safely fortified behind the cast-iron "Costumbres."

IV

A MOZO AND A TRIP

I thought I had heard of every loan known to man, even of the dire necessity of borrowing a broom, but to have reached the climax of borrowing a manservant was a supreme pinnacle of glory, to which even the loftiest flights of my vanity had never hoped to soar.

No high words nor outspoken disagreement ever occurred between the departing servants and myself, but the fact began to dawn upon me that they did not intend that their Mexican customs should ever be engrafted upon my American tree of knowledge.

Without a murmur of complaint, in almost every instance, these meek-voiced, studiously polite hombres would inform me that sickness in their families required their immediate presence. If I ventured to ask where their families resided, their replies varied according to the state of the weather or their good will to me. Frequently the answer would be, in Guadalajara, Zacatecas, or San Luis Potosí, neither of which places was nearer than three hundred miles.

In time I came to observe every mood and gesture, and could generally detect, some days ahead, the indications of a contemplated departure. I remember Don Miguel Rodríguez, as he called himself, who was determined to go away so silently that I should not suspect his heartless intention.

He had given me the gratifying information that he had no family, but, as the event proved, my hold on him was no stronger for this circumstance. He now looked at me as if to say: "Well, now, señora, you need not suppose that I do not understand your ways as well as our own customs. You have had no fewer than twenty mozos, and while they have all left you without the least disagreement,

I, Don Miguel Rodríguez, could explain all. I know why they have gone, but you don't. I am far ahead of you, poor ignorant gringo! Some day you'll know more than you do now!"

Each one in turn seemed to regret going, but at the same time showed plainly that my ideas of life, and of the management of a household were far removed from his own. But without a note of warning, or an intimation of his purpose, Don Miguel took his hat in hand, turned his head across his shoulder, while the most cynical expression that could have been depicted on the face of a human being, or of a mozo, played about his eyes and mouth as I anticipated his movements, and awoke to the certainty that another faithful one had gone to join the band of invincibles.

The word pues is thrown in between sentences so generally, and has so many significations, such as, "well," "then," "therefore," "since," "surely," and many others, that it is not always easy for a stranger to settle the point. The servants, however, in pronouncing this word make an amusing abbreviation of it into "pos." And so it was that Miguel only said, "Pos entonces yo me voy" ("Well, now, I am going"), but his face and figure spoke volumes. I learned from each one of them in a different way, the hopelessness and folly of any attempt to change their hereditary customs or invest them with new ideas. Good and faithful enough they were until the impression was fixed upon them that they were losing their national "costumbres."

A gentleman who often visited our house, and who had been long a resident of the country, and who knew full well the importance of the mozo, and that the respectability of our household was at a low ebb without that all-important adjunct, kindly loaned us one of his trusties. Many times we were the recipients from him of this order of hospitality.

I used to think there could be no better opening for a good, paying business than for some enterprising Mexican to establish an employment bureau for mozos, and exact of them that their families reside in the same city.

Cosme, our borrowed mozo, was duly installed, with highly gratifying results. He was several degrees above the common herd, and more trusty than the best, having been trained by Doña Angelina, the wife of our friend. Cosme had a most benignant face, with an open, beaming countenance, and every duty he performed was done with the zeal and alacrity which had characterized no other mozo, within the range of my experience. The wish in my heart that took precedence of all others, at this time, was, that I should not be forced to the necessity of hearing from him that forever emphatic avowal which had ere now well-nigh crazed me, "¡No es costumbre!" I knew, if he once began, my peace of mind and happiness were gone.

To prevent it, every species of a now highly cultivated ingenuity was called to my assistance. The possibility began to haunt me like a grim specter. It was ever present day or night, awake or asleep. It never relinquished its hold upon my faculties. It was written on the wall, look where I would. It stalked up and down the street defiantly. It was astride every burro, and waved its hands at me, every turn I made in the house. My brain was on fire, my senses dazed. Where fly for relief? One could hope for a respite from the haunting custom officials, but this, all-pervading, deep-seated, and irrepressible, had screwed its courage to the sticking place and would not down. My only hope was in Cosme.

Things moved pleasantly enough for the first few days, in which Cosme charmed us by his kindness and watchfulness of the premises. I let him have his own way, about the manner in which his various labors were performed. I remained away from where he was, and not once had the dreaded expression fallen from his lips within my hearing, prior to our trip to Palomas. "The things which try people show what is in them." It so proved with Cosme.

Business called us to Palomas for a day. It was settled

that we should go in a carriage drawn by a spirited pair of dark mahogany thoroughbreds, which had never been known to let anything pass them but a mozo.

Cosme was up betimes on this particular morning. He was more nimble and ready than ever before, in contemplation of the pleasure of an airing in the country. He gave his own characteristic toilet many extra touches. He washed his face and combed his hair, and even borrowed the blacking, in order, as he said: "Para dar negro a las botas" ("black his boots"). So excited was he that he partook of little breakfast. The gray dawn silently melted into bright streaks of purple and amber, and the gorgeous rays of the sun threw a genial halo over the quiet city, as he made his happy preparations. When the mozo is promoted to the honor of an equestrian, his name changes to that of "peón de estribo" ("slave of the stirrup"). This will better describe Cosme's services on this occasion than to be known as simply a mozo. His was no ordinary service.

Custom requires the mozo to lead the way for vehicles, to look out for intruders, ward off interlopers, and to be on hand in case of accident. During long journeys, where the travelers camp out, or stop in mesones, the mozo goes ahead and arranges for the accommodation of the entire party. Not even a drive within the city limits is contemplated without the mozo leading the way, although every route is thoroughly understood by the driver. He is to be relied upon in his representation as to the safety or expediency of any route or mesón.

On this particular morning we went all around our half of the castle, bolting and barring windows and doors, so that even a cat might not intrude during our absence.

A first-class riding horse of large size was scarce indeed, although it was hard to find a really bad-looking one, for, owing to their Andalusian blood, they were all graceful and spirited. It had been our good fortune to procure a large, magnificent animal to be used solely for this purpose. His flowing tail touched the ground, and his mane was long and glossy. He was docile, and frequently ate sugar or salt from my hand. At a moderate speed his gait was easy and comfortable for the rider, but when urged to unusual exertion, it became something terrible. This horse Cosme mounted. Never did mozo start out with prospects more flattering for a pleasant canter over the smooth roads, than did Cosme on that 18th day of September.

After passing through the narrow streets, our road lay for the most part across the usual Sahara-like expanse of country, only varied by the line of mountains on one hand, and on the other by several cotton factories, with their groves of cedar and other evergreens. They were not imposing, but by comparison with the neighboring monotony, to my tired eyes, were as interesting as the most famous castle on the Rhine.

Once or twice we passed strings of burros, overladen with marketable commodities—*pulque* in sheepskins, filled even to the feet with the favorite beverage; also wood, stone for building purposes; and whole families of human beings were sometimes perched upon one of these weary animals.

By far the most charming sights were several beautiful mountain cascades which gushed at intervals from the rocks in clear streams of sparkling purity. Far up in the ledge of a precipice or declivity, a spring burst forth suddenly, then dropping in a glistening fall, broke away down the scraggy mountain side in a foaming cascade, and, having disported itself in a thousand lights and shapes of beauty, quietly gathered itself together, and flowed away, a musical murmuring brook.

But Cosme took heed to none of these agreeable interludes in the monotony, nor of the monotony itself. He was otherwise engrossed. Intent upon keeping bravely in front of us, where custom had placed him, it became necessary for him to travel faster and faster, until his gallant steed was finally dashing along at the maddest possible rate. There was no restraining our fiery team, and, of course the faster they traveled the worse for poor Cosme. Ob-

livious to passing objects, the merciless animal bounced
Cosme up and down, but he held on bravely, his arms
broadly akimbo, his linen blouse floating out in horizontal
lines, his sombrero dancing up and down, as if to keep pace
with himself. He swayed backward and forward, jolted
and jostled as he kept up his wild career! Now and again
he ventured to turn and look back, as if to implore us not
to go so fast; but our horses' spirits could not be checked;
there was no help for Cosme!

Once, when hedged in by an impassable barrier of
stone on one side, and a line of determined burros on the
other, we were near enough to call aloud: "Cosme, go
more slowly! ride in the rear!" The temptation and
pressure of circumstances were too great, and once again,
after an interval of rest, my ears were greeted by the feeble,
halting voice of Cosme, uttering in hollow accents: "¡Pos
no es costumbre!"

That grim specter of departed mozos was again
thrust at me. But what recourse had I?—what vengeance
dared I seek upon this poor untutored boy, for his deep
devotion to what he considered the duty of his office? If
Cosme had died on the road, or a hundred robbers had
surrounded and threatened his life and property, except
he rode in the rear of the carriage, he would have forfeited
his all, and his body would have been found, where all
good mozos like to be—in front.

When Palomas was reached, and our horses were
reined in preparatory to halting in front of the house
where we were to spend the day, an amusing spectacle
greeted us. Faithful Cosme was lying on the ground. The
whites of his eyes only were visible; he quaked and shook,
as if in convulsion; his tongue lolled from his mouth, and
his whole attitude bespoke utter prostration. On stepping
from the carriage, I ventured to go near him, and inquire
as to the nature and extent of his injuries. Between chattering teeth and spasmodic jerks he raised himself on his elbow, saying: "El caballo anda muy duro" ("The horse
goes very hard")—"y tengo mucho dolor de cabeza"

("and I have a bad headache"). Shortly afterwards when he appeared before me again, he had a green leaf pasted on either temple—the sovereign remedy of the common people for headache.

Palomas is a small village, with little to recommend it save that it is picturesquely situated in a pass—Cañón de las Palomas (Pass of the Doves)—in the Sierra Madre Mountains, which here separate the valley of Saltillo from the tablelands leading to San Luis Potosí. It has a thousand inhabitants, consisting for the most part of persons employed in the cotton factory, the leading industry, shepherds and laborers on the adjacent farms.

Rising somewhere amid the heights which frown down upon the inoffensive village a stream of pure, sparkling water resolves itself into quite an imposing cascade, making, at one jump, a fall of perhaps fifty feet, thence flowing, broken and frothing, along its tortuous way through the pass. Here the stream is deflected from its natural bed into a ditch to furnish water power for a cotton factory of one hundred looms, and having served this purpose, it is taken through irrigating ditches, and spread over the corn and wheat fields of the Saltillo valley. The falling stream is hemmed in on one side by the jagged gray rocks, which rise up, naked and solemn, to grand heights—speaking, in their stern silence, unutterable things.

On the other side, we beheld the verdure of the native grasses, which lent beauty and color to the landscape after the destitution of the bare scenery of our monotonous sixteen-mile ride, and a touch of gentleness to this otherwise rugged and awe-inspiring scene. My imagination readily saw in the crags and serried peaks the likeness to some towering cathedral, and I almost heard the chimes from its turret. In fancy the silent multitude passed in and out at the doors of this imaginary temple, to whisper their petitions, and then disappear in the deep recesses of the rocks.

It was through the Cañon de Palomas that General

Miñon, who commanded a wing of Santa Anna's cavalry during the American war, was sent to flank General Taylor, from the Agua Nueva, on the day of the battle of Buena Vista. Had General Taylor met with defeat, this cavalry force would have been in Saltillo almost as soon as Taylor's army.

The neighboring mountains are covered with extensive pineries, yielding large quantities of lumber, tar, pitch, and turpentine, which find a market near home.

The house of the *hacendado*, where we spent the day, was typical of all houses in the towns and villages—a plain adobe structure, low, flat, and with simple pounded, earthen floors. We had scarcely entered the best room of the house, when one of my favorite Mexican processions approached the big door. A string of fifteen meek-looking donkeys laden with wood marched solemnly through the main hall just as they did in my own house, followed closely by the driver, uttering his characteristic "tschew! tschew!"—and punching them at every step.

The parlor had its line of plain home-manufactured chairs, arranged methodically around the sides of the room, as close together as they could possibly be placed. At the extreme end, farthest from the door, was a home-contrived sofa, or divan, which extended almost the entire length of the room. It was built into the wall, having only the front legs visible. Its height was nearly two feet from the floor. At either end were seven hard stiff cotton pillows elaborated with Mexican lace, the product of a universal feminine instinct. The covering was a gay chintz, which was fastened to the framework as a cushion, and the upholstering was completed below by a valance of the same fabric. The rocking chairs—home-manufactured also— occupied their normal attitudes as vis-à-vis, at either end of the sofa. I was tired from the long drive, and the rocking chairs had an inviting look, so without ceremony I ventured to take one. Instantly three women came to me, all laying their hands tenderly about me, and with one voice insisted that I must occupy the sofa. To ascend this wonderful structure—"la sofacita," as it was called—I found it necessary to give a spring and a leap, almost as if vaulting into a saddle.

An unusual bustle and commotion about the house, and the continual passing back and forth of so many people, made it evident that some exciting event was about to take place. Two doctors were to perform some surgical operations. About half a dozen girls were suffering from enlarged tonsils, which it had become necessary to remove. The girls belonged to different families, and this fact set me to speculating as to whether enlarged tonsils were contagious, customary, or due to the climate. Having already received so many proofs of their martyr-like devotion to their customs, I was prepared to adopt the second hypothesis upon the slightest evidence. When the surgeons were ready, the father of the oldest girl, with great tenderness, placed her in a chair. The mother fled to the corral to avoid the sight of her child's distress and pain. As soon as the girl was in a position ready for the instrument, she would jump, and wring her hands, crying and solemnly declaring, she could not, and would not, submit to the operation. All the neighbors came in to look on, and with difficulty she was finally held down by the strong arms of her father and one of the surgeons—and the work was done. The father with deep concern, murmured something, to my ear almost inaudible, but he kissed the girl again and again; and at last the words came: "My poor child! my baby! my sweet, good girl!"

The other girls were soon induced, by the gay spirits and complacence of the first, to be seated and have a similar operation performed. I thought of the well-known fable of the fox, when the tree had fallen on his tail, depriving him of that useful appendage, when with characteristic cunning, he told the other foxes that to wear no tail was the mode, and thereupon no-tailed foxes at once became the prevailing style. An old woman, who looked like a servant, came in and performed various, and, to me, amusing incantations with the forefinger of her right hand;

keeping up at the same time a continuous mumbling of some incoherences peculiar to her class.

The curiosity that was manifested by the crowd, and the earnest inspections that took place after the operations were made, and the vigilance with which the girls watched the disposition of their bereft members provoked a smile. It reminded me of childhood days, when we jealously guarded a tooth when it fell out, for fear that a pig might get it, and the dire consequence follow of a pig's tooth taking the place of the lost one.

If one thing more than another surprised me, it was the fact that almost without exception, all the family and the people gathered at the house of our host were afflicted with a distressing form of catarrh.

At such an altitude and in a clime so salubrious and bracing, high up in the mountains, with an atmosphere dry and pure, that either lung, nasal, or throat troubles should exist, afforded food for reflection.

Cosme, although sadly battered and bruised, managed to creep to the window, and look on at the result of the operations. On seeing what was going on, he muttered indistinctly: "¡Caramba!" "Good gracious!")—"¡Por Dios santo!" The painful experiences of his ride established a community of suffering between himself and the damsels, which gave intense pathos to his words.

About fifty persons had assembled in the house, or hung about the windows. I was so intensely absorbed in studying the strange dark faces and party-colored costumes that it was some time before it dawned upon me that I was, if possible, an object of still greater interest to them than they to me. I spoke to one or two of the women, and reassured by my friendly tones, they approached me. Soon others followed, when I became the center of an extended group—every one regarding me with almost unappeasable curiosity.

Everything about me, to the most trifling detail, filled them with childish astonishment. As their shyness vanished, they became as familiar as children. They toyed

with the banged hair on my forehead, saying in amused
tones: "¡Qué bonitas están!" "¡Qué chulas!" ("How
pretty they are!")

They took off my hat gently, and tried it on, one after
another. They felt the texture of my dress—a very simple,
navy blue nun's veiling—evidently regarding it as something unapproachably splendid. Then my fan caught their
attention. It was the color of the dress, and strewn with
red roses. They held it close to the dress, then to the hat,
comparing them, and the fact that all three corresponded
in color, struck them immediately as decidedly the proper
thing. "She has good taste!" they said approvingly to one
another—"Yes, very good taste!—very good manners!—
a very fine lady!"

One of them fingered a knot of red and blue ribbons
at my throat, saying: "From France? No such fine things
here!"—Everything fine, in their estimation, comes from
France. They seemed incredulous, when I patriotically
informed them that the United States, and not France,
had furnished me forth in all this astonishing glory. Before I knew it, one had picked the bow to pieces, and
drawn the ribbons out, to see how long they were. Another
called attention to the Newport ties on my feet, and compared them, with much curiosity, and some envy, with
her own shoes, which, after the fashion of the country,
were sharply pointed. All appreciated the greater comfort
of the American-made shoe, but ended by shaking their
heads—"Very nice—very pretty—but"—and what an
execrable *but*! "¡No es costumbre Mexicana!"

They were equally curious about my family relations,
asking me the number of my brothers and sisters, nieces,
nephews, cousins, and aunts—never stopping until I had
named them all, their location and business. When I mentioned a name, they immediately caught it up, and tried
to translate it into Spanish, showing much satisfaction
when successful. Their efforts in this direction were laughable.

They translated readily Willie, Guillermo; Fanny,

Panchita; Richard, Ricardo; Andrew, Andrés; but Walter was a stumbling block, they neither translated nor pronounced it. They asked me if in our country we had houses of adobe and windows like theirs with wooden rods outside? Their eyes opened wide and wider, as I described our houses as from two stories in height, to five, eight, ten and thirteen. They evidently thought I was drawing on my imagination.

When asked if in our country we used carriages, goats, and burros—had haciendas, ranches, factories, and mills, I described as well as I could our resources. They were convulsed when I told them that until I came to Mexico, I had never seen in my whole life more than six burros. They appreciated and sympathized with my lack of education on the burro question; for to be beyond the sight of a line of them was equivalent to being out of the republic.

Every one of the various persons with whom I chatted asked me if it were not very sad for me in their country. But I had not the courage to tell them it was sad for me; in truth I was so intensely interested in them, and their peculiarities, there was no room for dwelling on myself.

They evidently appreciated my friendly spirit and the willingness with which I allowed them to examine my toilet, not even resenting the liberty of one, somewhat more inquisitive than the rest, who lifted my dress a little to explore my hose, on which they murmured repeatedly: "She is very simpática," a word for which we have no exact equivalent in English, but which perhaps explains itself.

It was among these country people that I first observed any departure from the national type of feature and complexion. Some of them had glossy brown hair, gray eyes, and skin as fair as an Anglo-Saxon; while others had red hair, freckled faces, and pale blue eyes. The parents of one of these was pointed out to me. They were of swarthy brown complexion, with black hair, dark eyes, and in fact, all the characteristics which I had come to regard as typically Mexican. Among them all I observed the same gentleness of demeanor, and courteous bearing, which had already so forcibly impressed me in the city, among all classes.

Birth and education had nothing to do with it. It was an exquisite instinct, common to the people as a nation. Even here in Palomas, among a plain untutored population, of the laboring class, especially among the ignorant, wondering women who had dissected my toilet with such innocent complacency, it struck me, for in spite of their unconventional behavior, they were as gentle and courteous as royal duchesses.

About twelve o'clock, the family began making preparations for serving dinner, which I watched with keen interest. One of the daughters of the hacendado came into the parlor, and mounting a chair, on which she had placed a box, opened a small door high up in the wall, which I had not before observed. From this snug retreat—the alhacena —she carefully drew forth cups and saucers of exquisite china, as fragile as eggshells, and beautifully ornamented. When she had taken out four of each, she gently closed the door and left me wondering if it had an "open sesame" spring in the bolt; for I looked in vain for the little door, which when closed became invisible. I concluded it was a safe retreat for such articles of value in case of a revolution.

The table was spread in a bedroom. We took our seats, the host at the head, but his wife did not put in an appearance, nor indeed did any other member of the family. First of all, soup was served from the kitchen in quaint, glazed pottery bowls, elaborately ornamented on the outside with vines and flowers, and on top of each bowl was a hot tortilla. Next the national puchero was brought in on plates, the tortilla in this instance, being slapped down by our plates from a fork. This removed, a kind of stew, perhaps chile guisado, which I had seen in the market—was served on plates with a narrow green rim around them, and on each was placed another hot tortilla. The next course was roast mutton, served on plates which this time had a red rim—and again a tortilla. Next came a roast of pork, filled with spices and pepper. While hot enough to make one scream, it was nevertheless, delicious. With all these courses, we were served with salsa de chile bravo (green pepper sauce). Our host took great pains to initiate me into the merits of this sauce, but I could scarcely look at it without shedding tears copiously over its pungency. We had no vegetables, save the puchero which is described in another place; but when the last meat course was removed, we were served with a delicious quince jelly, which ended this excellent and hospitably served repast.

When dinner was over, and I was gratifying an idle curiosity by looking about the rooms, the eldest girl came in, and took her position on the floor, unrolling, as she did so, a handsome pair of slippers which she was embroidering. How strangely out of place they looked to me, in the hands of the girl seated on the earthen floor! I wondered who would be the one about those premises to wear them. But the design and the manner in which the work was executed would have been creditable in any country.

The extreme nicety and regularity with which the Mexican women, even in the plainest walks of life, carry out any contemplated design, with needle and thread, on linen or cotton, is quite remarkable. Time seems to have no value. It is the custom in many places for girls to learn all the dainty stitches, and while yet in their teens, begin to prepare spreads, table covers, napkins, and mats, which when they are married will constitute a part of their household goods.

When the wife of our host came in, she found me intently engaged in scrutinizing the bedspread, and began at once explaining its history. She said it was the work of her grandmother, who began it when a girl. It had been a part of her bridal outfit, and afterwards descended to her mother, then to herself. The material was bleached domestic, but the design was at once unique and ingenious. In the center was a large pattern of flowers and fruits,

with the daintiest vines, leaves, arteries, and traceries to
be imagined—all done by means of drawn threads and
spool cotton. Around the entire spread was a valance
wrought in the same exquisite manner. The space adjoining the border of plain domestic, above the valance, was
a kind of insertion, filled in with figures of girls and boys
swinging and dancing, women carrying water on their
heads, shepherds with their crooks, and donkeys with their
burdens—all truly represented by deft fingers, guided by
shrewd feminine observation. A long flat cotton bolster
had a case with several subdivisions at equal distances
apart, filled in with fine crochet insertion. The bolster had
first a covering of red, then the case stretched on, skin-
tight, thus exhibiting the pattern of the lace. Laid pyra-
midlike upon each other were ten pillows, each one a little
smaller than the other, and all decorated with the same
lace. The spread and pillowcases represented years of untiring, earnest labor, and also an inconceivable amount of
precious eyesight, which these people evidently regarded
as a mere nothing.

Altogether the day spent at Palomas was a most
agreeable one, and even now to recall it affords a high
degree of satisfaction. It opened to an appreciative eye
the inner workings of the home life of the plain country
people, in their original simplicity. Ah! peaceful Palomas!
—"Pass of the Doves"—name unique and suggestive, for
their soft melancholy coo! coo! coo! penetrated this
humble home from the clumps of trees near by. May no
ruthless innovator remodel your simple adobes! no insatiate gringo invade and despoil your sacred domain!
But throughout all time, may you and your honest people
continue to live out your lives, undismayed and undisturbed by any progressive, distracting or contaminating
influence! In primitive blissful ignorance and innocence
may your children live out their allotment of three-score-
and ten years, barefooted, bareheaded, and unsullied by
contact with modern galvanized institutions!

I watched Cosme with a humorous interest while he

was preparing for our return home. He looked at his valiant steed now and again furtively, shaking his head and muttering something about not going so fast on our return. Poor Cosme! It was the old story of man proposing and a higher power disposing. The air was fine and bracing, and when we were all in our proper places for the homeward journey, I will confess to no small amount of uneasiness concerning Cosme.

The numerous and long-continued adios of our kind host and his family, and their friends, were wafted to our ears by the evening breeze, and in a twinkling we were out of sight of the house and dashing along the highway toward home. The horses attached to our vehicle, were apparently fresher than when we started in the morning, and if we went out rapidly, the return was more rapid still. Cosme's horse dashed along before us with lightning speed, and soon made his hapless rider but a vanishing speck in the dim distance. The trip home was accomplished in almost half the time required in the morning.

On the outskirts of the city we halted for a few moments, in conversation with a friend, and Cosme, not knowing it, preceded us to the house. On arriving we found he had opened the great door, and there, on the bench in the hall, he was stretched full length, the most utterly exhausted, bruised and aching martyr that ever suffered for a cherished principle. In spite of the irresistibly comic nature of it all, I could not help feeling an acute sympathy for my poor servant, and Cosme, seeing it, was duly grateful. The horse he had ridden was walking about the court at will.

My dear little friend, Pomposita, had watched for our coming, and I had scarcely alighted from the carriage ere she came over and gathered me in her arms, saying that the day had seemed to her like a week, as she watched and waited for my return with feverish impatience. She clapped her hands, and laughed immoderately, when I related to her the amusing incidents of our trip to Palomas.

The next day Cosme appeared before me limping, while his countenance was indeed crestfallen and sorrowful as he said that he would have to leave our service, adding in a conciliatory way that it was not because he did not like us and our mode of life, nor that he would not willingly serve us until the end of his days, but he wished to learn the trade of a blacksmith.

The dreadful suspicion dawned upon me, that as I could not Americanize the mozo I would have to Mexicanize myself and household. Faithful Cosme! How sorry I was to lose him! At last I knew enough of the characteristics of the mozo to shrewdly suspect that his excuse was only a polite cover for his deep consciousness of the sufferings he had endured in our service the previous day. He did not intend to serve in a household where such an occurrence might be indefinitely repeated. He would be a mozo for the house; for the highway—never!

I made every effort to conciliate him—"never again would his services be demanded on such a ride." I walked about the court disconsolately, talking kindly to him. Nearer and nearer he approached the door. I followed, entreating him not to go; well knowing that if I lost Cosme—and all the other mozos had gone to San Luis Potosí, or some other faraway city, to see their families— not a shadow of opportunity remained to procure another.

An admirable feature in Cosme's composition was his love of truth. He had never heard the story of the cherry tree and the little hatchet, but his innate veracity was not to be outdone by anybody. Somehow I always felt that when Cosme did go he would express the real cause of his leaving and not quote, like his predecessors, a mythical family's imaginary demands. Nor was I mistaken. When the poor boy reached the door he halted, turned and looked mournfully at me, as though imploring me not to ask him to stay longer, while in pathetic tones he murmured, "Pos entonces yo me voy; adiós, señorita" ("Well, now, I'm going; good-by, señorita").

He stood on the threshold, perhaps for the last time.

when I again ventured to remonstrate, "Well, now, Cosme, why won't you stay?" Almost closing the heavy doors as if to prevent another appeal, and tossing his hat far back on his head, his eyes rolling, his face ashen but determined, he made the final *pièce de resistance* with admirable finesse. Catching the huge key and closing the door, so that he barely had a view of my face, while one foot halted on the threshold, with bent figure and eyes beaming kindly regret upon me, there came the inevitable movement of the forefinger before the nose as he faintly replied, "Porque tan fuertas son las costumbres Americanos me molestan y cargan mucho y tan pesadas que no puedo vivir bajo de ellos" ("Your American customs are too troublesome and too heavy a load for me to carry; I can't live under them").

The last that I heard from Cosme was one of the invariable parting salutations, "Hasta luego" ("I'll see you again"), followed by the invocation, "¡Queda con Dios! no puedo estar más" ("May God be with you! for I can't stay any longer").

V

THE CAPITAL

The City of Mexico is one of the finest and best built cities on the continent. The architecture is grand and massive rather than diversified and ornate. The monotony of solid walls and high-arched portals at first strikes the stranger with a feeling akin to disappointment, but familiarity brings only a deeper consciousness of the grandeur of the whole. A singular and impressive feature is the fact that not only is the site that of the ancient Aztec capital, but the general style of the buildings remains the same. The flat roof, the azotea, the square surrounding the patio, all belong to the past as to the present.

The Plaza Mayor, or Zócalo, is said to be unequaled anywhere. One entire side is covered by the cathedral, which occupies the site of the temple of the Aztec war-god. The National Palace, formerly the residence of the viceroys, covers another side, and stands on the veritable site of the Halls of the Montezumas. The other two sides are occupied by the shady portals.

The great causeways are still in use as leading high-ways, and the streets are laid out in symmetrical lines, running at right angles—north and south, east and west. Each side of a block has its individual name, but often the same is applied to three or four squares consecutively—as the three San Franciscos, the two Calles Plateros, "streets of the silversmiths," and the first, second, third, and fourth Providencias. A narrow street is called a calle-jón. An effort has recently been made to change this puzzling method by giving the same name to a street throughout its entire length.

I was much interested in the tradition of the "Calle del Indio Triste" ("Street of the Sad Indian"). A wealthy Indian cacique established his home there, and then became a spy upon his own tribe, steadily informing the viceroy of all their plans and intentions. He failed from some cause to make known to the latter a mutiny which was in process of execution. This gave the viceroy a pretext for the confiscation of his property. Poor and despised by his own people and held in contempt by the Spaniards, he took his seat on the corner of the street, weeping and distressed, refusing food or comfort, and finally, in this melancholy attitude, he breathed his last. His property passed to the crown, and with a view to teaching the Indians a lesson, the viceroy had erected the statue of an Indian weeping, in the same attitude as the real one, sitting with his back to the wall, which remained there until the house was demolished, when the statue was sent to the museum. But the street did not change its name.

The streetcar system is admirable. First- and second-class cars are yellow and green, and every ten, fifteen, thirty, or sixty minutes they leave the Zócalo all in a line, one after another, on their rounds, some of which include a radius of from ten to twenty miles.

Every moment in the day the ear is regaled with the unmelodious tooting of a cow's horn in the hands of the car driver. These men manage to extract more muscular exertion from their mulas than ever did a hard-hearted Sambo.

As the streetcar lines have their second- and third-class lines, with prices to correspond, so also is the cab system regulated.

The distinction in prices is indicated by flags. Carriages bearing a blue flag are first class, and may be had for $1.00 an hour, while a red flag is second class and costs 75 cents; a white flag shows a third class coach, price 50 cents an hour. No deviation from these rules is allowed save on feast days. But as those who dance must pay the piper, so, also, he who rides in a Mexican cab must pay the driver his fee of a medio for his pulque.

One great convenience in these cabs is a cord which is worn on the arm of the driver, one end being in the carriage, so that the passenger may at any time call an instantaneous halt without exhausting his lungs.

The ironhanded law at the Federal capital is unrelenting toward cabmen, and as the rates are posted in each vehicle and the drivers are all numbered, there is no necessity for an overcharge. Americans, with their profligacy in small change, are the most easily imposed upon, but if they make complaint the abuse is at once corrected, and the driver stands a chance of losing his position.

There is no fire department to speak of: as the buildings are either of stone or some other fireproof substance, a conflagration is of rare occurrence, and is a notable event of an ordinary lifetime. There is but one fire engine in the city, and perhaps in the republic, counting upon its venerable cogs and wheels at least forty summers.

Another machine, equally primitive, is the only water sprinkler. Its operations are chiefly confined to the Paseo; but it has many sturdy competitors in the mozos in white who throw bucketful after bucketful of water before their masters' doors.

No city is more peaceful after nightfall. Pulque shops, by order of the government, close at six o'clock in the evening, and are opened at the same hour in the morning. The city is so well patrolled that one may perambulate the streets at any hour of the night without fear of encountering rudeness. Little or no drunkenness is seen, though more than 250,000 pints of the beverage are daily consumed. The imbibers go at once to their homes, there to sleep off the effects of their indulgence.

The city lies in the lowest part of the valley of Mexico, like a deep-set jewel. From its location, and other unexplained causes, it has several times been visited with frightful inundations, which have threatened to wash it from the earth. The chief cause of these inundations is believed to be the proximity of the lakes, which lie at unequal heights around the city. When the summer rains filled the highest, Lake Zumpango, it would overflow into the next, San Cristóbal, and when that was full it in turn disgorged into a lower one, Texcoco, and so on until the waters overflowed into the plains of San Lázaro, and thence penetrated into the city. There is no danger from lakes Xochimilco and Chalco except in case of melting snows from Popocatepetl.

Seven times within the knowledge of man the City of Mexico has been inundated. Four times the calamitous visitation came in one century, twice in a brief interval of only three years; the latest occurred in 1629.

The finest engineering talent in the republic has been called into requisition to devise a system of drainage, but a wide difference of opinion as to the best means still prevails. Some favor a tunnel, but as the soil is spongy and treacherous, there could be no guarantee against its sinking. This, together with the prospect at any time of an earthquake, forbids the plan. Others recommend the extension of the Nochistongo, which is now utilized, and is partially effective.

Several engineering companies from our northern states have attempted to investigate the gigantic and dangerous task of draining the city, and if the problem be finally solved it will probably be by means of Yankee ingenuity and machinery.

When the great earthquake of 1882 visited the capital, it is claimed that the nearness of the water to the surface of the earth saved it from destruction. The opinion prevails amongst intelligent people that a thorough drainage of the city would increase the danger from this source.

The foundations of a large proportion of the houses are laid either in water or in marshy flats; and I have often seen a loaded wagon, carriage, or cart perceptibly shake a two-story house. The School of Mines, a massive and immense structure, has sunk more than six feet in the earth within forty years, so I was informed by Professor Costillo, of that institution.

Mexico has been termed the Rome of America, not only because of its temples and palaces, but also on account of its churches and other ecclesiastical buildings; but many of the latter are alienated from their original use, while of the one hundred church buildings, only half this number are now devoted to religious services. The grand Gothic cathedral rises majestically above all surrounding objects, the most conspicuous feature in the architecture of the metropolis. It is built of unhewn stone, and is five hundred feet in length by four hundred and twenty in width. The walls are several feet in thickness. This great building was completed in 1667, nearly one hundred years after its foundation, at a cost of two million dollars. Its exterior is majestic and imposing, and the interior gorgeously painted and decorated, its altars enriched with gold, silver, and jewels.

But with all its grandeur the cathedral is anything but a choice place for devotional exercises. True democracy is the rule, and the most degraded, unclean *lépero* has as much space allotted to him as the grandest lady or gentleman. This is undoubtedly the true spirit and intent of Christianity, but one cannot help being a little fastidious. I have seen men most earnestly engaged in their devotions, with dozens of chickens, and as many turkeys as they could carry, suspended from their persons; women with burro loads of vegetables on their shoulders, others with one or two papooses screaming and wiggling in their mothers' rebozos, all in such numbers as to forbid pious meditations.

Skirting the west side of the cathedral is a shady garden with fountains and seats, terminating in a most unique and choice flower market. At the corner, facing the Zócalo, there is a heap of curiously carved stones and broken columns, and, pushing aside the gorgeous screen of flowers and vines, the inscription may be read: "Stones from the bloody sacrificial altar of Huitzilopotztli, used afterward in the first temple that the Spaniards erected to the Christian faith."

The church of Santa Brigida (St. Bridget's) is the most modern in its interior arrangements, having comfortable pews and carpeted aisles. But Santa Teresa, with its exquisitely painted interior; San Hipólito, with the exterior of its dome of glittering porcelain mosaic; and grand old San Fernando, with illustrious memories and associations, whose timeworn floors have echoed the footsteps of generations—these speak volumes in their silence and mellow gloom.

Of public monuments and statues there are five— the most noteworthy that of Carlos IV at the head of the Paseo, which, with the exception of that of Marcus Aurelius at Rome, is perhaps the largest in the world. It was cast in Mexico, the first in the Western hemisphere. The statues of Christopher Columbus, President Juárez, and Cuauthémoc, the last of the Aztec kings, are all marvels of beauty and finish, and adorn the Paseo de la Reforma—the grand avenue or boulevard of the capital. This noble drive extends about three miles from the Alameda to Chapultepec, and is broad enough for six carriages to drive abreast. But usually they are driven in line, while the gayly equipped caballeros curvet in the opposite direction. Policemen are stationed every few yards. On either side the sidewalks are lined with pedestrians, in their "Sunday best"—groups of beautifully dressed children indulge in childish sports, the band plays, and all Mexico is jubilant.

There are five public markets. The principal one covers an entire block, but, despite its wealth of fruits, vegetables, game, fish, and meat, is a wretchedly forlorn place, having no building, but merely a collection of huts, booths, and tents, which are most uninviting to the stranger.

The public gardens number twelve, the chief of which is the Alameda, and are all laid out in truly Parisian style.

Excellent educational facilities are afforded at the capital. Among them are the School of Arts and Professions for Women, Industrial Schools for Men, the Academy of Fine Arts, Conservatory of Music, School of Mines

or Engineering, School of Jurisprudence, Military Institute, Medical Institute, Commercial College, Girls' College, Preparatory Institute for Boys (equal to one of our
best colleges), Deaf and Dumb, and Blind Institutes, the
National Museum, and a superb Public Library with one
hundred and sixty thousand volumes.

For the National Schools, President Díaz has pre-
scribed a course of study for seven years in agriculture and
engineering. The latter includes French, English, German, Greek and Latin roots, geography, drafting, mete-
orology, chemistry, botany, geology, architecture, agriculture, technology, surveying, bookkeeping, and political economy. The medical course also covers seven years,
and includes, in addition to the above, all the branches
requisite to the profession. Thoroughness is required in
everything, no diplomas being granted without proficiency.

I visited many of these public institutions of learning,
and found them admirably conducted. I was especially
interested in the School for the Blind, and surprised to
find the pupils outnumber the teachers only a little more
than two to one—the former numbering sixty-seven, the
latter thirty-one. The salaries of teachers range from
twenty to seventy dollars per month. On entering the
school a photograph is taken of each pupil and pasted in
a large book. By its side is placed a full description, with
age, date, and place of birth, and quantity and quality of
clothing. The object of the photograph is to prevent a possible substitution of one for another, and preserve the
identity of each pupil.

Musical culture is the leading feature here, as in every
institution of learning in the country. The orchestra
played, and a young girl of sixteen sang for us, in a rich,
mellow contralto which filled the building, selections from
"Il Trovatore." Another was asked by her teacher to read
for us. She began in a clear voice reading an account of the
entrance of General Scott into the City of Mexico. When
she read "he entered sin valor" ("without courage"), the
teacher gently interposed, and requested her to read in

another place, which she did, to my serious disappointment, for I was anxious to know in what spirit even a blind Mexican would read the history of that war.

The School for the Deaf and Dumb is conducted after the most modern methods, the pupils being taught articulation, only the older ones using manual signs. Many of the teachers have received a European education.

The noblest institution that I visited was the Escuela de Artes y Oficios para las Mujeres (School of Arts and Trades for Women), of which Juárez was the founder and benefactor. It gives to poor girls unequaled advantages for learning, without fear of the absence of their "daily bread," to make themselves independent of want. The government gives them comfortable rooms, two good meals a day, and furnishes many of the poorer pupils with clothing. Each girl wears a long, brown holland apron; their faces are clean, hair neatly braided, and every care taken that they may make, at all times, a neat appearance. Several hours daily are devoted to the acquirement of a practical education. Bookbinding, printing, bookkeeping, drawing, painting, music, embroidery are taught; also the manufacture of picture frames, and, on cunning little hand looms, cords and fringes of all colors for decorative purposes. The pupils upholster skillfully and artistically furniture that would adorn a mansion. There is a neat store in the building, belonging to the institution, in which the work of the pupils is disposed of for their benefit. They conduct a neatly printed weekly newspaper, consisting of four sheets, and called *La Mujer*.

In all the wise concepts of her Indian chief, Mexico has no higher monument to his greatness than this industrial school for the elevation of her women.

There are three hundred and sixty-eight pupils receiving the benefits of this institution, from misses of twelve years to demure matrons in middle life.

The public schools are numerous and well patronized. I was pleased to see the eagerness with which the pupils seized their opportunities for gaining knowledge. My American friend, Mrs. C——, has classes in English in several of these institutions, where I heard them reciting fluently in my own tongue. It is estimated that fully eight thousand people are now studying English at the capital.

The public charitable institutions are also numerous, and include the Insane Asylum, Foundling Hospital, House of Maternity, founded by Carlotta; Poor House, Leper Institute, and several hospitals.

The Monte de Piedad, or pawnshop, founded by Count Regla, is one of the noblest benefactions, enabling those whom misfortune has visited to realize or receive advances upon valuables without the risk of losing them. These pawnshops exist all over the country, and all classes can alike avail themselves of their advantages.

The city has four large theaters, the National being the second largest on the Western continent, but its interior furnishings are but a mockery in this age of elegance and luxury. Once gorgeous in their rich gildings and fanciful upholstery, they now appear in a sad state of dilapidation. There are many hotels, all kept upon the European plan, and the Concordia, which is the Delmonico of the capital.

The mercantile establishments do not generally possess in their exterior the attractions of those of our own cities. It is but a short time since a few of the leading merchants have had recourse to showwindows, but in these now are exhibited the choicest wares of home and foreign production—exquisitely set diamonds, rare jewels of all kinds, bronzes, statuary, and French china. Added to these are displayed laces, velvets, silks, and Parisian dresses, and an endless variety of foreign importations, including French dolls, the prettiest I ever saw. Once inside the stores, the activity and agility of the clerks, in their eagerness to wait upon you, are equaled only by their lack of system and business management. Be sure, however, that you will have an opportunity of purchasing some of the rarest and most costly dress fabrics upon which one's eyes ever rested.

The Monterilla, the stores along the portales, are the "Sixth Avenue" of the capital. The same classes of goods are kept as on Plateros, and for a much less price, a fact which holds in check the charges in the latter.

I saw comparatively few of our American dress fabrics in any of the stores; only domestics, prints, and goods of low grade. But there is no question in my mind that American silks, hats, ribbons, and woolens, as well as almost every kind of ready-made goods, would find a profitable market if only properly introduced. The portales is the place of all others to buy curios of every possible description.

A few practical words must be given as to the general lives of the people of the capital—the method of house renting, and the forms to be complied with before establishing a home there. Agencies for the leasing and renting of houses, accompanied by our modern advertising, are unknown. To secure a house, one must tramp up and down the streets looking for pieces of paper pinned to the iron rods of the windows. On finding one that suits, he must strain his neck out of the socket and wear out his shoes searching for owner or agent. Then he must procure a fiador—generally a merchant or man of business, who will act as security and assume responsibility in case of a possible delinquency. The contract is well worthy of attention. It is almost enveloped in stamps, and bulky enough for a treaty between foreign nations. After much delay and formality, this document is duly signed, and you are put in possession of your new domicile.

The familiar phrase, that "Three moves are equal to a fire," is here emphasized. One's earthly goods must be carried either on the backs of men or on the streetcars. If the first mode of transportation be resorted to, it is generally necessary to dispatch a trusty servant of the household with each load of goods, lest the cargador find it convenient to take his departure, with your valuables, for some unknown locality.

Houses are generally constructed on the vivienda

plan; that is, on one floor there may be from four to six establishments containing from two to six or eight rooms. But such smaller conveniences as closets are unknown.

Rents are high at all times, and in desirable localities excessive. Inside apartments, with five rooms facing the court, rent for $40 per month; of the same size, with one to four windows opening on the street, from $60 to $80, according to location. Houses are, generally, two and three stories in height, and the higher one goes, the more rent is demanded. For health's sake, the sunny side of the building is absolutely necessary—a fact considered by the owner in his assessment of rents.

Greater attention is now paid than formerly to the plumbing, ventilation, and general sanitation of the houses, but still there remains much to be desired. The drainage of the city is so very imperfect that it will be long, if ever, before the houses built many years ago can be made to fulfill modern requirements.

Many well-to-do families occupy apartments over business houses, and sometimes over pulque shops. The portero may be either a man or woman, who resides with his or her family in a little dark, damp apartment under the stairs. I have sometimes counted two or three turkeys, several chickens, a pig or two, dogs without number, and endless children, besides all the cooking and sleeping arrangements of the whole family, in one small room. When you ascend the stairs, the transformation is complete. Blooming plants, singing birds, carpeted halls and stairways, curtained windows and shaded balconies afford a striking contrast.

The climate, of which so much has been written, is exceptionally agreeable, yet difficult to describe. If one can conceive the delights of a crisp day in October, united to the brightness of a clear day in January, but without snow or ice, and, mingled with these, the lifegiving air of a balmy day in May, and then imagine twelve months of such weather, some idea may be had of this enchanting clime.

At the capital I observed the peculiar tints that settle over the mountain peaks in the late evenings. Looking upward from one street, the gazer sees a clear gray; from another, a liquid blue; from another, a bright rose or amber or gorgeous orange; all floating and blending together until the entire heavens are lit up by a bewitching roseate glow, which seems to vibrate gently to and fro in the thin air, while the whole superb canopy is gemmed with stars, which partake of the glowing tints surrounding them.

From my point of observation in the Zócalo, where both our modern gas and electric lights flashed their brilliant rays across the wide streets, I could see the sleeping place of a large proportion of the poorer denizens of the city—their roof, the broad expanse of heaven—their bed, the stone pavement, or at most a petate—the rebozo or serape forming their sole covering. Here, without inconvenience, these contented people slept, cuddled up, undisturbed by the gay throngs who walked back and forth around and among them.

Every climate in the world may be experienced between the seashore at Vera Cruz and the capital. Eternal snows lie upon the one hand; on the other, verdant plains and fertile valleys. Even the summer heat and drought on the tablelands are mitigated by the advent of the rainy season, which begins in May and ends with November. It is not continuous. The sun may be shining brightly, when suddenly the sky is overcast, and the rain descends in torrents, to be succeeded by sunshine. If two cloudy or rainy days come consecutively, the people find themselves quite aggrieved, and complain of the awful weather. But the rain usually comes late in the evening or at night; then the streets, ditches and canals overflow their banks and become merged in an open sea; but in the morning the water has disappeared; the sun comes out in all his splendor and cheering rays; the blue sky smiles, and all nature rejoices.

At the capital there are three distinct temperatures—

that of the sunny side of the street, that of the shady side, and that in the house. In the morning walk, as early as ten o'clock, on the sunny side of the street, the heat will be almost overpowering. On making a change to the shady side, the difference will be so great as to produce a severe cold, while the light wrap, worn with comfort in the street, will be found insufficient in the house.

On reaching an altitude of four thousand feet and upward, strangers, and especially ladies, experience a peculiar dizziness, which continues for several days, after which they usually return to their normal condition. At the capital the elevation above sea level is 7,349 feet, and during the first week after my arrival I was almost prostrated from this dizziness. Another peculiarity of the climate consists in the fact that it is considered by many to be dangerous to pass suddenly from a closed room to the white light and open air outside.

Still another climatic effect is, that the uncovering of the head is apt to produce a severe catarrhal cold. For this reason gentlemen never remove their hats for any length of time when out of doors.

According to the *Observador Médico*, the death rate of the city for 1885 was 12,008, of which 6,431 were females, and 5,577 males. The most frequent causes of death were pulmonary and tuberculous affections, which, with pneumonia and bronchitis, made up an alarming mortality of 4,292—about one-third of the whole. Contrary to what might be expected, only 179 deaths occurred from smallpox, while typhus and intermittent and malignant fevers claimed but a small number of victims. After lung diseases, diarrhea and dysentery were the most fatal, running up to 2,866. Allowing that the City of Mexico has a population of 350,000, the annual death rate is a trifle over 37 per 1,000. But if we consider that annually thousands of poor Indians from the hot regions come to Mexico and die from exposure and hardship, the real death rate will not exceed from two to three per cent. From its high rate of mortality arises the reputation of the capital for extreme unhealthiness; but with its primitive system of sewerage, imperfect drainage, and poor ventilation of the houses, no surprise should be felt. Any one who witnesses the repairing and cleansing of the immense sewer canals that are covered over in the middle of the streets, will certainly wonder that the death rate is not higher.

The number of funerals consequent upon such a large mortality is only equaled by the strange manner in which they are conducted. The highest dignitaries of the land and the humblest peon share equal honors in the mode of transit employed in conveying their lifeless remains to their last resting places. It was an astute nineteenth-century schemer who conceived the idea of employing the street railways as the best method of transporting the dead to the cemeteries. One man owned all the lines of street railway, and in order to carry out his purposes, he bought up all the hearses and their equipments, and thus compelled the public to accept his plan. It works admirably so far. The wealthy may indulge a hearse car, plumed, draped, liveried, and lackeyed, for $120, with an additional one, or perhaps two, for friends. The plainer cars, drawn by one mule, may be procured for $3, while others reach from $12 to $30, including one or two cars, neatly draped, for mourners. But to the stranger eye, accustomed to seeing the long cortege moving solemnly along the streets, with its hearse and weeping mourners, the Mexican plan seems repulsive and devoid of that respect which we pay to the lifeless clay of our loved ones.

A short sojourn, however, serves to convince the most skeptical of the "fitness of things," the Mexican method being far more expeditious and, it is claimed, less expensive than the old plan.

Any day in the week one may take a car for Tacubaya, and there see the Indians transporting their dead to Dolores Cemetery. I have seen four men bearing on their heads the coffin containing its dead occupant. For miles they tramp steadily along, themselves the only hearse, horses, cortege, or mourners. At other times one may see

a poor woman, bearing upon her head a plain little open
coffin, containing her dead child, with eyes wide open and
a profusion of gay flowers covering the tiny form.

VI

THE MEXICANS IN THEIR HOMES

Of the Mexicans Brantz Mayer wrote as follows: "I have found them kind, gentle, hospitable, intelligent, benevolent, and brave. . . . In fact, regard them in any way, and they will be found to possess the elements of a fine people, who want but peace and the stimulus of foreign emulation to bring them forward among the nations of the earth with great distinction. . . . There are of course in Mexico, as in all countries, specimens of egotism, selfishness, haughtiness, ill-breeding and loose morals, both among the men and the women; but, although we find these floating, like bubbles, on the top of society, they must not therefore be considered the characteristics of the country. . . . With domestic virtue, genius, and patriotism, no people need despair; and it should be the prayer of every republican that enough of these still remain in Mexico to reconstruct their government and society."

In speaking of their politeness, Mayer continues: "The 'old school' seems to have taken refuge among the Mexicans. They are formally, and, I think, substantially, the politest people I have met with. The respect for age, the sincerity of friendship, the results of reading and education, and the honest, unpretending *naturalness* of character, for which, over all other people I have ever met, I think the best of them are remarkable. . . . The fine benevolence of ancient friendship, the universal respect for genius, a competent knowledge of the laws and institutions of other countries, a perfect acquaintance with the cause of Mexican decadence, and a charming regard for all those domestic rites which cement the affections of a home circle may all be observed and admired within the walls of a Mexican dwelling."

Brantz Mayer, above all other writers, not even

excepting Madame Calderón de la Barca, has observed more closely and written more sympathetically and faithfully of Mexican characteristics. In dealing with this subject, it will be understood that reference is had only to the higher and more cultured classes of society.

During the more than forty years intervening since this distinguished writer gave expression to these views, ten years only of which have brought to Mexico the precious boon of peace, the changes occurring and the onward march of events in that country have proved the correctness of his assertions. With every possible distracting cause, calculated to foster and encourage ignoble traits and retrograde ideas, they have not only continued brave and patriotic, but their social and domestic institutions have remained sacredly intact. Let the unsympathizing comment as they may upon the hapless fate of poor Mexico, it is not to be gainsaid that perhaps no country in the world has politically presented a more desolate picture, nor yet one that speaks a nobler lesson.

But by sympathetic intuition a woman attributes to the women of Mexico that undercurrent of social and domestic regeneration which has purified and preserved her institutions. While the men have been engrossed in war and revolution, with their train of direful results, the women, in the seclusion of their homes, have kept an ever-faithful watch over the domestic virtues, and the happiness and welfare of those whom God has given them.

In repose, there is in the eye of every Mexican an expression of deep sadness which is hardly accounted for by recent history, however tragic, and must have been transmitted to the race through the miseries of martial conquests.

It has occurred to me that the women have inherited a larger portion of this constitutional melancholy than the men. I have been more convinced of it on meeting and conversing with them in their own homes. When the death of a member of the family was referred to, which had taken place years before—perhaps a son or a husband killed in battle—the grief seemed as deep and uncontrollable as if it had happened on that day. They are all patriotic, and if the country suffers, it is a part of themselves, and is reflected in their lives.

The Mexicans are by nature close observers of physiognomy, and, though shy, are sharp critics of the bearing of strangers. Their extreme isolation has probably added to the natural impulse. It does not follow that they criticise adversely; but they weigh one's lightest syllable in their own balances. Upon their first coming in contact with a stranger, they expect him to look them clearly in the face; and be sure they are watching every movement and expression with the keenest suspicion. Whatever may be their own failings, they are wonderfully endowed with the power to "fix you with the eye"; and you are expected to meet it bravely, and not to quail under the penetrating glance. To an infinite degree are the women expert in reading character, probably more so than our own more world-experienced and educated countrywomen.

It is no matter of surprise that they are distrustful of strangers, when the most they have known of them has been in the way of armed forces seeking to crush out their national existence. Their hospitality, too, having so often met with unwarrantable criticism personally and in the press, they cannot be expected to welcome the stranger over their threshold without caution and misgiving.

A kindly and sympathetic warmth is always heartily reciprocated, while coldness at once repels. To desire their friendship is to deserve it, especially if the wish be tempered by the observance of the golden rule. No people are better aware of their national, political, and social defects, but, being sensitive, nervous, and very proud, an adverse criticism from the thoughtless and ungenerous stranger naturally wounds, and induces that reserve which is so largely national, and which it is so difficult to overcome. When a disposition is manifested to meet them on equal terms of friendly good will, and proper deference is shown to their customs, it will be found that no people are more delightful, socially, more faithful as friends, or more ready to serve the stranger from whatever land, than the Mexicans.

Hospitality is one of the national characteristics, but it is of a nature peculiar to itself, and, contrary to our customs, the latchstring hangs on the inside, for the court circles of Europe are not more exclusive than the higher classes of society in Mexico. The architecture of the houses —their barred windows and well-guarded doors, which prevent intrusion from prying curiosity—together with the climate and customs, conspire to incline the people to lead exclusive lives. It is manifested even in the choice of vehicles, closed carriage being almost invariably used, though with such air and skies the reverse might naturally be expected. The first aspiration, with them, is to make home beautiful, and to this end every element of a cultured and refined taste is duly provided and cared for within the massive doors. The exquisite beauty of the rare and gorgeous flowers in the patios affords constant pleasure by day, while by night they have only to glance upward to obtain wondrous visions of a star-gemmed firmament.

Letters of introduction, even, will not always secure access to the inner circle of the home life. Comparatively speaking, few are accorded this privilege. But when once admitted by personal friends, especially if accompanied by them on the first visit, all formality and reserve are at an end, and the most gracious attentions are freely bestowed, the veriest stranger feeling that he is no longer such. A genuine glow of pleasure has often been mine on finding that their inborn distrust of foreigners had melted away in my first intercourse with them. On passing many handsome houses in the large cities, and halting to admire the beauty and luxuriance of the flowers in the court, on seeing me the gentle voice of the dueña de la casa (lady of the house) would bid me enter and inspect them to my satisfaction. When this was done, and my hands filled with flowers, I was invited to the sala, chocolate ordered, and on departing—certain we would never meet again—

a warm embrace, a cordial shake of the hand, and a "¡Vaya V. con Dios!" ("God be with you"), heartily given.

They are endowed by nature with a highly nervous and sensitive organization, with jealousy for a birthright; and amongst intimate friends of their own nationality they are easily offended, but less so with foreigners. And I have observed that the higher the altitude the more evident are these tendencies, attributable, probably, to both climate and elevation.

Much as the Mexicans love their homes, their language contains no word expressive of the meaning of the word "home." They have only casa (house), and hogar, but little used and lacking euphony. Another fact—the absence of chimneys, depriving them of the pleasures of the fireside, renders it only natural that they should seek diversion outside. The balmy air invites them to life al fresco, consequently the morning promenade, which usually includes the mass at church, the afternoon drive, and perhaps the theater at night, constitute their chief sources of outdoor recreation and amusement.

No people more eminently possess the faculty of entertaining their friends in a royally hospitable way. An assemblage of five hundred guests is as well taken care of as fifty, and no one feels neglected. They are convivial and joyous, mingling freely with one and all; gay sallies of wit and sparkling repartee rule the hour. But, at the same time, a remarkable dignity characterizes their every movement.

In the majority of the towns and cities the ringing of the cathedral bells, at ten o'clock, calls the people from their places of recreation to their homes, and the streets become as quiet and silent as the campo santo (graveyard).

In all their professions of friendship, I have found them frank and sincere, and untiring in their demonstrations to the favored person who has won their regard. While this sincerity is unquestionable, they are yet gifted in a high degree with the pretty art of evasion. Let one who has had trouble confide in them, and let them be but fully convinced that they are the trusted custodians of such confidence, and nothing can induce them to betray the trust so reposed. The penalty of severest punishment cannot wring from them a secret intrusted to them. But by the dainty manipulation of their admirable tact and diplomacy, the inquirer is satisfied and not one syllable betrayed. As well try to make an incision in the side of Popocatepetl with a penknife as extract from a Mexican what he does not want to tell you.

It is asserted by some writers that there is no middle class. It is my opinion, founded upon careful observation and inquiry, that there is not only at this time a very large and influential middle class, but that every year it gains large accessions from the humbler class, who are making giant strides to a nobler place in life through the fine educational advantages now afforded them. In this connection I must say that, while access to the higher strata of society is difficult, the middle class vie with them in their hospitality, never turning a stranger from their doors, and some of the most delightful acts of courtesy and kindness that I ever met with in that country have been extended me by the ever faithful and gentle middle class. With them letters of introduction are unnecessary.

They may not own their homes, but there is an air of pretty neatness about their houses; an unobstructed freedom, a gentleness of manner, which I say unqualifiedly is not equaled anywhere. It is from this class that are springing up every year men of genius and talent, of unremitting toil and study, which will enable them to take that honored station in their chosen field of labor which, in all countries, is the reward of untiring patience and fidelity to any cause.

The forms of greeting and salutation are numerous, and among them none is so distinctively national as the abrazo. Men fall into each other's arms and remain thus for several minutes, patting each other on the shoulder and indulging in all sorts of endearing epithets.

Another form, rather less diffuse, may be seen any

time on the street and promenade, not only among men, but also between friends of opposite sex. In the quickest, most spirited manner, the arms of both parties are outstretched; they rush together for a second, their breasts barely touch, and while the observer is watching for a kiss to follow this ardent salute, they separate and the abrazo is finished. The extreme frankness accompanying it compels one to rather admire the custom; for it means no more than handshaking among Americans.

A mere introduction between men assumes elaborate proportions. Señor Calderón says: "I have the honor to present to you my friend, Señor Ojeda, a merchant of this city"; whereupon Señor Ojeda replies: "Your obedient servant. Your house (meaning his own) is in ———— Street, where I am at your orders for all that you may wish"; or, "My house is muy a su disposición" ("entirely at your disposal; make yourself at home").

From this profusion of politeness, doubtless, has arisen the impression that the Mexicans are devoid of sincerity; when in truth the recipient of such offers would alone deceive himself should he suppose that the Mexican proposed to make him a gift of his house.

Handshaking goes to extremes. If friends meet twenty times a day, the ceremony must be gone through as often.

It is not sufficient for gentlemen merely to touch the hatbrim, in passing each other or any friend; but the hat is removed entirely from the head, whether driving, riding, or walking. I noticed a little pantomime they go through when one gives a light to another. He draws his right hand quickly to his breast, in a second extends it outward, tipping his hatbrim three times, which is all repeated by the one who has lighted his cigar.

I saw on Calle Plateros, one day, two splendid carriages each occupied by one man. On seeing each other, the carriages were halted, both alighted, removed hats, shook hands, embraced, talked for a few moments, again embraced, shook hands, bowed, took off hats, and each entered his carriage and went his way.

Among women the salutation assumes a more confidential form; the stranger receives a gentle tap of the right hand upon the left shoulder, and then a generous shake of the hand; while more intimate friends not only tap each other, but also kiss, not on the lips, however, merely laying the cheeks softly together. The Mexican mode is to be commended.

A lady admires some ornament or article of wearing apparel; instantly the possessor gracefully informs her it is "muy a su orden" ("at your orders"). Changing residence requires that cards be sent announcing the fact, and placing it "muy a su orden," otherwise visiting ceases. Young babies are also placed "muy a su orden." In writing notes of invitation, the Mexican lady always closes with, "We will expect you here, at such an hour, at your house."

A vein of sentiment and poetry, however, runs through every detail of their lives, which forms the motive power of that fastidious nicety which regulates social intercourse. A spray of flowers sent as a token will be first pinned over the heart, the pin left in it, indicating the pledge as a part of the personality of the donor, hence more sacred; or a note may contain a pansy, with a dainty motto inscribed on its petals.

In letter writing or in making a formal acknowledgment, politeness and high-bred courtesy govern; even the President would make himself the individual under obligation.

No gifts are made at Christmas, but on "El Año Nuevo" ("The New Year") tokens of all sorts and kinds, and cards, are sent to friends, with "felicitaciones."

Visiting is the same as in all well-regulated society, except that strangers must send their cards and make the first call. A short visit is not appreciated, as it would indicate coldness and formality. Everything is given up to the guest, let the time be long or short, and a Mexican lady never continues the performance of any duty, however urgent, or engages in anything that would distract her attention from her guests.

On entering a Mexican home, after an absence of

months or years, if you are an old friend, the reception you meet with is overwhelmingly joyful. Every member of the household in turn gives you an embrace; you are seated on the right-hand end of the sofa, and then a thousand kind inquiries follow in regard to relatives, and many interchanges of thought and incidents that have occurred in your absence. You are allowed to do nothing for yourself, for the entire family, from the least to the greatest, perform a part in entertaining and making you feel at home.

But it is a difficult point in Mexican etiquette, that of seating visitors. Guest and host vie with each other in politeness, and sometimes several minutes are occupied in this courteous contest.

On leaving, the visitor is always entreated to remain longer, but when he must go, they "speed the parting guest" with all the fervor with which he is received.

Gentlemen bow first on the street, but ladies have the advantage in the house; for even if the President were to call, the lady of the house is not expected to rise from her seat to receive him.

In walking, ladies hold the right arm of the gentleman. The right-hand side of the back seat of a carriage, and the right-hand end of a sofa, are the places of honor reserved for the guest.

At balls introductions are not necessary for gentlemen to ask ladies to dance, and in private houses all are supposed to be ladies and gentlemen.

A lady retains her maiden name in marriage, and her visiting cards are engraved with her own name with the prefix of *de* before her husband's—as, Josefina Bros de Riva Palacio. Madame de Iturbide, as known in the United States and Europe, in Mexico is simply Alicia G. de Iturbide.

It is better for foreigners to have visiting cards engraved after the fashion of the country if they intend mingling with Mexican society.

Mexicans are as fastidious in the style and quality of

paper and envelopes as in everything else; even the minutest detail is *de rigeur*. In high society, only the finest paper, with monogram in gold or silver, or elaborately engraved with the name inside the monogram, is selected. Some of the daintiest informal little notes I have seen passed between lady friends—written on the finest paper, and then by deft fingers folded in the form of a leaf or flower, with the address on one tiny petal. In all correspondence the rúbrica or firma must be used; neither the nature of what is written, nor the name, has any significance without the peculiar flourish beneath. This is taught in the schools, and the more elaborate the better. The rúbrica is a receipt, a part of every business obligation or social correspondence. Every public document closes with "*Libertad y Independencia*," or "*Libertad en la Constitución*," and in sending an agent to a foreign country, every document relating to the business bears his photograph—perhaps a wise precaution.

In exchanging photographs, it is customary to dedicate them with a pretty sentiment or verse, and the date— not infrequently the age, also—is added.

Smoking publicly is not now customary with señoritas, but I have been told they indulge in this harmless and, with them, graceful pastime in private. Matrons smoke without reserve, and as a matter of course, men are habituated to the indulgence everywhere—no place in the house being exempt from the odor of the cigarette. Pipes are not used, and a delightful offset to smoking is that there is no chewing.

Many of their forms of daily and general politeness may seem empty and meaningless; but there is no more insincerity intended than in some of our own social small coin. It will be borne in mind also that these are not the characteristics of cities or city people, but belong equally to smaller towns and villages. In mingling with the people, their hospitalities and courtesies should be received in the same kindly spirit in which they are given.

Even in the country, on lonely haciendas, everything

is free and openhanded. Your servants have the freedom of the kitchen and stables, the host gives up to you his place at the table, and often, on resuming the journey, will ride half a day, to lead you safely through some mountain defile or dangerous, bandit-infested place—and then the parting is as earnest and as zealous as word and manner can make it.

Natives of climes more frigid may contrast the formal bow, the restraint and stiffness of a possible shake of the hand, and the greeting commonly observed by their own countrymen, with the native ease and graceful cordiality to be met with here. Hence, an introduction into a select circle in Mexico makes a never-to-be-forgotten episode in the life of the favored stranger, cementing the ties which bind him to the country.

Wherever the fates may direct him, he will often experience a yearning to revisit a land where he was ever the recipient of a gracious courtesy scarcely to be found elsewhere. But few Mexicans, save those in diplomatic service, take up their permanent residence in other countries, especially among the Anglo-Saxons. The coldness and formality they there encounter freeze their own warm and cordial manner.

Like the Frenchman, the Mexican talks quite as much with hands and eyes as with his tongue. He shrugs also, but not so unceasingly as his brother Latin.

These gestures are rendered very attractive by the appropriate and graceful manner in which they are used. They are seen as much in the street or horsecars as in the house.

One of the prettiest and most cunning of all the hand motions is called beso soplado, throwing kisses by gathering the fingers of the right hand in a close group, touching the lips, then throwing them out fanlike, at the same time blowing on the hand as it is outstretched toward the object for whom the demonstration is intended, thus indicating that five kisses are given at once.

An irrevocable edict has gone forth when that

prophetic forefinger goes upward and outward before the end of the nose. The laws of the Medes and Persians may be evaded, but "no es costumbre" never.

In no country are family ties stronger. The thought of separation is to them fraught with unspeakable anguish, and even after marriage it is not unusual to see half a dozen families living in the same house, daughters with their husbands and sons with their wives remaining under the paternal roof. The time never comes in the lives of the parents when the children are not more or less amenable to them. Grown sons and daughters do not forget the respect and obedience that were expected of them when children. The reverence for parents goes with them in their wedded lives, and even increases with the lapse of years. A man never grows too old to kiss the hands of his aged parents or to visit them every day if they reside in the same city, and the daughters do the same.

When the martial knot is tied, the women accommodate themselves to whatever fate may have in store for them with that grace and fortitude which belong to them, rarely equaled and never surpassed. The time never comes in which they feel their burdens too great to be borne with patience.

They go but little into society or mixed assemblages, consequently their earthly happiness is summed up in home, husband, children. Their outward deportment corresponds with the interior calm. Whether riding, driving, or walking, they always retain a decorum and dignity of manner peculiar to themselves. To express emotion or surprise in public is not considered becoming.

In all my intercourse with them, I have seen but two who used the trenchant weapon of sarcasm; in their hands it cut like a two-edged sword, and in each case their own countrymen were the victims.

Among the earliest lessons of Christianity inculcated by the Franciscan missionaries were love, charity, and self-denial, and the outcome of these teachings of nearly four centuries may be seen today in the beautiful graces and charities of the Mexican women. These high lessons, exemplified in the lives of the teachers, were received gratefully and practiced faithfully by the warmhearted people. To feed the hungry, clothe the naked, relieve the distressed, and entertain the stranger—surely there is no nobler mission!

Although there are hospitals, homes, and public charities in every city, still there are not only numerous beggars, but blind, maimed, and distressed persons—real objects of charity—seeking aid from the more fortunate members of society. Assistance is never denied; even little children take by the hand, with the sympathetic "¡pobrecito!" ("poor creature"), and lead into the house, some poor creature to be fed and cared for, having been taught to pity and never to ridicule or despise personal afflictions.

The housekeeper is supplied with home remedies, that she may give effect to her charitable interest in the sick and miserable. In many places, ladies of high position on a saint's day will unite in giving a dinner to the poor. Each one contributes to the feast, and then, with her daughters and friends, waits on the squalid guests. Theatrical and musical entertainments are also frequently given for charitable purposes.

Poverty, while greatly to be deplored, is not considered a disgrace. Almost every wealthy family has its full quota of poor relations, who in many instances fill the places of housekeeper or upper servants. But at the same time they are provided for comfortably and kindly. Even where means are limited, it is common to see in a household several children outside the immediate family taken from time to time, and cared for by the tenderhearted lady of the house.

Two of the most interesting young people whose acquaintance I made at the capital were the descendants of a humble Indian woman. With her sick babe, only a month old, lying in her rebozo, homeless and unfriended, she trudged through the rain at dusk. A charitable lady, from the interior of a luxurious home, witnessed the scene, and calling the woman, took the babe to her heart as if it were her own. She proposed to her to adopt the child, promising a mother's care. The trust was sacredly kept, and although this lady afterward became the mother of fifteen children, the poor waif was one of the many, and developed into a lovely woman. She married an accomplished gentleman and bore several children, but to the day of her death she knew nothing of her origin.

The religious observances, as well as the customs of the country, are kept up mainly by the women. The men naturally become more cosmopolitan through travel and contact and intercourse with the outside world. But whatever the cause, scarcely a man of education can be found who does not proclaim himself a deist or an atheist.

But if a long illness ensue, or death appear inevitable, the priest and the holy sacrament are at once ordered. So I have come to the conclusion that they consider the expression of irreligious sentiments when in health indicative of liberal ideas, and showing a sympathy with the "advanced" thought of the age. While they adopt the theory that "the first requisite of man is to be a good animal," in the hour of trial they fall back on the time-honored consolations.

But, despite their lack of creed or religious faith, there is one respect in which husbands of other nations might learn from them a profitable lesson. They generously believe that their wives are fully entitled to an equal share of their business profits and to the expending of their income. The wife is not subjected to the humiliation of begging a pittance, but the whole matter is left to her own good judgment.

It is only justice to say that courtesy and kindness are almost invariably with them the rule in the family.

It is a knightly spirit which impels the men to the belief that their women are not capable of sustaining the burdens of life. And when a man marries, if his wife have a widowed mother and sisters without means of support, it never occurs to him that it is not his duty to keep and maintain them. These offices they cheerfully accept as an hereditary right, without regard to the attainments or accomplishments which might be turned to account.

This chivalric conduct extends still further, in view of the fact that estates of orphans and widows are administered with much care and honest effort. No dread Nemesis pursues the Mexican in the form of a mother-in-law, for, even if there be room for criticism, she may counsel, but she never interferes.

In many homes I have seen the husband regularly, three times a day, bring from the courtyard a flower to lay on the wife's plate. And such little attentions are not meaningless. I have also known many instances where the husband fondly insisted on the wife placing herself at the table, so that she might be excused from serving either the soup or coffee—saying, "The care of the children was enough for her."

There is little or no intoxication among them. At the club or in their homes they may imbibe too freely, but the effects are never apparent in the street.

In social life there are certainly no more agreeable companions than educated Mexican gentlemen, and they are still more delightful when one comes to know them intimately upon the basis of friendship, time and means being alike at one's disposal; and wherever fate may lead, they follow the fortunes of their friends.

One American family whom I knew were kindly conveyed on their journey of five hundred miles, over a rough and barren country, and nothing would induce the generous Mexican to receive one cent in compensation; and further, the mozo who drove them, and the one who rode ahead to ward off interlopers also declined any compensation, saying, "It was the master's orders."

Some of the grandest public benefactions that I have ever seen were endowed by Mexican men; not only hospitals of every kind, but also institutions of learning. An instance I recall, is that of Evaristo Madero, ex-Governor of Coahuila, who devoted his entire salary during his term of office to establishing public schools in his State.

The taste for ceremonious display and profusion is national, and enters into all arrangements, whether of house, dress, or equipage, being limited only by the means for its indulgence. If rustic chairs, cornices, or brackets are used, the dainty fingers of the housewife adorn them, until they lose the rough, unpolished appearance of the native boughs, by means of gilding, bronze, and gay paints, the whole combined into a brilliant mosaic.

Pots containing their lovely plants are draped with mosses peculiar to the country, exhibiting only the beautiful. But in striking contrast to these natural flowers blooming the year round I have frequently seen in handsome houses huge artificial plants in pots, with exaggerated coloring in foliage and flowers.

A love for all bright and lovely objects is innate with these children of the sun. Gorgeous flowers, trailing vines, Chinese lanterns, paintings hung in corridor or patio, brilliant-hued singing birds, all combine to form a scene of Oriental richness and beauty.

Notwithstanding the apparent tendency to prodigality, the utmost care is taken in every detail of domestic economy.

The carriage, with its silver mountings bright and glistening, stands in the zaguan ready for the drive at a moment's notice, but when not in use, carriage, horses, and harness are all in their proper places, in the best possible order.

On the first visit, a guest is cordially shown through the house by its mistress, who may well take pride in its spotless condition. The Mexican housekeeper dreads nothing more than an insignificant particle of polvo (dust) in any part of her domain.

Great care is bestowed on the marking of household linen, the husband's initials or monogram being exquisitely embroidered on each article. Merely to write the name in ink does not suffice, not being considered in keeping with a refined taste.

The bedsteads are of either brass or iron—in wealthy families of the former—and almost universally single. Much ingenuity is expended in the draping of filmy laces in canopies of various shapes, daintily caught back with bright ribbons and flowers, while the greatest pains are taken in the execution of elaborate embroideries, laces, tatting, and crochet for coverings, those with drawn threads being the most distinctively national. But with all this industry piled up, I have never seen in the country our well-known, if homely, patchwork quilt.

Pillows are more numerous than with us. I have counted thirteen on one bed, made of either wool or cotton (feathers are limited to the few), very thin and narrow, graded and piled up, pyramid like, and all trimmed uniformly with lace.

Lace curtains are prime essentials of a well-arranged home and adorn every opening, but I have seen none of our gay chintzes or cretonnes used in this way. Mirrors are indispensable, and with the careful forethought of the housewife, one invariably occupies a place over the sofa, while another hangs on the opposite wall, directly before you.

On entering the *sala*, the most noticeable feature is the sofa, with its invariable accompaniment of four chairs —two large and two smaller ones—placed at either end of the sofa, parallel to each other and vis-à-vis. The unusual number of chairs in most of the houses is surprising, and suggests occasions of reunion as their *raison d'être*; and regardless of wealth or station, the method of arrangement is the same, extending around the room in unbroken lines, except when met by the sofa or the triangular tables that fill the corners. The parlor furniture of the wealthy is extremely handsome; upholstered in damask, either pure white, or in shades of blue, pink, or crimson, supported by stately frames of gold or silver; with carpet corresponding in style. But the furniture in more general use has wooden frames covered with bright reps; the cushion of each, with its dainty, home-wrought lace cover, tables with the same, all fitting to a nicety make a unique and harmonious effect. Plainer houses have the same unbroken lines of homemade chairs (the sofacita before described), with the same tables and arrangement. Here one will see as pretty homemade laces and drawn-thread work as in the grand houses.

Surrounded by so many evidences of a refined and luxurious taste, the absence of books and pictures is conspicuous. Private collections are few, but in every large city there is a public biblioteca (library), of which the men and boys avail themselves, but the desire for knowledge is not yet sufficiently urgent for these institutions to be much patronized by women.

On the great Tacuba highway, at the eastern extremity of the Alameda on the right, at Mariscala No. 2, stands a mansion typical of the wealth and luxury of the capital. This stately edifice is the home of General Vicente Riva Palacio, the distinguished statesman, soldier, and littérateur.

The house is entered as usual through the zaguan, from which a spacious stairway, branching to right and left, leads to the principal apartments. A bronze statue of Guerrero, a leading hero of the Independence war, who was grandfather of the owner of the house, now stands [at the head of the stairway]. The stairs and floors of the corridors and halls are of the finest Italian marble; while around and on either side are tropical plants of every shade and tint; and on the north side swings an aviary filled with bright-hued singing birds.

The house contains about fifty rooms, including three parlors, a grand salon and two smaller ones, all fitted up luxuriously. The oratorio (chapel) is impressive with its altar handsomely draped, and the picture of the Virgin Guadalupe in the center—crosses, silver candelabra, kneeling stools in plush and gold, magnificent vestments, and I was surprised and pleased to see, on either side, American mottoes—"In God we trust," and "God bless our home."

Quite near the chapel is the comedor grande (large dining room), which is, perhaps, 100 feet in length and 50 in width.

The furniture is of native rosewood and mahogany, wrought in most tasteful designs, while the floor glistens like glass, in its varied mosaics of rare and peculiar woods. Mirrors alternate with the massive side boards, with their rare marble slabs from the quarries of Puebla.

In different receptacles were no fewer than 3,000 pieces of china, many of them hand-painted in the flowers of the country, 2,000 pieces of crystal, and silver that for quantity, variety, and brightness was truly dazzling. Included in this was the magnificent silver service sent by Francis Joseph, Emperor of Austria, engraved with the royal arms, to Mariano Palacio, father of the present owner of the house, as a token of gratitude for his voluntary and noble defense of Maximilian.

Smaller rooms are used by the family informally.

The table linen, of finest texture, includes cloths with monogram elaborately embroidered at either end, and napkins for every possible use, many representing the talent, industry, and ingenuity of the women of Mexico, being hemstitched, embroidered, or ornamented with that original lace—the drawn-thread work—for which they are famous.

While on the subject of needlework, I must mention that I was shown about thirty of the most elegant bedspreads on which my eyes ever rested. They consisted of velvet, silk, satin, plush, lace, crochet, with various kinds of embroidery as centerpieces; all quite adequate to arouse feelings of lively admiration. The sheets, of snowy linen, are hemstitched and embroidered, sometimes several inches in depth. The pillowcases correspond in style, the whole forming a collection of rare needlework which seemed to amount to thousands of pieces.

The sleeping apartments, in addition to every article of luxury and ease, are furnished with single brass bedsteads, over each of which is suspended a canopy of delicate lace, caught up with flowers and bright ribbons, forming a veritable bower.

The sala grande bears evidence of an immense expenditure, every thing being of European importation. In size it corresponds with the dining room. The carpet is shaded from pale pink to bright crimson; the furniture in frames of gold, upholstered in the same shades of the carpet. Grand chandeliers costing thousands of dollars are suspended from the ceiling; mirrors and sconces are arranged on the walls, and lace curtains of daintiest weft shade the windows. In this apartment I again encountered the beautiful hand embroidery of Doña Josefina, the noble and lovely wife of General Palacio, in the chairs, ottomans, and hassocks, all executed in the finest Japanese designs, some of which she told me had occupied her time for six months.

I must also mention the ceilings of this mansion. Some 30 feet in height, they rest on heavy beams of wood, laid crosswise of the room, each one perhaps 18 inches in depth, the whole giving an effect of massive grandeur. The beams are tinted to correspond with the ceilings and walls, and ornamented with lines of gold. These lines also panel the walls, and outline doors and windows.

The azotea, a notable feature in the architecture of the Aztecs, still adorns these square-topped buildings. At the capital they are constructed of brick, and form a delightful promenade at all seasons. As the houses are joined together, one may walk over the entire square, as I had the pleasure of doing.

The study of General Palacio contains, perhaps, one of the finest collections of books and manuscripts in the republic. He possesses a large number of the original documents of the Inquisition handsomely bound; also a valuable foreign library, comprising books in many languages. The door of the case containing the books of the Inquisition opens over a winding stairway, and the carpet is fitted to a nicety over the semicircle which opens and closes with the door, giving ingress and egress to the private study below. When the General opened the door of this case, I came near going headlong below, and the thought flashed through my mind that I was verily descending to the vaults of the Inquisition, not knowing that the door of the book-case was also that of the dark stairway. I was, however, rescued by my friends, and made the descent in the usual way. I would here remark that these spiral stairways are a prominent feature of Mexican architecture.

In the room below there is a handsome case containing the swords of General Francisco Xavier Mina and Vicente Guerrero; the feathers—pink and white—worn by the Emperor Iturbide on his hat when entering the city in 1821; a bronze cast of Napoleon; and the original sentence of Picaluga, who betrayed Guerrero into the hands of his enemies, besides many Indian curios and bric-a-brac. In another room were the chair of Hidalgo and the saddle that Maximilian rode the day he was captured.

Some idea of the immense collection of books, manuscripts, legal documents, and literary works of General Palacio may be gained, when I say that eight handsome rooms in this grand house are devoted exclusively by him to his scientific and literary pursuits—the large study upstairs, from which we descended by means of the winding stairway, and seven rooms on the ground floor, running from the front windows on the sidewalk, along the patio, far to the rear. On the opposite side is the family theater, capable of seating two hundred persons, beautifully arranged and decorated. The drop curtain and scenery are painted from native subjects. In the season a select company occupy the boards—sometimes varied by amateurs —and play to crowded houses of friends.

In the rear zaguan, a carriage is ever ready for the drive, while immediately behind this is an exquisite fairylike grotto, with its fountain, creeping tropical vines and gorgeous flowers, distinctly visible from the sidewalk through the open doors. On one side are various baths, and still beyond, sewing rooms; while on the other are the numerous servants' rooms, all neat and well kept. Beyond these is the vast laundry, then the stables containing stalls for many horses, all sleek and shiny, with vehicles of various kinds, the premises extending until halted by the rear street.

It may be interesting to know that the number of servants constantly employed is thirty-five—among them three housekeepers—to say nothing of many extra ones who come in on special occasions. The family to be waited upon by this array of domestics consists of, at most, six members.

Externally the mansion presents the semifeudal appearance so often seen here—a mass of solid, gray stone, indicating little of the extent and magnificence of the interior.

The love of music permeates all classes, and is cultivated equally by both sexes. Thoroughness is the rule, and memorizing is always required; the most difficult and prolonged recitals being rendered with brilliant execution without the score or a break. When asked to play, the musician complies at once, and if the guest expresses pleasure, will continue playing indefinitely.

On marriage the beautiful art is not given up; on the contrary, is practiced quite as much as before. In some delightful homes I have been agreeably entertained for hours at a time by the choicest musical duets rendered by an elderly man and his wife, the sons and daughters, and even the grandchildren, taking their places alternately at the piano.

I heard but little classic music, but the opera is popular and understood by all. In this, public taste is quite critical, Italian opera taking precedence. Opera bouffe is regarded as highly immoral, although the ballet is universally popular, and introduced between the acts of grand opera. English opera is regarded as a compromise between them. A young Mexican friend of mine quaintly classified Italian opera as blanca (white or pure); English, color de rosa; and opera bouffe, muy colorado (highly colored).

An enterprising manager, not a great while since, attempted to present on alternate nights grand opera and opera bouffe. On grand opera nights every seat and box was filled with the wealth and fashion of the capital, while on opera bouffe nights they sang to almost empty houses. If any laxity of morals exists in private life, immoral and corrupting plays are certainly discouraged on the boards.

The native airs breathe a passionate sweetness, uniting with the tender minor tones the high staccato movement and the short, quick rest—a style to be observed both in the voice and instrument.

A marked difference may be noted in the melodies of the plains and low country and those of elevated and mountainous regions—the former being soft and pathetic, while the latter breathe the exhilarating spirit of the hills.

The finely attuned national ear for music assists greatly in the acquirement of foreign languages, for which their aptness is remarkable. I have been in families where English, French, and Italian were spoken quite as fluently as the native tongue. In this respect they excel our own country people. Their linguistic culture is practical, while our students generally neither have nor make opportunities for speaking in foreign tongues.

Closely connected with music and languages is the poetical faculty, which seems equally inherent. It comes out on any occasion, with surprising readiness, in little tender sentimental effusions, or graceful compliment—tone and gesture having added emphasis in delivery.

Diminutives are universally employed, and the *cita* never sounds so sweetly as when murmured by infant lips in mamacita and papacito (dearest or darling mamma and papa). The names we are accustomed to use in a formal manner sound sweet and pathetic in their simpler adaptation, as heard in Mexican homes. Aunt Julia, in our prosaic idiom, becomes Julita—pronounced Hulita, little Julia—tia (aunt) being entirely omitted. Everybody is called by the Christian name, regardless of age or position in society.

Nothing is more melodious in Mexican homes than

the terms te and tu (thee and thou). The pronoun you, usted (written V.), is not used in the family, nor with intimate friends, te and tu being expressive of confidence. I have been corrected by heads of families for thoughtlessly addressing some of them as *you*, instead of placing myself in their inner circle, sharing its most sacred privileges.

In the endearing expressions, " ¿Tu me quieres a mi?" ("Lovest thou me?"), "Yo, te quiero a ti" ("Yes, I love thee"), the pronouns are repeated for emphasis.

Another way of putting it is, " ¿Me quieres tu?" ("Lovest thou me?"), "Si, te quiero" ("Yes, I love thee"). Still other loving expressions which are heard in Mexican homes every day are, "Luz de mis ojos" ("Light of my eyes"), and "Ídolo mío" ("My idol"), "Mi corazoncito" ("My heart's treasure"), and "Vida mía" ("My life"), all having an added zest by the speaker's tender manner.

In the baby language of mothers, nothing is sweeter than these expressions. Intonations vary in different localities. At the capital the rising inflection is generally heard, the voice running on an upward sliding scale—the marked rising inflection—with pleasing effect.

Great delicacy is always exercised in speaking of ages. In one part of the country, one a little advanced in years, or even quite old, is called viejito (a little old). In the choice society of the capital this term is considered wanting in good taste; un poco grande, or grandecito (a little large) is usually employed, but the phrase carries conviction with it.

One highly commendable trait is, that Mexicans will not say disagreeable things to you, either on their own account, or repeating what others may have said. I have been told that the women are much given to gossip; but if true, I have not heard them, as they are careful never to speak unkindly or slightingly of their countrywomen in the presence of strangers. The possible failings of their own people are carefully held in reserve; and the most critical remark I heard one woman make of another was, that she was "muy buena, pero para pura buena no sirve" ("very good, but to be purely good, and no more, was of no value"), a nice discrimination between negative and active goodness!

"Muy mexicano" ("Very Mexican") is another phrase used in the same way, referring to something slow, or out of accord with the feelings and sentiments of the speaker.

"Muy mal criado" ("A very bad servant") expresses great contempt. Sometimes, however, it is used humorously, as when a child teases its mother, or a friend insists on the conferring of some little favor at an inconvenient season.

In the arts of the toilet the señorita is fully up with her Anglo-Saxon sisters; indeed, it may truthfully be said she is ahead of them. Paint, whitening lotions, and dentrifices are used freely. But no women excel them in the care of the hair, that "glory" of woman, and its wonderful length, its silky, luxuriant softness, amply compensate them for their pains.

Houses built before the days of modern conveniences are not provided with baths, but comfortable and luxurious public baths—warm and cold—for all classes exist everywhere. It is here the señorita, at least once a week, uncoils her lovely tresses, and washes thoroughly both hair and scalp, then, with towel pinned around her shoulders, and hair flowing in unconfined ripples from crown to tip, goes through the streets to her home with no more concealment that if returning from church.

Señoritas are universally known in plain English as chickens. If very young, they are pollitas (little chickens). If twenty or more years, the graver and more prophetic term polla (grown or big chicken) is applied.

An opportunity was given me of hearing an amusing adaptation of the term.

A number of ladies were arranging to give an entertainment for a charitable purpose. All had stated what they would contribute, save one, who had remained silent throughout. But when a lull came in the conversation, she quietly remarked she would bring the pollas y pollitas. The merriment spread like contagion, for she had three marriageable daughters.

On another occasion, at a fashionable dinner party which I attended at the capital, Guillermo Prieto was also a guest.

The venerable poet sat at the extreme end of the long table beside a blooming señorita, who was evidently entertaining the old gentleman to the best of her ability. A charming, middle-aged señora sat near me, and when the conversation flagged, she turned and said, naïvely, "¡Oye! oye (hear! hear)! Guillermo! You like those pollitas much better than the pollas!" To which he replied, "Naturalmente (naturally), there is nothing prettier or sweeter than a pollita!" An expression of taste which could not be described as national.

But these lovely pollitas never experience the pleasures of our debutantes. From thirteen years of age they may be candidates for matrimony, but such an event crowning their entrance into society as a winter in Washington would be as foreign to their ideas and impressions of real young ladyhood as their Romeo and Juliet lovemaking from the balcony or barred windows to our young ladies. So they are always out, and yet never out!

Solteras or doncellas viejas is the term applied to old maids. While no derogation attaches to this position, yet often much sport is made at the expense of those who may in any way render themselves odious and disagreeable. "Muy fastidiosa" ("very fastidious," or "a little difficult to please") is politely applied; or "Very good to dress the saints," meaning, that they are always at church, and, having nothing else to do, dressing saints is a proper occupation for them.

Thirty years are allowed a señorita ere she is launched on that monotonous soltera journey; and they are to be found as often in wealthy as in plainer families.

Bachelors are quite common, and they also have

their special names. Sometimes solterones, at others, solterones perniciosos (bad or pernicious unmarried men). A Mexican lady said to me, "Life to the solterones is never bleak nor desolate. They keep up their houses and have everything about them that contributes to their happiness!"

Young marriageable men are called gallinos, older ones, gallos (young and old roosters). And those tireless, idle young men who stand on the streets habitually, watching the señoritas on their way to mass or to shop, are called by the appropriate name of lagartijos (lizards), because they are always in the sun.

Foreigners are not long in sorting these out from the multitude, as they make it a rule to stare one out of countenance.

They compare with the idlers of all countries, and are not a whit behind them in deportment and dress— even the eyeglass is not wanting.

A natural and, it would seem, national source of pride to the Mexican, is his small and elegantly formed foot, and, not satisfied with its original graces of slender form and arched instep, he compresses its size by wearing tight-fitting, high-heeled, and pointed-toed shoes.

Apropos of this little display of personal vanity, shared by both the sexes, I may repeat what a lady of great culture and refinement told me in plain words, that while her husband was handsome, good, and kind, yet, had he not possessed the most perfect foot she ever saw, never would she have married him!

The women are by no means migratory in their habits. Indeed, with few exceptions, they do not travel in their own country. They have no seaside resorts nor watering places kept solely for recreation; the change to a hacienda or to a quiet village being the chief portion of their knowledge and experience in that line.

The increased facilities for travel do not offer sufficient inducements to them to leave their homes.

One charming woman, whose acquaintance I formed

at Morelia, said to me that she had never been ten miles beyond Morelia but once in her life. This was a trip to the capital after her marriage. Then she only remained one day, which was spent in weeping so violently, and in entreating her liege lord to take her home again, that he was only too glad to do so without delay.

The boardinghouse, as it is known to us, is entirely unknown in Mexico, so that in cases of financial difficulty or other misfortune, ladies do not assume the care and management of such establishments. I only know of one instance where a lady, suddenly reduced from affluence to poverty, had recourse to this method of gaining a livelihood. Now and then one may encounter a casa de huéspedes, where furnished rooms are rented, but this is the extent of such business by women. And it is safe to estimate that scarcely one out of ten thousand señoritas has ever found herself inside either a hotel or boardinghouse.

Indeed, so deeply rooted is the feeling against any kind of publicity in the domestic life, that it is not considered etiquette for a lady, married or single, to visit in hotels.

Foreigners are attracted by the tender, kindly manner of the señoritas, and frequently choose their life partners among them. But, though loyal and devoted wives, as is well known, the fewest instances are on record where they have been successfully transplanted to another soil. They will not quarrel to carry their point, but sooner or later they will and must return to their native land. The women of other countries may fill a wider sphere, but there is no climate nor customs like their own.

A parallel is found by transplanting the American woman to Mexico, and the Mexican woman to the United States. The one sighs over her lack of freedom, while with the other, the excess of freedom is an untold burden. No charm or attraction can exist for her beyond the barred window and the circumscribed limits of the promenade, accompanied according to custom, by some female relative or servant.

The foreigner who contemplates seeking the hand of a señorita, should first arrange all business matters in his own country, bid adieu to kindred and friends; for when the event takes place linking his fate with that of the object of his affections, he must become in word and deed a Mexican, and be one of the family in every relation.

One noble trait is exemplified in the life of the Mexican woman who shares her worldly goods with either a foreigner or countryman. He may bring into his house his parents, his aunts, and his cousins, even as remote as the twenty-ninth cousin, and his wife will feel it only her duty and pleasure to be kind and tender, dividing with them her wordly possessions.

According to law, a girl is eligible for matrimony at fourteen. She is then as fully developed as an American girl at eighteen. Maturing thus early, marriage takes place, and from twenty-five to thirty-five, the piquancy of youth waning, they arrive at a faded and premature age. The dearth of intellectual pursuits and the climate do their part in the metamorphosis.

The fine physical development among the women is particularly noticeable at the capital. Their beauty, however, grows upon and impresses one by degrees; their glorious soft eyes, glossy black hair, exquisitely shaped hands and arms and small feet are more admired the longer we observe them.

It is a pleasure to chronicle the fact that the government is now thoroughly aroused to the importance of giving educational advantages to the excellent, honest, and kindly disposed middle class. Nothing will tend more to make Mexico strong in herself and the sooner place her in the foremost ranks among nations, than the disposition she now manifests of being deeply interested in the education of the masses, and especially in that of the women. Industrial and normal schools and colleges are now in successful operation at many central points. In these they receive not only a practical education, but also instruction in the various branches of art by highly qualified masters.

Treated heretofore more like dolls, or ornamental adjuncts—and in a state of dependence—now, without fear of misconstruction, they may enter such avenues of art and industry as will support them independently. Every latent talent is being fostered and encouraged by the administrators of the law. Poor young girls, as well as boys, are pensioned by either their own state or the federal government, and only a few years more will witness an upward and onward progressiveness heretofore unknown.

At home, also, their range of accomplishments is extended. Where formerly señoritas employed themselves in lacework and embroidery, they now cut, fit, and make their own dresses with taste and skill, copying closely European and American fashions, and taking much pleasure in the selection of the various styles.

During my sojourn at the capital, one young señorita graduated in dentistry. She began at once assisting her father, who was a dentist, in his office, the fact being announced in all the leading daily papers.

Happily the class which most needs this aid and encouragement is the one most benefited by it—the excellent, faithful, and hospitable middle class.

It need not be inferred that husbands interdict their wives from sharing intellectual enjoyments. Yet one—a distinguished man of letters—remarked to me that it was all very well for American women to walk along with the men in science and literature, but it would never do for Mexican women to know any place aside from the home, with its relation to husband and children. If so, they would at once grow unhappy and discontented.

A Mexican gentleman, who had lived a great deal in the United States, and appreciated the Americans as a people, freely admitted to me that he had made the "double mistake of marrying two American women." If this remark savored of a a lack of gallantry, it bore, however, a general truth, for the races are not, as a rule, suited to each other conjugally.

But some of the most majestic old dames it has ever

been my fortune to know are among the Mexican women. They step as if descended directly from Montezuma, and the manner in which they uphold the dignity of their homes is something well worth seeing.

In neither six is the slightest effort made to conceal age. Even young ladies on the shady side of an "uncertain age" do not seem aware that the least derogation attaches to that fact, but with a quiet unconcern state the exact number of their years.

Having so many servants, the lives of the women are much easier with regard to household labors than with us. There is no hurry—no necessity for it; but, though custom yield to *négligé* in the mornings, sacques and skirts, loose low shoes, and no corsets, hence no inconvenience as from the more formal toilet of our women, their maladies are quite as numerous. The lack of exercise, and excessive indulgence in rich, highly-spiced peppery food, may account for many ailments.

Children sum up, generally, ten, twelve, and sometimes as many as fifteen to eighteen in number, many not reaching maturity. In few instances do the mothers nurse their babes, the wet nurse being "the power behind the throne."

I was agreeably disappointed, however, to see so few instances of personal deformity. Nearsightedness is prevalent all over the country, and is accounted for by the excess of light outside and its deficiency, with lack of ventilation, in both homes and schools.

Mexico is an earthly paradise for children. The little monarchs hold high sway in the affections of the people; and from the moment they see the light it is a long heyday of enjoyment and child play. Expressions of the tenderest love are lavished on them without affectation, whether in the street, the house, or the shop, and, regardless of how many may have preceded him, the new baby is hailed with delight, and takes superior rank in the household.

No country can produce more marvelously beautiful, brighter, or more precocious children. They are happy by nature, and, though indisposed to quarrel with each other either in the house or street, yet somehow they manage to assert their rights.

The childish prattle in the sweet baby Spanish is melody itself, coming from these winning and most lovable little creatures. Beautiful Alfonso, the baby boy of Señora Calderón—a little more than two years old—came tapping at my door one day.

Opening it, I asked, "What do you want, precious one?" Taking my hand and looking archly in my face, he said, with baby incorrectness, "Sabo inglés" ("I know English"). "Well, then," said I, "speak to me in English." "Gooch," he replied, laughing, shaking his head, and, as I caught him in my arms, patting me on the cheek. My name was the only word he knew, but he had rehearsed it with his nurse until his pronunciation was perfect. After this, every visitor was made aware of his proficiency in English, the whole family entering into his own enjoyment of his knowledge. No wonder these darlings are so little under control when they are so cunning and interesting!

National tastes and characteristics are early developed. Among the first is, that noise of any kind—laughing crying, and walking heavily—is rude and unbecoming.

Babies do not creep because always in the arms of the nurse, who does the greater part towards amusing them. They are so tractable that in sitting for a photograph they naturally take a graceful, easy position, upon which even the artist cannot improve.

Clinging as they do to inbred traits, the universal habits of all children exhibit themselves. If they are not given the drumsticks of the fowl, I have seen their great luminous orbs gather moisture until tears would overflow in distress at the appropriation by some one else of this important appendage. No child is excluded from the table or asked to wait; even on ceremonious occasions their places are reserved. They are admitted into the full confidence of the family circle, and such interesting events as births, marriages, and deaths are discussed in their presence with the utmost freedom.

Boys begin to smoke about ten years of age, but never do they indulge in the presence of their elders—not even an older brother. Few games and but fewer outdoor sports have been provided for them; and until within late years, bicycles or gymnasiums were unknown. But they are grand little horsemen, when fully equipped in the national dress; though sometimes rather grotesque when mounted on a hard-mouthed "billy goat" instead of a horse, accompanied by a train of boys. One rides, another leads, and still another uses the lash. I have seen two boys on one "billy," and this usually obstreperous animal yielded quite kindly to the caprices of the riders.

Girls have quite as little diversion, and often I have seen them playing self-invented games, in close imitation of church scenes—with altar, candles, and swinging censers—the boys acting as priests, while the girls, as nuns or plain worshipers, would file into the imaginary church.

The home discipline is of the mildest. If a correction be necessary, it comes in the form of an appeal, both parents showing tender leniency. An infraction of the household laws brings no punishment from the mother, and if persuasion and tears will not avail, the culprit goes free. At school the discipline is of the same character. No scolding, no correction or use of the rod is ever permitted. The laws of the country are express and explicit on this point, and even a parent so inclined could not grant this privilege to the teacher. But parents and teachers vie with each other in inculcating all the laws of politeness and courtesy.

I wish I could tell half I have seen of the graces and courtesies of these children. In the Alameda, with kindly deference, they will always yield to elderly and infirm persons their own cozy and shady seats. On entering a sala, where there are few or many guests, these exquisitely polite little gentlemen will go all around shaking hands with every one present. They never break into the conversation, but when addressed will modestly join in it; then, wishing to retire, will say, "With your kind permission," and again shaking hands, move gracefully from the company. Girls are no less imbued with the same spirit of courtesy.

A Mexican boy never thinks himself too near manhood to pay the compliment to his mother of kissing her hand every time he comes into her presence. But I have sometimes seen evidences of a double motive in this pretty custom. Every one of these lads loves to patronize the dulce vender, and to do so he must keep in the good graces of his mother. While he stoops to imprint a kiss upon her hand, he whispers in her ear, "Give me a medio, dear mamma, I want some dulces." This appeal is never resisted.

Children are entertained by their mothers with an inexhaustible supply of tales and legends. Kings and queens are generally the subjects of these stories, and while their origin is Spanish, much Mexican sentiment is ingeniously interwoven with them.

Something more must be said about the dear babies and their clothing. In the Aztec country, baby's wardrobe is an unpretentious affair. The custom prevails of supplying only a very few simple articles. A square yard of flannel and one of muslin, hemmed all around and edged with lace or embroidery, known as pañale, are wrapped around the infant's body and worn for three months, when little drawers—calzoncillos—are substituted. Dresses are held in reserve, to be worn on special occasions.

In wealthy families now, however, European wardrobes for babies are used, yet many still adhere to the original mode. At night the nurse wraps a small rebozo tightly about the arms and hands of the little one. She explains that baby will become frightened at his hands and scratch himself with his nails. In some families the rebozo is kept wrapped around the little one's arms and hands, both by day and night, so there is no danger of his taking fright at his own development.

Poor little babes! They do look so uncomfortable,

inveigled in the folds of the relentless rebozo, their bodies straightened out full length, so that neither arms nor legs can toss about if colic or other baby malady should overtake them.

VII

Fasts and Festivals
and Social Forms

It is not my purpose in this connection to dwell upon the
past history or present status of the Church in Mexico, except as it is connected with the actual lives of the people.

The propriety of blending social events, household
customs, and religious ceremonies, as one subject of description, may seem questionable to the uninitiated reader.
But when it is understood that the feast days of the church
are holidays for the people, and that these feast days are
numerous, and without these holidays there would be but
little social life, the harmony of these subjects will be at
once understood.

The November feasts, beginning with All Saints' Day,
were the first of interest that I witnessed, and the brilliant
capital never saw a finer inauguration of these festivities.
The rainy season was ended, the atmosphere was bracing,
as is always the case at that time of the year, and these
happy effects harmonized with the smiling faces of the
multitude, as they moved back and forth, bearing in their
hands flowers as lovely and delicately tinted as though
blushing from the kisses of angels.

Strains of delightful music were wafted to my ears
upon the early morning air from organ and choir, and the
stronger and more martial notes of stringed and brass instruments. Hundreds, even thousands, of women and
children in their best clothes wended their way to the
various churches. Business was suspended, even the school
children having a holiday; though the public schools, fostered by the government, make no allowance for holidays
in their regulations.

The Alameda, the great central figure of every outdoor social event, presented a picture that the mind loves
to recall. The great central pavilion was illuminated by

iridescent lights, which were rendered more fairylike and bewitching by numerous moss-draped mirrors, Chinese lanterns, brilliant growing plants, the magnificent fountain with its silvery showers, and the basin with its dainty, bright-colored fishes, streamers and flags with the national ensign, the whole making a gorgeous Oriental picture, vibrating under the modern electric light.

The Zapadores, of Exposition fame, assisted by other bands, played alternately on Tuesdays, Thursdays, and Sundays, and on special feast days. At night grand concerts took place, which were enjoyed by the most cultured and elegant society. Occasionally benefits were given for charitable purposes.

The play of Don Juan Tenorio, known throughout Spain and Spanish America, comes in among the November celebrations, being placed on the boards on All Souls' Day, and kept there as long as public taste approves.

But to return to the feast. The highest testimonials of remembrance were on that day given to the beloved dead. Every cemetery was filled to its utmost capacity with mourning relatives and friends. The humblest grave at Dolores (cemetery of the poor) was not forgotten, and at the French cemetery the scene was most impressive. The clergy celebrated mass with full orchestral accompaniment; lights burned everywhere, while the glorious tropical sunshine was shut out by the towering forest and ornamental shade trees.

Pictures of deceased friends and relatives were placed at the headstones, while garlands, wreaths, and floral emblems encircled them, almost concealing the tomb; and as the priest passed from grave to grave, with solemn intonation and pathetic music, there were few dry eyes in that vast concourse.

The most touching mass that I witnessed that day in the French cemetery was celebrated before a monument that had been erected to the memory of "All the mothers and the fathers who have died in other lands, when separated from their children, who lived in faroff Mexico."

The American dead were not forgotten, and the last resting places of the humble and unfortunate, as well as the wealthy and influential, were overlaid with lovely floral tributes.

The Alameda, with its indescribable attractions, continues nightly, throughout the month, to be filled with an elegantly dressed crowd, who revel in this gorgeous and bewildering realm of beauty. The holiday look everywhere is kept up in anticipation of the most universally celebrated of all the feast days of the country, that of the Virgin de Guadalupe—the patron saint of Mexico —which takes place on the 12th of December.

She is venerated in all Spanish-America, and the story of her mysterious appearance to Juan Diego is firmly believed by thousands of every grade and class. The most ignorant Indian may not know of the President, Congress, or machinery of government, but he is sure to be well informed as to the merits of "Our Lady of Guadalupe." No doubt the tradition with its fascinating sentiment has been the means of inducing many wandering and scattered tribes of Indians to enlist themselves in the service of the Church.

We are told that when the patriot Hidalgo placed the image of the Virgin Guadalupe on his banner, the royalists bitterly persecuted those who worshiped at her shrine; and at once stamped on their own banners the representation of the Spanish Virgin, "Nuestra señora de los Remedios."

These two ladies, as representing the different causes, were bitter rivals throughout the War of Independence. But the native blood and determination were the stronger, and when Augustin de Iturbide became Emperor, the Indian Virgin resumed the absolute sovereignty which she this day holds. So dear is her name that thousands of children are annually christened by it.

For days before the inauguration of the festivities in honor of Guadalupe, both the capital and the highways leading to this sacred shrine were alive with people making preparations for the occasion. Platforms to be occupied by bands of music were erected at every prominent street corner, and every garden and plaza showed signs that something unusual was about to transpire.

Indians had tramped a thousand or more miles in order to be present. They had brought with them the various wares and products of their own labor peculiar to their respective sections, and sold them through the streets—among them many articles of rare, beautiful, and skillful workmanship.

In the Zócalo the palm huts and rush-covered booths suggested an affinity between the native Indian and the banks of the Nile, but the novelty and variety of the surroundings precluded prolonged speculation. The bazaars, shaded by cypress boughs, were presided over by Indian maidens endowed with great versatility of talent and with an abundant supply of small talk for every customer. Their stock in trade was unique—Nacimientos, representing the birth of Christ, in figures of wax, candy, and clay being the principal ones, though one may also find many other specimens of curious and ingenious handicraft.

Everything and everybody took on a holiday look in their new clothes, which none had omitted except the Indians. The azoteas were also enlivened by thousands of people, who enjoyed the brilliant display of pyrotechnics, and every imaginable species of illumination.

A party of Americans of which I was one, with a few Mexican friends, went to Guadalupe the night before the grand fiesta was to take place. To adequately describe the scene would require the pen of a Dickens. The poor, the lame, the halt, the blind had been here congregated, as well as the hale and hearty, with their petates, vessels of pottery and other things needful for the occasion. While the architectural beauty of the cathedral was displayed, the grotesquely attired multitude was also thrown into relief.

Inside the inclosure of the church the stillness of death marked the sleeping multitude. Overcome, perhaps, by the fatigue of the long journey from their homes, hundreds of women and children slept peacefully, undisturbed by the gaze of the curious foreigners who stepped over them to enter the portals of the cathedral.

It seemed to me that hundreds of poor women, wrapped only in their rebozos, with occasionally a blanket, were asleep, and in their immovable postures, transfixed to mother earth. Now and then one might be seen upon her knees, devoutly offering up the prayers of her faith, while tears stole gently down the weather-beaten faces of others. Here as everywhere, making himself conspicuous and well known, was the ever-present, insatiable papoose.

Within the cathedral, the soft tones of the organ, aided and enhanced by the youthful voices of the choristers, filled the vast temple with solemn harmony.

An indescribable multitude of worshipers had assembled there, among whom Indian women on their knees, with candles in their hands, and children strapped to their backs, moved down the grand old aisles murmuring their "Ave Marias."

A contrasting scene was presented as we passed through the great doorway on our way out. Two men— one of them very old, with a pair of green spectacles which looked as if made by a blacksmith—were deeply engaged in singing from a home-manufactured book, as I discovered by peeping over, a rude chant, without rhyme, reason, time, tune, or ending. They sang with *gusto*, oblivious of the interest with which we regarded them, and each utterly regardless of what the other was singing. It was the strangest duet that was ever framed—two cracked voices, in utter discord, the singers as serious as pictured saints. The faces of the men, the spectacles, the book, the rattling discord of the duet, seen and heard by the dim light of a tallow dip, flickering in the December wind, formed a woebegone scene that should be painted by a Hogarth.

The chapel on the hill of Tepeyac can be reached only by a tiresome tramp up, perhaps, two hundred steps, cut in the side of the mountain, and here we were held in unbroken admiration of the scene below. The valley, bathed in the chastened light of a glorious full moon, lay serenely at our feet and stretched beyond to its mountain limits in the dim distance. The air was sweet, balmy and refreshing, even on that mid-December night. All this was the handiwork of nature in her sublimest moods. But what a contrast when we turned to the little plaza in front of the grand cathedral and beheld the multitudinous assemblage of human beings on grand parade, in fatigue suits and undress uniforms! True, the mellow moonlight was over them, as over us; but nearer were the flare of torches; the flickering of campfires, by the lights of which the crowds moved about like characters in pantomime, and with the Babel of voices, the songs of the Indians, the firecrackers and skyrockets, suggested to us on the height, instead of a vast religious congregation, rather a demoniacal pandemonium. Now and again the swelling notes of the organ were heard above the din, but these were soon lost in the pealing of bells from the towers as they revolved rapidly in the gay lights of the national colors, until the valley was filled with their deep-toned utterances.

We went down the steps and were soon lost in the variegated concourse, but our interest was undiminished. Confronted on every hand by gambling booths, tents, palm huts, and a motley multitude, cooking, eating and drinking, to open the way for our exit required the strength of a Hercules. We had glimpses of men and women in the booths who played on harp, guitar, and bandolin, and if their faces had been carved from wood or stone, they could not have been more immobile or expressionless.

The defects, by nighttime, in a picture so realistic, were concealed in a measure by the glamour of moonlight and torchlight, but the longing of unsatisfied human nature urged us to return on Sunday afternoon to take a more prosaic view of it in the broad, open daylight. It was a cruel and a crucial test. An army of beggars in rags, hundreds of children—faces unwashed, hair unkempt—

sallied around, gnawing on great chunks of meat, playing in huge basins of soup, scooping up frijoles with tortillas, or screaming and fighting with the myriads of dogs. Gambling was in full force; women were cooking in every way known from the time of Adam, selling everything, screaming their prices, and, like the tireless venders they are, seldom failing to secure a purchaser. Some presided in booths, gayly lined with fruits and flowers, and danced, sang, and patronized you, while generously overflowing with pulque. The air was filled with an indiscriminate jangle of most unearthly sounds, from a variety of very earthly instruments, which, with the dust, the odor of meat cooking, and the fumes from the crowd added, made us hurry along to the chapel on the hill, where a treat was in store for us. The Indians from the fastnesses of the Sierras in the far north were to dance in their peculiar costumes.

Animated by insatiable curiosity, and anxious to witness the entire ceremonials, I pressed through the crowd of pobres to the inner circle. What a scene! The wildest, most fantastically decked beings that mortal eye ever beheld were in the inner space. The old men, adults, and boys, with their immense panaches of variegated colors that towered to startling height; their curiously wrought dresses that were strongly marked with the national colors, somewhat resembling the kilt of the Scottish highlanders; their ornamented moccasins; the women and little girls with their curious masks of coarse gauze, in black and white, crowned with immense wreaths of feathers, of every variety, intermingled with flashing tinsels, with tawdry dresses of many colors, and in fashion not unlike the kilt of the men and boys, made a scene that was grotesque and fantastic beyond description. Then the dance! They formed circles—the men on the outer circle and the women on the first inner circle—and again other circles of the younger Indians of both sexes, forming one within the other. The everlasting jangle and trum-trum of the ghastly jarana covered with the skin of an armadillo, looking like an exhumed skeleton, with the finery of

flaunting ribbons floating around it, its harsh notes mingling with the drowning wail of the wild musician who
played as though in a frenzy, were in keeping with the whole
scene. The circles, with all their varied colors, danced in
opposite directions with a slow, bouncing step that was
half a waltz, half minuet, and as they proceeded they grew
more excited—more frenzied—the musician seemingly
more infused with his awful duty, and the dancers stepping
higher and higher, the circles wheeling more rapidly, until
the ear was overpowered and the eye confused with the
endless changes of faces, colors, and sounds. It was the
wildest, most mournful dance that mortal could invent;
and it seemed as if the souls of the devotees were in the
movement. It was a sort of paroxysm of physical devotion,
and seemed to exhaust its votaries.

Having concluded the dance to the honor and glory
of Guadalupe, they filed into the church chanting a low,
monotonous hymn. I was the first to enter after them, followed closely by my friends. When they reached the altar,
where a large picture of the Virgin was suspended, all
dropped down on their knees in regular lines of fours, and
began crossing themselves and murmuring their *pater-
nosters*. Catching the spirit of the occasion, and unwilling
to wound their acute religious sensibilities by the close
proximity of idle sightseers, we followed their example and
knelt for a few moments. But so absorbed were the devotees, or so natural our movements, that we remained
unnoticed among the worshipers.

The man who played on the jarana recited prayers,
the other responding. After this they sang a litany, accompanied by low moaning sounds, as if in anguish of
spirit, while every eye was fixed steadily upon the patron
saint in mute appeal, and tears streamed spontaneously
down these bronzed and hard-used faces.

After a half an hour thus spent upon their knees, they
arose, and still accompanied by the strange music from
the ghastly instrument, that seemed to have taken on a
more unearthly character, moved backward, making a

low courtesy at each step, and, as they filed out noiselessly in their strange tongue, sang in chorus:

I.

From Heaven she descended,
Triumphant and glorious,
To favor us—
La Guadalupana.

II.

Farewell, Guadalupe!
Queen of the Indians!
Our life is Thine,
This kingdom is Thine,

III.

Farewell, Guadalupe!
Queen of the Indians!
We who leave you today
Know not who may come again.

When they withdrew from the church, our party following closely, the dancing was resumed with added fervor. Before I was aware of the fact, my feet were going up and down, out and around, in imitation of the Indians, and greatly to the amusement of my friends and the spectators, some exclaiming, "¡Qué chula! ¡Mira la niña bailanda!" ("How pretty! Look at the child dancing!") which broke the spell, recalled me to myself, and joining my party, we went down the hill. But before we had gone down ten of the almost countless steps, one of the most picturesquely attired of all the Indians was walking by my side, making a bargain with me for the sale of his crown and feathers.

While the scene I had just witnessed had, at times, an effect to excite merriment, the contrary feeling of sadness and almost reverence prevailed. I could not but feel awe in the presence of those dark children of the wild mountains as they performed their mystical devotions and sang the rude barbaric songs that had in their tones the strangeness of another world. They were so earnest, so devout, so loving to the Mother of the shrine, and their grief so deep, when they plaintively looked on her image, and bowed in a sorrowing farewell, that they excited a sympathetic feeling in the coldest heart.

At the sacred shrine of Guadalupe, eight days after the feast has been duly celebrated by the Indians and common people, the wealth, beauty, and fashion of the capital wend their way thither to tender their renewed obligations to the patron saint.

I was a guest at a sumptuous celebration in honor of the Señora Doña Guadalupe Bros, who invited me to participate in the ceremonies and festivities of her día de santo.

At seven o'clock in the morning mass was celebrated in the chapel, with the administration of the Holy Communion, followed by an impressive sermon from the young cura of the church of Santa Vera Cruz—Daniel Escobar. A full orchestra dispensed the sweet and solemn strains of Mozart.

Many distinguished society people were there, among them the wife and daughters of General Corona. The ladies all wore black dresses with lace mantillas.

The numerous lighted tapers were gifts from foundling and orphan institutions. of which the Señora Doña Guadalupe is a benefactress. All were deeply moved by the solemnity of the services, the more evidently so that their noble hostess and relative was weak and infirm in health.

After mass a light breakfast was served in the grand dining room, consisting of coffee, chocolate, and breads in great variety. The sumptuous and elaborate dinner took place at three o'clock in the afternoon. The orchestra in the corridor, supplemented by the singing of birds in the aviary, filled up the pauses with sweet sounds. Covers were laid for a hundred guests, the elite of society, among them many of the most distinguished men in Mexico—writers, orators, statesmen—including Altamirano and the venerable Guillermo Prieto.

In the evening a brilliant ball was given in the sala grande, and for several days dinners and balls and general rejoicings followed. The gifts received by the Doña Guadalupe were numerous and elegant, and had the additional charm, in most instances, of being useful, handwrought articles of every imaginable kind. One chair alone, the gift of Doña Josefina, had required six months to embroider.

General Palacio and wife, the noble Josefina, gave their aunt a *función particular*, in the way of a theatrical performance in the house, which was again a brilliant affair. Three short plays were presented, a melodrama, a tragedy, and a comedy.

The players were amateurs, friends of the family, and acquitted themselves admirably. I was particularly impressed by the talent displayed by a young comedian, Francisco Cardona, who continually brought down the house with his hits on the times.

The feasts of Guadalupe at Morelia were unusually brilliant. Thousands of the faithful attended the matins in the cathedral. The houses were decorated and the pyrotechnical display was very fine. At sunset, and as soon as the bells chimed, an allegorical car, representing the apparition of the Virgin of Guadalupe, started through the principal street from the portico of the cathedral toward the San Diego Church, followed by great crowds. Fireworks crossed the sky, giving it the appearance of a dome of fire.

In Querétaro these feasts were equally splendid. The city was converted into a great garden. Triumphal arches spanned the streets. The capitol was covered with fluttering streamers, banners and bunting of tricolor, stretched from balcony to balcony, from post to post and from roof to roof. At night the illumination was general. Querétaro seemed wrapped in a mantle of fire. The towers of its church and the roofs of its highest buildings were crowded with flames of different colors that oscillated in the winds. Fireworks were kept up till midnight.

A Mexican Christmas is very unlike one in the United States. No merry jingle of sleigh bells is heard in this sunny land where the rigors of winter are unknown, and the few lofty peaks, where alone snow is ever seen, would hardly tempt the most adventurous tobogganist.

As there are no chimneys, Santa Claus is deprived of his legitimate and time-honored entrance into households, so the delightful and immemorial custom of hanging up stockings is unknown to Mexican children. But perhaps they enjoy themselves quite as much after their own fashion as ours do. One circumstance in their favor is the long-continued celebration, which, beginning on the evening of the 17th of December and continuing till New Year's Day, is one long, delightful jubilee.

The celebrations in honor of Guadalupe extend from the 12th until the posadas, or nine days' festivities. The last prayers on the lips of the faithful and the last tones from organ and choir in praise of the patron saint, hardly die away ere the Christmas rejoicings begin.

The word posada signifies an inn, and the whole observance is a relic bequeathed by the Spaniards. The celebration is limited almost exclusively to the capital and the larger cities, and may be considered more as a social feature than belonging specially to the Church—though really combining the elements of both. It is a reminder of the Nativity, based on the Gospel narrative, but with additions.

The first act of the posada represents the journey of the Virgin Mary and Joseph from Nazareth to Bethlehem, and the difficulties they experienced in finding shelter. The family and invited guests march in procession through halls and around corridors, holding in their hands lighted tapers and singing solemn litanies. Before the procession, the figures of Mary and Joseph are borne along by servants or young boys. Each door they pass is knocked upon, but no answer or invitation to enter is given, and so the procession continues to move around, singing and knocking, until, at last, a door is opened, when they all enter and mass is said and hymns are sung with all possible solemnity, after which the other interesting features of the posada are presented, as hereafter related. Sometimes a burro is introduced to represent the faithful animal that carried the holy family in their journeyings.

All over the city is heard the litany of the posadas, sung in a hundred homes, as the pilgrimages wind in and out of the rooms and round the improvised shrines. Venetian lights hang in the patios, and fireworks blaze skyward in every direction. One of the most interesting features is the infantile resort set up in the southern part of the plaza. The Zócalo is a bewitching place; lights flash through the branches of pine and cypress, and the place is alive with children of the first families of Mexico.

The breaking of the piñata is the chief sport of the posada. The piñata is an oval-shaped, earthen jar, handsomely decorated and covered with bright ornaments, tinsel, gay flowers, and flaunting streamers of tissue paper. The common people are experts in the manufacture of these curious objects, and when a vender of them is seen perambulating the streets, it is worth while stopping to examine his stock in trade. There are turkeys, horses, birds, monkeys—in fact, every beast, bird or fowl of the air that is known. In addition, there are children almost life-sized, and even brides, with the trained dress, veil and orange blossoms. But oh! the hapless fate of these earthen brides! They are soon beaten and smashed into atoms by the fun-loving crowd.

The holy figures are left in the chapel after the litanies are ended, and then, either in the patio or a room selected for the purpose, the fun of breaking the piñata begins. It is suspended from the ceiling, and each person desiring to take part is, in turn, blindfolded. Armed with a long pole, he proceeds to strike the swinging piñata. Often a dozen people are blindfolded before the final crash comes, and the dulces go rattling over the floor. Then such racing and chasing!

The first posada that I attended was impromptu without the procession, litany, or Mary and Joseph; the piñata was a monkey, and my young Mexican friends insisted I should be the one to break it. Being duly blindfolded, and armed with a long pole, while the crowd of Spanish-speaking people looked on, asserting that I could and would not fail in the effort, I set confidently about my task. But no sound came of broken crockery or falling dulces.

The rule was, that every one should have three trials. After the third stroke imagine my chagrin, when the handkerchief was removed, to see the monkey above my head, slowly descending, grinning and wriggling his tail. A wild and clamorous burst of laughter went up when I discovered the trick. They insisted that I should have another stroke at his monkeyship; so, acting on the rule, "If at first you don't succeed," blindfolded and pole in hand, I advanced, and with one vigorous stroke, shivered it, amid shouts of laughter and rounds of applause. No dulces were ever so sweet to me!

A happy event for me was an invitation from General Palacio's household to attend the posadas in their house, affording me the opportunity of witnessing a distinctively national custom in all its true elegance.

Mary and Joseph were represented by two wax figures, placed upon a flower-wreathed, moss-embowered vehicle, made for the purpose, and propelled by an enthusiastic youth. The procession, consisting of the family and invited guests, formed in the corridor, which had been profusely decorated for the occasion. The posada began with the singing of a hymn, in which all participated with due solemnity. We marched around the corridor, with candles in our hands, preceded by the images, knocking at a door each time, but were always refused admittance by some one inside the rooms. At last we knocked at the chapel door, where we sang a petition, as if Mary and Joseph themselves were imploring admittance. Questions from within called forth the natural responses from the wayfarers without, who sang, "The night is cold and dark, and the woman who seeks a night's lodgings is the Queen of Heaven, having not where to lay her head."

The door at once opened, the weary pair entered,

and the procession moved into the chapel singing a ringing anthem, which to me had the spirit of our ever-familiar
"All hail the power." The litany and prayers followed,
after which we went downstairs to the theater, where the
fun and merrymaking began in earnest, leaving Mary
and Joseph alone in the chapel.

Once seated in the theater, two of the gentlemen
guests, dressed in the uniforms of *gens d'armes*, presented
themselves, bearing silver trays—one loaded with brilliant
badges in the national colors, and the other with handsome finger rings, ornamented with settings of various
stones. These badges and rings were passed to each guest
with the most courtly grace by the pompous, sham gens
d'armes, who could ill conceal a smile on their sober faces.
My ring was of seed pearls and sapphires.

A long chitchat followed, as we adorned ourselves
with badges and compared rings. The ladies were seated
in a circle, and the men passed around in groups, or singly,
and all being acquainted, the liveliest sallies and repartee
were heard on every side, and good humor and mirth to
overflowing filled every heart.

At length a bell rings, the curtain rises, and an enchanting scene greets our wondering gaze: a vine-embow-
ered stage covered with a wealth of tropical plants and
flowers; mossy grottoes, sparkling fountains and mimic
cascades, which seem a part of nature's own handiwork;
oranments of precious metals wrought in most elaborate
patterns, gorgeously attired characters; all under the blaze
of the dazzling lights, form a scene which might have been
produced by the Genii of Aladdin's Lamp.

Two gentlemen in costumes of the time of Louis XIV,
richly overlaid with gold and silver embroidery, were discovered. One was dressed in blue coat, with white knee
breeches, while the colors of the other were pink and cream
color. Both wore flowing, curled wigs. They stood on opposite sides of a richly carved table, on which was a glittering display of magnificently wrought silver, comprising
not only the plate of the Palacio family, but also the service

presented by the Emperor of Austria. Two servants dressed as pages in satin suits, wigged and powdered, stood near the cavaliers, and with profound respect presented salvers loaded with fruits and flowers.

The tableau was broken by the cavaliers and pages passing down from the stage and serving each guest with liqueurs and wines in tiny glasses, and delicious sweets prepared in the household.

This posada sprang from the fertile brain of the General himself, and all the actors therein were members of the household and invited guests. He proved himself an adroit "stage manager," as few of the participants knew the extent of the varied and humorous programme.

Two young ladies of the household, dressed as nuns, then presented us with those curious and grotesque rag dolls—the invention of the natives—almost as large as real babies.

We had scarcely recovered from the effects produced on our risibles by the dolls, when the gens d'armes entered bearing trays. On one, dainty little parcels were arranged, tied up most artistically in bright-colored silk handkerchiefs. The other contained lovely bouquets and *boutonnières*, and cornucopias of what we supposed to be sugar plums, but on our opening them proved to be hairpins! The silken bundles enveloped the homely peanut and tojocotes, the most insipid fruit in Mexico.

Thus did our genial host keep us constantly amused and entertained with his rapid and ingenious transitions from the grand and gorgeous to the mirth-provoking and ridiculous.

One of the elegant courtiers who figured upon the stage, came to me at this moment stating that in the patio there was another posada of a still more interesting nature, and he wanted me to witness it. We there found assembled a crowd of excited children with the servants of the household, in addition to those who came with the guests, all eagerly enjoying the sport of breaking the piñata, which was in the form and about the size of a five-year-old girl. This figure was clothed in a white dress of some diaphanous material decked with tinsel; long black hair, plaited and tied with ribbon, hung down her back. Suspended by wires she swung in mid-air, calmly unconscious of the severe castigation in store for her. I was politely invited to join in the drubbing, but all my efforts failed to demolish her. When she finally became dismembered, I was presented with the legs to take off as souvenirs of the occasion.

On our return to the theater we heard in the distance a peculiar music. As it approached, the unusual sounds were accounted for by the appearance of a band of forlornly dressed Aztecs with their ancient musical instruments, followed by a train of attendants of the same race. In the rear came a hand wagon laden with boxes of bonbons, fruits and sweets. When this singular band entered the brilliantly illuminated theater, the contrast excited boundless merriment. Our host appeared at the door and was greeted with shouts, when he entered and made a humorous little speech. The Indians continued their earsplitting strains in stolid impassivity, apparently quite unconscious of the grandeur of their surroundings. To look on their emotionless and expressionless faces would extract a smile from an Egyptian mummy.

At this juncture General Palacio whispered in my ear that very soon he intended to give an entertainment más serio (of a more dignified nature), in order that I might witness in his own house every form of social life known to the capital. The Velada Literaria, mentioned in the chapter on Mexican literature, will give some idea of the elegance of this convivial reunion.

The scenes were interspersed with dancing, and now the witching strains of the danza again rose from the orchestra, and away went the gay señoritas and caballeros, responsive to its intoxicating measures.

This ended, again the curtain rose and our eyes were greeted by the representation of statuary by several of the gentlemen guests. Their superb physique, clad in stockinet, posed in the most graceful manner, imitated to perfection the sculptured forms of the Dying Gladiator, Brutus and the Conspirators, and many other classic and historical groups.

A señorita then entered, dressed in one of the prettiest costumes of the country, called La China poblana. Nothing could have been more striking and brilliant or more becoming to her dark, rich beauty. A bright crimson skirt, embroidered with white, reached partly to the waist, where it was supplemented by an upper portion of green. The bodice was simply a white chemise, exquisitely wrought, leaving neck and arms bare. Around her form was twined in graceful fashion a silken rebozo, combining in its gay stripes the national colors which marked the rest of her costume. Green slippers were on her dainty feet, and white silk stockings showed to where the petticoat began below the knee. She was a harmony in red, white, and green—a patriotic symphony.

She held one end of a long pole, while a friend, also in national costume, held the other. Dozens of pretty little baskets decked off with gay ribbons were suspended from the pole. Each guest was given one, nobody suspecting its contents, until a live chicken made its presence known by fluttering in its futile efforts to escape.

At that moment General Palacio appeared at the door, when the company greeted him with much applause, singing out, "Long live Riva, Riva Palacio!"

The next scene revealed to us a single carved column, surmounted by a richly ornate capital. It seemed singular, and we wondered what it meant after the splendid scenes we had just witnessed. Suddenly, as by magic, a swarm of mockingbirds emerged through the top of the column, each decorated with ribbons of the national colors, and fluttered through the hall.

Little shrieks of delight went up from the ladies, and all eagerly pursued the frightened birds, making captures. Order being restored, we turned our eyes again to the stage to behold the mysterious column slowly opening, revealing to our astonished vision exquisite articles of virtu, bric-a-brac, curios, and magnificent ornaments of every description, all glittering against a crimson background. These were distributed as regalos to the guests.

The entertainment closed with a finale grande. Upon the stage were assembled in one heterogeneous but effective tableau, gentlemen of the court, nuns, la bonita China poblana, pages, flowers, silver, grotto, and, in the background, our genial host. This was the prelude to a recherché collation in the comedor grande.

Dancing was kept up until sunrise, but those of us who reluctantly withdrew were gently reminded by our host that we were expected to carry home our chickens.

On that glorious Mexican, moonlit night, with all our bundles, regalos, and chickens squawking at every step, we must have looked like the remnant of a Mardi Gras procession, as our figures were thrown full length on the broad street in exaggerated silhouette.

Posadas on so grand a scale are given in comparatively few houses. But the litanies, wax figures and procession are generally a part of the programme, varying according to means or taste.

Every night for more than a month, and for a month longer, at regular intervals, in this hospitable mansion, entertainments of various kinds were given—grand balls, dinners, and brilliant theatricals. My invitations were as numerous as the entertainments, where, whenever possible, I found myself, ever at home, an honored guest.

In rural districts, where posadas are not given, one of the chief Christmas recreations is the pastorela. This signifies an idyl, and is used symbolically to represent the announcements of the birth of Christ to the shepherds. A little girl dressed in white, with wings attached to her shoulders, represents the angel, while the shepherds are furnished with crooks, with which they beat time to their chanting. The infant Jesus, represented by a doll, is rocked in a cradle or swung from the ceiling, and on Christmas eve is baptized, the godfather and godmother being selected from the company.

This pastoral is much in use on the Rio Grande frontier, where there is a dearth of amusement, and generally among the plainer population. When practiced by the wealthy, it is enlarged upon until it assumes grand proportions. The pastorela begins sometimes a week or more before Christmas.

The Feast of the Epiphany, known in Mexico as the Fiesta de los Tres Reyes (Feast of the Three Kings), which comes on the 6th of January, has connected with it an interesting social event. This is known as the Baile de los Compadres. It is not so commonly observed now as formerly, but is none the less interesting.

A coffee cake is made, in which is placed a bean, and at the dinner which follows mass on that day this cake is placed under a napkin and then cut by some one of the guests. The one who gets the bean is known as king; if a woman, queen. If the former, he drops the bean into the glass of the lady whom he selects as queen. If a lady gets the bean, the same process is gone through, with the difference of sex in the selection. They embrace a la mexicana, becoming at once compadres. The king makes the queen a present, and must also give a ball within the month of January.

At the ball the names of all the ladies are put into a hat and the gentlemen draw. The lady whose name the gentleman draws becomes his compadre for the evening, and much merriment follows.

El Candelario, or the feast of Candlemas, comes on the 2d of February. It commemorates the purification of the Virgin, and is the occasion on which the candles are blessed and consecrated, to be used the ensuing year, in extreme illness, death, earthquakes, and thunderstorms.

The day is celebrated at Tacubaya in a novel way. The streets are filled with gambling booths, where all kinds of games of hazard are played by the common people; not only by the men, but women also of every age yield to this fascinating pastime.

On the 5th of February the Church celebrates the death of Mexico's only martyr, San Felipe de Jesús. He was martyred in China, and his baptismal urn stands in a wooden frame in the cathedral beside the tomb of the Emperor Iturbide.

The carnival season comes with its throngs of gay, promiscuous maskers, but without a representation of our King Comus. Some of these are said to represent the spies sent out by Herod in search of Christ; if so, they seem to enjoy themselves amazingly.

Lent is duly observed, especially by ladies, who perambulate the streets dressed in black, on their way to and from church. At this time the Zócalo has two of its sides adorned with booths and rustic tents, in which various delicious drinks are sold by captivating Indian maidens. In accord with the season fewer toys are sold in the streets, but as the people pass they halt to partake of a drink of *agua de chía*, *agua de piña* and *horchata*.

On Palm Sunday large quantities of palm, plaited in every imaginable form and tied with ribbons, are taken to the church and blessed. They are then placed on the iron rods outside the windows to protect the house from lightning or any other dread calamity.

During Holy Week, bells, organs, and choirs utter not a sound, the stores are closed, and the world has a holiday. On Holy Thursday it is customary for both ladies and gentlemen to turn out in their new suits. The ladies appear in handsome toilets, the result of weeks of labor for the dressmakers, while the gentlemen display a corresponding industry on the part of the tailors.

Good Friday sees an entire change. The whole republic is in mourning, and the smiling faces of yesterday are superseded by downcast eyes and sober mien, as the vast concourse of people pass silently on their way to church.

In the afternoon is celebrated the feast of the Tres Caídas (Three Falls), which commemorates the three falls Christ suffered on his way to Calvary. After each fall the priest preaches a short sermon. Then follows the ceremony of the Tres Horas (Three Hours), when the scenes of the Crucifixion are represented in pantomime and with effigies. On the evening of the same day there is a service called pésame, a visit of condolence to the Virgin on the death of her Son.

The last day of Holy Week, Sábado de Gloria, or Saturday of Glory, is devoted to the death and disgrace of Judas. Effigies of the traitor are hung all over the streets, and, being filled with powder, burst as they fall to the ground. This catastrophe is celebrated by the rattling of myriads of matracas, wooden rattles, that make the head ring, mingled with the shouts of the populace.

Numerous and grotesque paper effigies hung across many of the most prominent streets, and the Judases, filled with bamboos of powder, were tied to the balconies, roofs of buildings, and lampposts. Many of them had silver coins pasted upon them, representing the thirty pieces of silver for which Judas sold Christ. When the Judases burst, the eager crowd gathered up the coins and then proceeded to tear into shreds the effigies, in order to avenge the treachery of Judas.

On the 16th of April, the annual Fiesta de las Flores (Floral Festival) is inaugurated on the Viga Canal. None of the feasts of the capital affords more pleasure to its citizens. The paseo is deserted, while the boulevard beside the Viga is enlivened with hundreds of elegant equipages, filled with the elite of the capital, as well as pedestrians and horsemen, who repair thither to witness the festival of the Indians. The canal itself is literally overspread with boats large and small, some with a covered space in the middle and a deck at each end, all manned by swarthy Indians. Indian women and girls in their well-befitting costumes, with wreaths of poppies on their heads, and garlands around their necks, guitar in hand, sing in every imaginable key the madrigals of their people, dancing as they go. On the shore the best bands play, and the same scene of animation is presented for days.

The 24th of June is the Fiesta de San Juan Bautista (St. John the Baptist), the patron saint of all bathers. This is a day on which the Catholic world of Mexico bathes and puts on clean clothes.

Small boys dressed up as miniature soldiers, with imitation swords and guns, parade the streets. It is a holiday that any mortal who cares for St. John may enjoy inexpensively.

A legend received by the common people has it that ablutions made in honor of the Herald of the Saviour "give beauty to the maiden, vigor to the matron, and freshness to the old maid."

Regardless of the truth of this, the bathing establishments everywhere are liberally patronized on this day. Such pushing, jostling, screaming, and lofty tumbling as these devotees of St. John do!

The public is entertained with as much freedom as though it were a bull fight, and it shows a generous appreciation in long and continued applause. In one tank one hundred and fifty or more bathers may be seen at once, throwing themselves head first, diving and swimming, or standing half-submerged, or perhaps jumping from the springboard.

To all these gyrations add the screams of the multitude, the shrieks of the bathers, and the people on shore selling a thousand and one articles beneath the rays of a scorching sun, to complete the scene. Though many pursuits and avocations are carried on, the dominating and supreme desire of the crowd is to get wet.

This feast of water costs but a *real*, and on that day the populace shows its appreciation of the opportunity for so insignificant a sum to be made wet from crown to sole.

Superb masses, probably not surpassed anywhere in the world, are celebrated for the dead. A very grand occasion of this kind was when the Spanish colony honored their dead king at the Profesa Church. This was the most imposing church service that I witnessed. The interior attested the faultless taste of the decorator. An immense catafalque stood in the center with white and silver drapings. The bust of Alphonso was wreathed in immortelles, the whole surrounded by the arms of Spain. Columns were draped with black and great black streamers were suspended from the dome and gracefully festooned from the altars. Wax candles of remarkable size and length were lighted all around and throughout the church, while clouds of incense floated over all. Each one in the large congregation was provided with a candle two feet in length. The music, both orchestral and choral, was grand. Chairs were provided for all, and the floor was handsomely carpeted. The best of society was represented, and I never saw a more elegant assemblage, all in deep black. President Díaz with his cabinet occupied seats near General Jackson and his friends, so there was a commingling of nationalities as well as of tears on that day.

Funeral cards are elaborate both in style and diction. The following will give an idea of the forms in general use:

"Died yesterday at half-past twelve, Señorita Dolores García. Her mother, brothers, and relatives, in informing you of this sad event, beg that you will lift your prayers to the Eternal for the repose of her soul, and be kind enough to attend her funeral, which will take place today at four o'clock at the Church of Santa Vera Cruz."

The sending of cards or letters of condolence follows, as a matter of course, and where families have an extensive circle of acquaintances, every day in the weeks finds them writing to their afflicted friends.

Below will be found another still more poetic in its language, which was sent me upon the death of the gentleman named, who was the father of Señor Alberto Bianchi, the well-known author and journalist:

A la sombra del árbol santo de la Cruz, ayer a las ocho de la noche, voló al seno de su Criador el alma del

SR. D. ALBERTO BIANCHI

(PADRE).

Sus atribulados hijos piden para él oraciones a la piedad de sus hermanos en Jesucristo.

México, Setiembre 23 de 1886.

(Translation.)

Under the shade of the holy tree of the Cross, yesterday at eight o'clock at night, ascended to the bosom of his Creator, the soul of

SR. D. ALBERTO BIANCHI

(FATHER).

His afflicted children ask for him prayers from the piety of his brethren in Jesus Christ.

Mexico, September 23, 1886.

The wearing of mourning is universal, not only for near relatives, but also for friends. A young lady dies, her companions don the somber garb for thirty days; if the father or mother of the girl should die, it is worn for fifteen days. By this time some other relative or friend may die, when the custom is again in force, and may be indefinitely prolonged. During all this time they seclude themselves from society. On visiting a house of mourning, likewise, custom prescribes a black dress; and for these ever-recurring occasions mourning costumes are an essential part of every lady's wardrobe.

Ladies do not attend funerals, but visits of pésame (regret) are made immediately after death, and for nine days those who cannot call send letters or cards of condolence.

The national feasts are those of the 16th of September and the 5th of May. Differences of opinion may exist upon every other subject; but on those days, the former recalling the grito (call) of Hidalgo for Independence, and the latter the victory of the Mexicans over the French at Puebla, all hands and hearts are united in giving them a fitting and enthusiastic welcome.

Courtship is something of a serious matter as undertaken under Mexican auspices. The probation may extend from five to ten years, or may even exceed that of Jacob, and at the end of this period the devoted Romeo has perhaps never entered the house—possibly not even spoken to his Juliet. Patience is a virtue all possess; and as time is of no consequence, they content themselves with waiting for something in the future. The lover walks slowly back and forth before her house for hours at a time, days and nights alike. Perhaps it is from this fact that he assumes the unromantic appellation of haciendo el oso (playing the bear). He may also play the bear on horseback, and his "ladye faire" knows by intuition when he will pass, and, securely screened from public gaze remains behind the curtain on the balcony and merely shows her head or salutes him with her fingertips. She goes to church or on the plaza, sure that he is not far away, and though they do not speak, a glance or smile each day is worth a lifetime. But frequently tiny billets doux find their way to the angel upstairs, by means of strings, and the family is none the wiser.

I remember to have seen one young man "playing the bear" until my deepest sympathies were enlisted in his behalf. Day by day he repaired to the same spot, on the corner of the street opposite my window, at No. 6 la Primera de la Providencia. For months the trying business had gone on, until he was reduced to a mere skeleton, and his hollow eyes had that expectant expression which marks the victim of love in Mexico. So interested was I that I determined to know something of the fair creature to whom the luckless swain was yielding up his mental, moral, and physical strength.

The father of the girl was so much opposed to the match, the young man being only a medical student, he forbade his going nearer than two squares of the house.

Having seen the effect of "playing the bear" on this lover, I was curious to see how the girl sustained the ordeal. Directed by his fixed and steady gaze upon the house, I found her standing on the balcony with only her head visible. Her eyes were fixed on him, and now and then the dainty little hand made motions towards him. After a few months thus spent, the poor fellow disappeared from the corner, which was perhaps the end of their love-making.

I was told by several English-speaking Mexicans that the larger proportion of the young men of the country greatly prefer "playing the bear" from the sidewalk, to entering the homes of the señoritas, even if permitted by custom.

I witnessed the opposite of this in the case of a young Mexican girl who had been reared by an American sister-in-law. Lupe was pretty and attractive, and naturally at an early age was the recipient, from the young men who had come within sight of her, of numerous bearish favors; but two of them, Fernando ———— and Julio ————; became more deeply enamored than the rest; but the sister was determined there should be no "playing the bear," so she invited the young men to call at the house. I have seen as many as ten or twelve in her parlor in one evening, all animated and interested—each one being only too pleased to take his turn at a few moments' conversation with the señorita.

But a denouement, quite unexpected, came. One of the young men who had become desperately enamored of the girl found he had a rival in one of his friends. A dispute arose, some of the boys espousing one side and the remainder the other, until bloodshed seemed inevitable. No case in chancery ever required more skillful diplomacy than this, calling for the good offices of at least half a dozen outside friends to adjust the matter and prevent a catastrophe. The rupture between the boys was never healed, but neither of them won the señorita. So, after all, perhaps it is better that they should have "bear playing" in order to win their wives. I confess that after witnessing these love affairs I was for once, as our latter-day politicians say, "on the fence," and quite as ready to fall on the "bear side" as on that of our less conventional, more modern lovemaking.

A Mexican lady related to me a method of courtship

somewhat different. A señorita is sometimes made aware of the interest a young man takes in her, by being continually followed when walking along the street. In the course of time he writes a letter which he leaves with the portero, and it is always necessary to enlist the interest of these men by the bestowal of a little cash. She pays no attention to his first letters, but after a while she may perhaps notice his advances. He goes to the house each day and finds out her movements from the portero, governing himself accordingly. At last, accompanied by a responsible friend, he makes bold to call on the father and asks her hand in marriage. Then the father asks the girl if she is willing to marry the young man. She replies she cannot say until she has met him. When at length he calls, every member of the family, and even the servants, have the privilege of being present. After this, he is the novio oficial (accepted lover), but even if the marriage be postponed six months or as many years, he is never left alone for a moment with his fiancée.

Once admitted as novio oficial, it may be imagined that the fervor of his devotion will find vent in many lover-like expressions. As indicative of their warm, poetic imagination and passionate Southern nature, I append a few of the most characteristic of these phrases as used by both sexes:

¡Niña de mi alma!	Child of my soul!
¿Me quieres?	Dost thou love me?
¡Te adoro, te idolatro!	I adore thee, I idolize thee!
¡Me muero por ti!	I die for thee!
¡Eres mi dicha!	Thou art my happiness!
¡Te amo mas que a mi vida!	I love thee more than my life!
¡Eres mi único pensamiento!	Thou art my only thought!
¡Me mato por ti!	I kill myself for thee!
¡No te olvides de mi!	Do not forget me!
¡Siempre serás mi!	Thou wilt always be mine!
¡Tú serás mi solo amor!	Thou wilt be my only love!

¡No me engañes!	Do not deceive me!
¡No sabes cuanto te amo!	Thou dost not know how much I love thee!
Oye, hijito, ¿me quieres de veras?	Say, my boy, dost really love me!
¡Que feliz soy a tu lado!	How happy I am by thy side!
¡No dejes de escribirme!	Don't fail to write me!
¿Vienes mañana?	Will you come tomorrow?
¡Ingrato, Ya lo sé todo!	Ingrate, I know all!
¡Pero hija, eso no es cierto!	But daughter, it is not true!
¿No me crees?	Dost thou not believe me?
¡Perdóname corazón!	Pardon me, heart!
¡Adiós chula, hasta mañana!	Good-bye, precious, until tomorrow!
¡Sueño contigo!	I dream of thee!

The señorita is not intentionally, or by nature, a flirt. She would scorn to inveigle in her meshes the affections of her admirer. But, in addition to her irresistible eyes, there are certain little social and toilet graces which she unconsciously employs in a most expressive manner that never fail to bring him to her feet.

The most effectual and indispensable toilet accessory is the fan. Of every size, style, and color, it is often an expensive item in a fashionable lady's outfit. When manipulated by the fair owner—opened wide and waved in graceful challenge, raised to eyes or lips in witching coquetry, or even when peacefully folded in jeweled fingers—its language is varied and expressive.

Great care and attention is bestowed upon the pañuelo (handkerchief), which plays, too, an important part, second only to that of the fan.

For a young man of moderate means, matrimony is a serious undertaking. He not only furnishes the house and home, but the bridal outfit as well. But in some of the wealthier families parents furnish the greater part of the latter themselves, restricting the purchases of the groom-elect to perhaps the bridal dresses, the jewels, and other accessories. An ivory-covered prayer book is an indispensable offering from the groom. The bridal tour is one expense from which he is now exempt, but as facilities for travel increase, perhaps in the near future, this item may be added to his already long list of expenditures. I believe the event of matrimony is no less troublesome than the long and tedious courtship. The war of reform made three marriage ceremonies necessary. Two months before, the young people must register at the cathedral, giving date of birth, in what city or country, vocation, etc., whether widow or widower. After this, the priest registers the same at the civil office, and their intentions must be placed on a bulletin board outside the office for twenty days. For five Sundays the priest publishes the bans. After this, accompanied by the notary public, he goes to the house of the bride, where she is asked if she acts of her "own free will and accord," and other necessary questions are put with as much freedom as though the subject were a transfer of real estate. A few days prior to the church wedding, the judge of the court, accompanied by six witnesses, the priest being one, performs the civil marriage. The dress worn on this occasion is presented by the groom.

I witnessed a church wedding at "Santa Brigida," and the Mexican ceremony is a pretty one. The groom passed many coins through the hand of the bride, indicating that she is to handle and control the household funds. They knelt at the altar with lighted candles in their hands, emblematical of the Christian faith, and a silken scarf was placed around their shoulders, after which a silver cord was put around their necks, and the ceremony was complete.

An American who contracts marriage in Mexico, regardless of faith or creed, must have three ceremonies —two in Spanish, and one more in either English or Spanish. This is the invariable rule even when marrying his countrywoman. He must, besides, make public notice of his intention by having it announced on a bulletin board for twenty days. He may evade or escape the latter by the payment of a sum of money—it is said from $60 to $150; but in any event, he must have resided one month in the country. The three ceremonies consist of a contract of marriage—civil marriage, the only one recognized by law since 1858—and the church service, which is not compulsory with Americans, and may be celebrated in their own homes. The first two must take place before a judge, and four witnesses, at least, including the American Consul. The contract of marriage includes a statement of names, ages, lineage, business, and residence of the parties. The ceremony of the civil marriage—the legal one—is always in Spanish.

The length of time required for the completion of one of these marriage arrangements may be from one or two days to three months, as the parties understand facilitating such matters. But once such a knot is tied, it would be a difficult task to have it loosened by even the expert fingers of a Chicago lawyer.

Weddings are not generally widely announced. Intimate friends are invited to the marriage in the church, and afterward participate in the festivities that follow at the house. After the wedded pair are established in their own home, they send cards which read:

"Tirso Calderón y Julia Hope

tienen el honor de participar a Vd. su enlace, y se ofrecen a sus órdenes en la casa, número 6 a de la primera Providencia." In other words, you are considered a friend of the newly-wedded pair, and they will be happy to see you in their house.

Cards announcing a birth are thus expressed:

"Tirso Calderón y Señora

tienen el gusto de participar a Vd. el nacimiento de su hijo, y lo ponen a sus órdenes," which means, in few words, that this gentleman and his wife have the pleasure of announcing the birth of their son, and place him "at your orders."

Baptism occurs within ten or fifteen days after birth, and, as is customary in the Catholic Church, children bear the name of some saint. Birthdays are not noticed, but the celebration of the día de santo, or day of the saint for whom the child is named, is the most important event in his life. Cards are sent announcing baptism.

When ten or fifteen days old the infant is taken in charge by the padrinos (godfather and godmother), and after much elaborate preparation is carried to the church and baptized. These godparents are called comadre and compadre by the child's parents, in preference to their legitimate names.

The names of children of both sexes are identical, by simply changing the termination of *a* or *o*, and often even this is not done. José María is the same for both, but Pomposa is the feminine for Pomposo.

Within a reasonable time a great dinner follows, at which many handsome gifts are displayed for the young innocent. Cards of congratulation are sent, if nothing more, but more frequently it is some delicious article of food or drink, or a piece of jewelry.

Social usages show no signs of change or relaxation, even with the advancement so manifest in every other direction. Many of them may seem formal and useless— based on the tedious Spanish etiquette—but they are not without charm as well as meaning; and in comparison with our own rather free and informal ways one might wish that a happy medium might be found. Many of the customs are admirable; and always the culture, ease, kindliness, and elegance with which they are observed must commend themselves to our brisk, business-loving and energetic countrymen.

Those agreeable features of American and English home life, informal luncheons, teas, and the unceremonious happening-in of a few friends to a "feast of reason and a flow of soul," or perhaps games and music, and whatever else may be, are wanting among the Mexicans. The merienda, a mid-afternoon luncheon, which takes place after the siesta, consists of a cup of chocolate or coffee with some sort of fancy cake or bread. It is the only small social feature of everyday life, and a friend may drop in and partake of it without ceremony. But they are happy in their own way, and a departure from it would be rather painful than otherwise. The love for pomp and ceremonious display leads them to discard simple and unoestentatious entertainments, which makes a narrow limit to their social existence. Hence, if the wealthy indulge but seldom, those of less means, being unable to cope with them, though in comfortable circumstances, abstain from any, except on occasions of domestic festivals—christenings or weddings. But there are many smaller hospitalities which always prove acceptable. One is scarcely seated before being asked to have something, and generally delicious chocolate is served *sin ceremonia*.

A high estimate is placed on dress and external appearance. The taste for rich and gorgeous clothing belongs to them by heredity—Montezuma himself giving an example. We read of his mantle of the plumage of rare and brilliant-hued birds, his gold-embroidered clothing, that "his half boots were set with jewels, their soles being of solid gold"; and that he always allowed four days to elapse between the wearing of each suit.

In these latter days the taste displays itself in every way to be imagined, and they judge others from their own standpoint. Quickly is the dress of a stranger summed up, even before an impression has been made as to his face, being able to give a minute description of his clothes, even to the pocket handkerchief and shoes, two articles of dress in which every Mexican takes pride.

To enter the higher strata of society, one must give external proof of his fitness by his dress. After this, his merits are duly weighed. The first appearance of a stranger, both in dress and manner, makes his future position. I have often been amused at seeing the very dignified and quiet manner in which the inspection is made, the distinguished invited guest never for a moment supposing himself a subject of scrutiny. But however incorrectly he may speak the language, under no circumstance will he encounter a smile, and he is kindly assisted in mastering its many difficulties.

The last decade—the period of railways—has marked a new era in dress, for even in the smaller cities and towns the people are leaving off to some extent the ancient styles of their progenitors and are donning the newer modes. The old-fashioned silks that stand alone, the laces and shawls, worthy heirlooms, have been relegated to the silent shades. Even the black lace mantilla is no longer used except for church. On Sunday mornings in the alamedas of all cities, hundreds may be seen, but the graceful devotees have already attended morning mass, and now the assembled sightseers may view them in the national mantilla.

Later in the day, and on all other occasions, Parisian hats are worn. But the señorita is never so charming, so fascinating, so haloed by mystical romance, as when her glossy tresses are crowned with the graceful mantilla.

No people on the continent indulge more in the luxury of fine clothes than those of the Mexican capital. Here the votaries of wealth and fashion receive their toilets direct from Paris, from the king of dressmakers, M. Worth; while the men are fully up to the standard of either Europeans or Americans.

But the gentleman of ease and wealth, supported by the profits of his landed property, is one thing when in the city, clad in European dress, and quite another on his hacienda arrayed in the native garb he so delights in. The swarthy complexion takes on a different cast enhanced by color. The suit of cloth or buckskin, trimmed with a profusion of flashy silver ornaments, a red sash about the waist and full, loose tie at the throat, a gayly bedecked though very heavy sombrero, all go to make up a costume eminently becoming to the dark beauty of the wearer.

Mounted upon his gorgeously caparisoned steed, whose equipments sometimes cost thousands of dollars, he presents a striking picture of a "gay cavalier."

No more charming feature exists in Mexican life than the brilliancy and variety of color in the costumes of the hacendado. The effect of this picturesque attire is most pleasing, not only from its intrinsic beauty, but also for the novelty of English and American eyes, accustomed only to dull, conventional garments worn alike by all our classes. May the hacendado never change his colors!

Sisters have a fancy for dressing exactly alike, so that not a button, hook, or article of jewelry varies. I have counted in one morning six of them promenading arm and arm and talking in a low, confidential manner.

The prevailing style of dressing the hair is the plaited coil low upon the neck and the crimped bang across the forehead. But fashionable society belles have long since adopted the more modern high coif. The men universally appreciate the value of exposing the entire brow, consequently their hair is invariably arranged á la pompadour.

Mexican gentlemen manifest their appreciation of feminine beauty by gazing intently at ladies whether in the Alameda or at the theater. This custom, which would be generally resented as impertinent by our fair ones, is there well understood and accepted, as it is meant—a flattering tribute to their charms. Between acts at the theater or opera the men rise to their feet and with leveled glasses pay admiring homage to the señoritas whose dark-eyed beauty has attracted their attention. The pretty language of the fan then comes into admirable play, and the maidens nod gently to each other in appreciation of the gallantries of these knights, and with blissful memories to carry away, the evening ends happily for all.

It has been said that the gallantry of these caballeros is rather wearisome and tedious, but I scarcely imagine that any lady of refinement could feel herself otherwise than honored at being the recipient of their courtly attentions. They are punctilious to the last degree in observing the most insignificant courtesies of daily life. If ascending a stairway accompanied by a lady, she always takes his arm, and in descending he precedes her a step or two, holding firmly her hand so as to avoid a misstep. This attention is even offered to strangers with as much naturalness and with far more regularity and promptitude than our own countrymen relinquish to us a seat in the streetcar.

In saluting ladies, gentlemen still observe the Spanish form, "A los pies de usted" ("at your feet"), the response to which is "Beso a usted la mano" ("I kiss the hand to you"). And in closing a letter they always add "B. S. M." —"Beso sus manos" ("I kiss your hands").

A few current complimentary phrases in society are: "Tan hermosa como siempre" ("As charming as ever"); "Es Vd. muy simpática" ("You are very captivating"); "Soy su más humilde servidor" ("I am your most humble servant"); " ¿Puedo tener el gusto de bailar con Vd. esta pieza?" ("May I have the pleasure of dancing this piece with you?") To this last remark the answer generally is, "Si, señor, con mucho gusto" ("Yes, with much pleasure"). Not to be outdone, the gentleman replies, " ¡El gusto es para mi—cuanto honor, señorita!" ("The pleasure is mine—what honor, Miss").

On retiring from a visit, as long as in sight, the salutation with the hand, the bow, the "A los pies de usted, señorita," are continued, until one feels as if transported to the days of chivalry.

All Mexican cities have their social organizations, which on one evening in each month give a handsome ball that is attended by the elite of society. With all their tropical embellishments, growing plants, and sparkling water from the fountains in the patio, singing birds, brilliant flowers, and salons of grand proportions and magnificent furnishings, added to the elegant costumes of the guests, it makes a delightful event in the lives of the people and an enviable one for the stranger.

But dancing is an inherited accomplishment with the native Mexican, the younger members of society learning from those more experienced in the ways of the world. Grace and ease of movement are inseparable in the Mexican make-up, but nevertheless as a rule they do not dance as gracefully as one would expect. Teachers of Terpsichorean art have not, from some cause, with their divine talents, penetrated that country. But unquestionably they will follow in the wake of railways and other attendant comforts and perhaps give a strong contest for precedence over the time-honored customs.

The danza is the most distinctively national of all the dances, and bears a strong resemblance to the Habanera, as known in Cuba. Its slow and rather pathetic music, played by native musicians on national instruments, renders this dance fascinating to both natives and strangers. The latter find some difficulty in catching the time, but a little practice soon makes them perfect.

Beyond all things it is a boon to the Mexican lover, for it is only when treading its slow, dreamy measures that he can without restraint convey to the dark-eyed darling of his heart the thousand tender utterances that glow afresh at every motion. They can with propriety dance together every danza on the evening's programme and excite no comment.

The danza, though resembling in some respects our waltz-quadrille, differs greatly from it in many essential features. The "sets," if they may so be termed, consist of but two couples. The first figure is a "ladies' change"; next, the lady with her right hand on the gentleman's left shoulder and his arm around her waist, the couples balance four times to each other; then, joining hands, they again balance, go partly round a circle, then back again, after which they waltz away. This waltz may be continued *ad libitum*, the waltzers pausing at any moment in their revolutions to go through the same graceful maneuvers with any other couple similarly disposed. They generally make a point of not dancing twice with the same couple during one danza.

In a country so favored by climate, the stranger is early impressed by the limited amount of outdoor amusements in which the women participate; in lawn parties, picnics, or riding they rarely indulge. The men are understood, of course, to ride almost unceasingly, but señoritas, though graceful equestriennes, seldom do. At the capital riding is more frequent than elsewhere, and some of the most bewitching beauties—whom Hebe herself might envy—I saw on horseback enjoying the lovely environs of Mexico.

I recall a gay party of twelve señoritas near Tacubaya, ambling along on the broad avenues lined with great trees which stretched out their friendly arms to ward off the scorching rays of the sun. With navy blue and plum-colored habits, big white straw sombreros, their horses handsomely equipped after the fashion of the country, they made a striking picture. Two brothers and three mozos attended them, and they laughed and had a good time.

The tamalada is an outdoor diversion somewhat corresponding to our picnics. It usually occurs in the afternoon, in some quiet wood or beautiful garden, and begins with dancing, which is kept up throughout the afternoon and evening. The refreshments are tamales, after which the entertainment is named—atole de leche and chougas. The latter is simply sliced bread with piloncilla (syrup made from brown sugar) and grated cheese thickly spread over each piece, the whole arranged in pyramid form, and is a most delicious dish. Un día de campo (day in the country) with a gay tamalada party, is a most agreeable recreation. Pity that it occurs so rarely!

One of the most brilliant national and social events at the capital in which I had the pleasure of participating was the annual distribution of prizes, on the night of January 30th, to the cadets of the Military Academy, at Chapultepec.

The National Theater, where it took place, was gorgeously decorated with banners, streamers, and military emblems. Flowers were everywhere—wreathing the cannon which lined the entrance, surrounding trophies of war, combining with the white moss of Chapultepec and dark evergreens, in festoons from light to light—even cannon balls reposed on them and bayonets were converted into bouquet holders.

In the patio electric lights, in the form of stars, shed their white radiance over the scene and mingled with the lights from a thousand Chinese lanterns and Venetian lamps which swung between the flag-draped and flower-wreathed pillars.

The main entrance was lined with soldiers who, with the cadets, presented arms when President Díaz, accompanied by members of the Cabinet, entered and passed through to the great stage reserved for the presidential party and high army officers.

The interior of the theater presented a grand spectacle; every column was covered with national colors arranged diagonally; flags of all sizes and the ensign of the Republic were draped artistically on the walls and hung from every available point. Three hundred gay and gallant cadets were ranged with military precision on either side the grand aisle, forming a guard of honor, themselves the motive and main feature of the occasion.

Boxes were filled with people prominent in fashionable and public life, a central one being reserved for Madame Díaz. An excellent orchestra and pupils from the Institute for the Blind furnished the music.

The prizes were handed to the cadets by the President.

In the literary exercises poems appropriate to the occasion were read by Juan A. Mateos and Anselmo Alfaro, but the most noted was the official address delivered by the "Poet Laureate" of the Republic, Guillermo Prieto.

It would be a graceful compliment for the students of Chapultepec Military Academy to be invited to participate in our competitive interstate or national drills.

VIII

A Glance at Mexican Literature

Like New York, the federal capital of Mexico is the center towards which all the genius of the provinces, whether literary, artistic, or scientific, gravitates. For there, as in the metropolis of the United States, all brain workers expect to gain, at least, appreciation, while many hope to win renown.

The principal cities of Mexico, such as Toluca, Morelia, Guadalajara, Guanajuato, Puebla, Mérida, and many others of like size, have their literary associations, but *El Liceo Hidalgo*, at the capital, ranks highest; and is, in fact, intended as a National Institute. It was established on the 15th of September, 1849, and has known many vicissitudes during this time, but of late years it has renewed the original designs of its founders.

On each recurring Monday evening the society meets at its handsome hall, and it is then the brilliant genius and flowing wit of the members may be fully enjoyed. Scientific essays and literary productions are read before this Lyceum, and nothing that is unsound, unscientific or weakly sentimental, can escape the censorship and rigid criticism of such able men as Riva Palacio, Ignacio Altamirano, Vigil, Pimentel, Juan de Dios Peza, Juan Mateos, Ramón Manterola, Ireano Paz, Francisco Sosa, and others.

The meetings are well attended and appreciated, not only by the cultured part of society, but also by many of the plainer and less educated of the population. Not infrequently bevies of ambitious college boys are numbered among the most attentive listeners to all discussions and debates, giving expression to their enthusiasm in rounds of applause. The aim of the society is of a pure and lofty nature, its sole ambition being the encouragement and development of native talent, and right royally is it succeeding.

The name of Vicente Riva Palacio occupies an exalted place in the history of his country. It would seem, therefore, an act of injustice to place him only among the writers, when he has played so grand a part among the gallant heroes in "grim-visaged war." For, from the age of twenty-three to the present time, he has filled almost every place of honor that could be bestowed upon him by his people. A man of brilliant genius and liberal ideas, he enjoys the reputation of being the most humorous and versatile of Mexican writers. It is somewhat surprising that, although by profession a lawyer, we yet find him, also, a statesman, a leading politician, a soldier, a poet, a journalist and dramatist, and in each position he has reached high distinction.

As a politician, he has filled acceptably not only the office of governor of several states, but has also been Justice of the Supreme Court and cabinet minister. From 1870 to 1879 he was Minister of Fomento (public works, commerce, industry, and colonization), during which time he used signal efforts for the development of the country in the extension of railways and telegraph lines, the improvement of public buildings and roads. Like others of his countrymen, he has suffered imprisonment, but his confinement was cheered by the muses, and some of the sweetest poems he ever penned was when behind the prison bars.

As a writer, his works are not only extremely popular in his native land, but throughout the whole of Spanish America. By request of the federal government, he edited the national history entitled "*México a través de los siglos*" ("Mexico Viewed through the Course of Ages"). Among the most popular of his novels is that of *The Hill of the Bells*, which is a thrilling and faithful account of the last days and execution of Maximilian.

At this time Riva Palacio is enjoying the honor of Envoy Extraordinary and Minister Plenipotentiary from Mexico to the court of the noble Queen Christina of Spain.

As his time is not fully absorbed in his diplomatic duties, he is now writing a historical brochure, and will also soon publish a volume of Mexican legends in verse.

General Palacio's magnificent mansion is the grand center and rallying point of all toilers after lore, and it is there his courtly hospitality shines resplendent, dispensed with equal impartiality to all, whether they be distinguished and acknowledged in the world of letters or only humble aspirants for fame. They here meet together, a common brotherhood, and among them all the host is himself the most brilliant and witty.

An entertainment, probably not excelled intellectually and socially by any given in a private house during the winter, was the *Velada Literaria* (Musical and Literary Reunion), given by General Palacio on the first night of the New Year, and of which he had previously given me a hint.

The house throughout was a grand scenic illumination, of which the center was the sala grande, with its brilliant assemblage of elegantly dressed people. Diamonds shimmered and flashed, adding to beauty which might be sufficient of itself, the charm that jewels and the accessories of wealth can give, and lighting up the faultless Parisian toilets.

Several ladies were present whose jewels summed up from $100,000 to almost double that amount.

An unusual feature was the reading of a beautiful poem by Señora de Flaquer, the editress of *El Álbum de la Mujer*—the only paper at the capital edited by a woman and devoted to the interests of women.

All the leading writers of the city were present, and each one read an original poem written specially for the occasion. With something of the enthusiasm of the time, I recall a charming poem by Juan de Dios Peza. His rich, soft voice is wonderfully effective; its sonorous intonation and smooth inflections, added to the eloquent gestures of the reader, carried his hearers along with rapturous enjoyment.

But Altamirano, Francisco Sosa, Juan Mateos, and others, as they stepped before the audience with dignified and graceful bearing, received an equally hearty greeting.

Our distinguished host read a poem full of dramatic effect, based upon the tales of the pirates of the Gulf. A most weird and peculiar effect was added to this reading by a piano accompaniment composed and dedicated to the author by a señorita, a musician of great celebrity. The voice of the reader and the tones of the piano flowing in admirable accord, now moved the audience to tender sympathy, again aroused soul-thrilling emotions or blood-curdling horror at the will of poet and musician.

Among the many brilliant renderings of musical compositions, was the remarkable performance on the violin of two boys of twelve and thirteen years. Without book or break they played throughout the music of "Il Trovatore" with marvelous technique and admirable expression.

The exercises of the evening closed with a superb banquet given in the comedor grande. The flow of wine was only equaled by that of wit. The Mexicans seldom indulge to intoxication; their frequent potations "cheer but not inebriate"—only add brilliancy to their conversation without clouding the intellect.

One of the most erudite and brilliant of the literati in Mexico is Ignacio Altamirano, who is also an eminent jurist, and was at one period a judge of the Supreme Court. Altamirano is a corresponding member of the Spanish Institute, also of several literary societies in France, England, and Germany.

He is a pure descendant of one of the Indian races. He won the prize in his municipality in Oaxaca, and his education was completed at the "Instituto Literario" at Toluca. On going there, some one observing his marked Indian parentage, laid his hand kindly on his head and said: "Nothing will ever come from this brain." The utter fallacy of the prophecy is too well known, both in this country and in Europe.

The most popular poet in the republic is the venerable

Guillermo Prieto, who may justly be styled "the Mexican Béranger." He has also been called the Robert Burns of the republic, and, like the Scottish poet, he sings the songs of the people. Identifying himself with them in feeling, he is able to express their every emotion, and in their own tongue. Not even the despised léperos are neglected, but with that exquisite "touch of nature" that he possesses, he finds and acknowledges kinship with these degraded pariahs. Guillermo Prieto is not merely a poet; he has served his country on many battlefields, and was the chief counselor of Benito Juárez during the most perilous days of Mexico's national existence.

Prieto's *Romancero Nacional*, published about a year ago, is a collection of historical incidents related in verse, and is so highly appreciated that the federal government has ordered it to be used in all the national colleges.

Even now, at the advanced age of eighty-one years, Señor Prieto holds the position of Professor of Ancient and Modern History in the Military College at Chapultepec, and has not only compiled a history of Mexico, for the cadets, but has written an excellent work on political economy for the instruction of his pupils.

"The Mexican Longfellow" is Juan de Dios Peza, whose exquisite poems are best appreciated by the aristocratic and cultivated classes. Señor Peza has now in press a volume of Indian traditions.

The distinguished philologist, Don Francisco Pimentel, is also a *littérateur*, but, with a noble and holy object, has devoted the greater part of his life to the study of the native Mexican languages, and now speaks twelve of the Indian dialects. Señor Pimentel has greatly encouraged the study of the Nahuatl and Otomí languages in the Government School of Agriculture, because he fully coincides in the opinion of the great educator and philanthropist, Señor Herrera, who maintains that the only way to elevate the Indian races is to learn their native dialects and then go to their pueblos, or tribal settlements, to instruct them in those matters most essential to their mental and moral development. Señor Pimentel is a member of various scientific and literary societies in France, Germany, and the United States.

Alfredo Chavero, although more generally known in Europe and in this country as an archæologist, is not only a literary man but an eminent lawyer, and is today president of the Chamber of Deputies. His quota of that invaluable history called *México a través de los siglos* has just been published.

Señor Chavero has written numerous dramas and *zarzuelas*, several of which have been enthusiastically applauded in Cuba and the principal cities of Mexico.

Chavero's most important work, entitled *A Study of the Aztec Calendar Stone*, has created quite a sensation among archæologists. He maintains that this relic was an altar dedicated to the "Sun God."

An entire volume might be devoted to the poets of Mexico, most of them rarely gifted men. The poems of Manuel Flores, entitled *Pasionarias*, equal some of the best productions of Byron. José María Ramírez, a popular poet during the second empire, edited *La América Literaria*, *La Tarantula*, and contributed to other journals. Later in life Ramírez professed atheism, and styled himself a philosopher.

I must not omit to mention Señor Ignacio Mariscal, Minister for Foreign Affairs, who, in addition to his diplomatic abilities, has shown marked literary talent. Sharing the poetic gift common to his countrymen, he is not only the author of many meritorious works in both prose and poetry, but has also made fine translations of Longfellow's *Evangeline* and Poe's *Raven*.

Manual Acuña was an impassioned writer of great talent, and among the modern writers none have made a stronger or more lasting impression. His betrothed becoming the wife of another during his prolonged absence was more than his soul could bear, and he took his own life, which had been rendered unendurable by her faithlessness. His poem, *A Rosario*, expresses the keenest pangs of

disappointment mingled with undying love for the faith-
less one. The closing verse is eloquent of his utter wretch-
edness. He says: "But now that a black gulf has succeeded
the entrancing dream—farewell! Love of my loves, light
of my darkness, perfume of all flowers that bloomed for
me! my poet's lyre, my youth, farewell!"

Mexican journalists are a bold and fearless set of men
and express their disapprobation of any public cause with
but little regard to consequences. Therefore the best of
them may any day find themselves political prisoners in
Belem.

There are but two American newspapers published
in Mexico—the *Two Republics*, a daily, and the *Mexican
Financier*, a weekly. The first is owned and edited by Mr. J.
Mastella Clarke, the latter is the property of Boston capi-
talists, and ably edited by Messrs. Levy and Guernsey.
These gentlemen are on very harmonious terms with the
native editorial fraternity, and belong, with them, to the
"Mexican Press Association."

The Mexican newspaper reporter is not so ubiquitous
and persevering as his American brother. I have known of
houses being entered by lightning rod men, sewing machine agents, and other inevitable invaders, but an "inter-
viewing" reporter penetrating the sanctities of a home is a
thing unheard of. The rattle of the family skeleton is not
a healthy subject for the versatile talents of a knight of the
quill. The costumbres del país, backed by the powerful aid
of barred windows and heavy doors, forbid all such inves-
tigations, and he would as soon think of leaping into the
Gulf of Mexico as daring to break through those Mede-
and-Persian laws or storming those forbidding portals.

The Liceo Morelos is also an institution of merit. It
unites with readings, recitations, and scientific discussions,
amateur theatricals, tableaux vivants, and other social
features. The latter entertainments are generally given in
honor of some of its members, which include the most brilliant men of the capital, among them many journalists.
Ladies, also, are numbered in its membership.

Social reunions are held in compliment to various members of the society, and every eulogistic speech relates to the person thus distinguished.

At these reunions the versatility of talent of Mexican writers is remarkable. One of them delivers a eulogy in prose upon some prominent person. The enthusiasm runs so high, knowing the genius of the speaker, that he is called upon, amid storms of applause, to transpose the speech into poetry, which is done upon the spot, without a moment's preparation. In the theatrical entertainments, each one takes a part, and they often play to crowded houses of friends.

Among her women writers, Mexico may well be proud of such poets as Esther Tapia de Castellanos, Señora Castro, Isabel Prieto de Landázuri, Laura Klinehaus, Refugio V. de Ortiz, and of such prose writers as Señora Flaquer, all of whose productions are an honor to their sex.

IX

More about the Common People

Whether seen beneath the brilliant white sunshine of a cloudless day on his native plains, or under the mellow effulgence of the peerless Queen of Night in the valley, consecrated by the shrines of his forefathers, the "Silent Aztec Child of the Sun" presents a picture unique in the history of the world. He is the primitive man, unmoved by the march of civilization around him, but in every lineament and movement, reflects the griefs and struggles of past centuries. He lives surrounded by the traces of those mysterious races which preceded him. All speak of the mutations of the world—the subjugation of mighty powers—and he has accepted the inevitable with a sad and unresisting stoicism.

He is ever picturesque. In his mountain home enraged in pastoral pursuits, in holiday attire on his patron saint's day, or in rags under the electric lights of a great city, the traditions of the past hang over him, investing him with the interest attaching to the pathetic last man.

Today men and women may be found with accredited documents proving their descent from Montezuma and the princes of Texcoco, but owing to inertia their claims are unasserted.

The conquest and Spanish domination wrought a metamorphosis in the life and character of these Indians. Vast estates were once theirs. Their flocks and herds roamed at large upon the plains of their fathers. The blue sky, the shining lakes, the forests, and mountains belonged to these children of the sun. Today they are in dire poverty; the lands once tilled by their vassals they now till for others. They are the patient burden bearers of this once grand Indian empire. If their yoke is not easy, nor their burden light, we hear no complaint.

If we compare them with our North American Indians, we are struck with the contrast presented. At one fell blow the Aztecs were conquered, their spirit of independence crushed out. We have contended with our Indians for more than two hundred years.

The Mexican Indian leads a peaceful life and remains on the same soil, even though it be his no longer. He is satisfied, feeling the worst is past and perhaps a better day in store for him. Shut up in his hut of adobe or palm, without either light or air, the chase and the camp have no charms for him. It troubles him little that he belongs to a conquered race. The independence of Mexico has not yet accomplished much for these people, yet they are content.

The Mexican Indian is by inherent custom an agriculturist, and notwithstanding the fact that the conqueror imposed upon him burdensome and distasteful labors—among them that of mining—he at the first opportunity returned to his favorite vocation, to which he still adheres at the present day.

He is an uncompromising antagonist to any change of locality, and clings to the place of his nativity with unwavering fidelity. There is but little mirthfulness or merriment in his composition. An intense believer in the supernatural, it cannot be better illustrated than by the fact of Montezuma, in spite of all his splendid resources, yielding with so little resistance to Cortez' small band of four hundred and fifty men; for he must have felt convinced that the Spanish conqueror was the one designated by prophecy and tradition to possess the land.

"According to what you declare," said he, "of the place whence you came, which is toward the rising sun, and of the great Lord who is your King, we must believe that he is our natural Lord."

Without being inventive, they are great imitators and marvelously ingenious in the construction of the infinite variety of curiosities of the country.

Straw, wax, wood, marble, grass, hair, and mother

earth are all successfully treated by these dexterous brown fingers. True to life are these imitations, even the tiniest wax figures not more than an inch in length, representing venders of vegetables, fruits, or other commodity. But to me the most wonderful are the productions of the Guadalajara Indians in clay and glazed pottery. Of the latter, their pitchers, vases, water jugs, animals, and toys of all sorts are beautiful, while in the former an extraordinary artistic conception is evinced. In an incredibly short space of time they will model for you a lifelike bust, either from the life or from a photograph. The strength of expression and fidelity to the subject are remarkable.

Their plumaje (feather work) is delicate and artistic. Cortez and his men were much interested in the cloth woven of feathers, so intricate, multicolored and beautiful. They no longer manufacture feather cloth, but expend their skill in this line in the representation of cards of all kinds of animals, birds and landscapes.

On feast days these ingenious people have their stalls on the Zócalo, with their street agents, and business is animated. Each one of these days finds still another variety of toys, and some of them are indeed laughable. For the 1st of November they have crossbones and skulls, funeral processions (calaveras in wood), and death's heads in imitation bronze, with glaring eyeballs and grinning teeth. All these are arranged on a miniature table, with a small bottle for pulque, and on one corner a cake or piece of bread of the kind the dead may be supposed to like.

Their rag figures and dolls are a comical invention. They make baskets with taste and ingenuity, from the size of a thimble to one or more yards in height. They excel in frescoing. They manipulate tissue paper into decorative forms, and in numberless ways display aptness and imitative skill.

In brief, these productions of their natural ingenuity would require, in other countries, years of patient toil and study, if they could even then be reproduced. But I have been told that any attempt to educate them in their peculiar branches of art would be the means of losing their entire knowledge. This wonderful skill is purely the result of an artistic tendency—a faculty handed down from his ancestors.

But, as may be seen in other avenues of business in this land of rest and romance, they work on insignificant articles for days or weeks, seemingly to the exclusion of all else, and then dispose of them for a mere trifle.

The Indian voice is soft and low, almost flutelike in its sweetness, in this quality contrasting with the shrill tones frequently heard in the higher ranks of society. Their step is light, even catlike, in its softness—a characteristic of all classes, regardless of station.

On días de santo and other feast days, outdoor gambling of every description is indulged in by this class, while bullfights and pulque drinking constitute their principal pleasures.

The love for spectacular display is also a predominating characteristic with them. It is shown in the pleasure taken in skyrockets and all pyrotechnics, especially if accompanied by a band of music.

Their taste also finds expression in the universal love of flowers. Not only are the humblest homes embellished with such gay and gorgeous flowers as would constitute the choicest treasures of a northern hothouse, but in the streets and markets, edibles and other commodities are exposed for sale side by side with them, and for a tlaco or medio one may buy a lovely bouquet.

They are also great admirers of pictures, and groups may be seen any day in the principal cities, gazing intently on those exhibited in the windows. But I have caught glances, pathetic to the last degree, as they peered through windows where shoes and stockings were exposed for sale.

The laboring class rise early and work late, rarely going home before the close of the day. Their wives bring them their dinner, and the whole family sit down to the bread of contentment upon a curbstone.

The large number of unoccupied and nonproducing

among the common people may to some extent be accounted for by the bounty of nature and the cheapness and great variety of food products. It is little wonder that they have no ambition to rise higher in the social scale, when the luxuries of life, without the least adulteration, may be obtained for a mere song. The idle, indigent, and thriftless have equal advantages in the food they eat, with the toiling and industrious. The atole of all kinds, the barbecued meats, soups, beans and rice, together with the great variety and cheapness of fruits and vegetables, render their dietary one to be envied. From six to twelve cents will purchase a substantial and well-cooked meal, and it is an interesting event in one's experience to see the motley assemblage in the market place, and to hear their gay sallies at the mid-day meal; so that in many respects they have decided advantages, so far as relates to food, over even people of affluence in some parts of the United States.

The climate, also, brings its blessings to the poor. They may sleep in a house, if it can be afforded; if not, their lodging may be in the streets, the recesses of the churches, or any place that Morpheus may overtake them.

Clothing may be domestic or muslin, with a blanket or rebozo, and no special inconvenience is experienced. But, however poverty-stricken and wretched their condition, the women are always expert and canny with the needle. A woman with scarcely a change of raiment will embroider, crochet, and do plain and fancy sewing that would put to the blush our most dexterous needlewomen. She sits on the sidewalk from morn till eve, selling a basket of fruits, but not a moment does she lose from her stitching.

One fact worthy of being chronicled is, that the common people are making a considerable effort toward advancement in learning to read and write, even while employed as servants in families. I saw several at the capital who, unaided, were studying Spanish one day and English the next.

Mexico has a population of about 10,000,000, of which one and a half are pure white—Americans, Germans, French, English and Spaniards—and two and a half mestizos—leaving about 6,000,000 of Indians.

It has been estimated that there are five hundred different dialects in the country. The Indians have, in the main, retained their own race and tribal characteristics. Spanish is the language of many of them, but numerous tribes are to be found who speak purely in their own tongue, and cling to their own traditions, dress, and, to some extent, their own peculiar forms of religious worship, seldom intermarrying with others.

In the sixteenth century, according to *México a través de los siglos* the types were classified as follows, and, barring the natural increase of population, they remain about the same today:

Children of *Spaniards* born in the country are called *Creoles*.

”	*Spaniards* and *Indians*	”	*Mestizos.*
”	*Mestizos* ” *Spaniards*	”	*Castigos.*
”	*Castigos* ” *Spaniards*	”	*Españoles.*
”	*Spaniards* ” *Negros*	”	*Mulattos.*
”	*Mulattos* ” *Spaniards*	”	*Moriscos.*
”	*Negros* ” *Indians*	”	*Zambos.*

Occasionally race characteristics, after lying dormant for perhaps generations, crop out unexpectedly in families, causing quite a shock when they appear. A dark, or as is sometimes the case, black child makes its appearance, and this is called salta atrás (a leap over several generations).

The mestizos are the handsomest, and the zambos must rest content with occupying the position of the ugliest and most unattractive of the races.

As to the real merits of this classification, it is not possible for me to speak. I only know how the various shades and complexions impressed me as a subject for study. The dark, olive-tinted types seized upon my fancy from the date of my advent into the country. I felt a deep and sympathetic interest in them, as being the more directly connected with the aborigines. In their quiet and humble manner I read the history of a conquered people.

In these dark shades there exist at least two different types. The pale though dark, swarthy, bloodless face, with melancholy, expressionless eyes and dejected bearing, indicates the one, while the other, the type above all others pleasing and interesting to me, possesses a rich brown skin, with carmine cheeks and lips; glistening, white teeth, united with great, wondering, half-startled, luminous eyes, soft and shy as those of the gazelle. Even their forms and gait are different, the one thin and shambling, the other, plump, full-blooded, graceful, and active. Their politeness and humility, even among the most ragged and degraded, are touching. This is not confined to their bearing toward superiors, but is also shown to each other.

The salute of the poorest to his bronze-colored compatriot as they pass, makes the air musical with their liquid Indian idiom. Their code of etiquette is expansive enough to cover that practiced in the grandest homes in our American cities. In this respect the wealthiest hacendado has no advantage over the humblest peon who toils for him a natural lifetime. They are strictly careful never to omit the Don and Doña to each other, and "where you have your house," and "muy a su disposición,"—terms synonymous with the higher classes—are in no way modified by the lower. Even their children are taught to say, on being asked their names, su criado de V. (your humble servant).

The talent for music is even more striking than that of the cultured higher classes. It is no unusual thing to hear every part of an air carried through in perfect harmony by full, rich, native voices, entirely ignorant of the first principles of the art which they so successfully practice.

The government is now doing a great work by granting pensions to all meritorious persons in the cultivation of any talent. I saw in the Conservatory of Music, in the capital, two Indian girls who had walked from Querétaro, a distance of one hundred and fifty miles, to present themselves as pupils in that admirable institution. I heard them sing selections from Italian opera, and the sweetness, strength, and range of their voices were far beyond the average, and produced a profound impression upon the audience.

The brass bands, with which travelers' ears are regaled everywhere in the country, are composed of this part of the population. It is no uncommon thing to see bands composed entirely of young boys, from twelve to eighteen years, who render the music in such a manner that a master from the Old World would find but little to criticise and much to commend.

Their music is of a sad, melancholy kind, even that danced or sung at their fandangoes. *La Paloma* is a universal favorite, and as they sing it, often their bodies and faces look as if it were an appeal to the Virgin or some of the saints, rather than an air for enlivenment or amusement. In this way the sentiment and deep-toned pathos in their natures find expression.

The large class of useless, lazy, indigent, ragged, and wretched objects in the streets of a Mexican city impresses the stranger that there is no good among them. But there is a large and industrious population possessing kindly and gentle impulses, the women practicing, as far as possible, the tender charities of the cultured higher classes.

Even the lépero, the representative of the very lowest and most degraded of the male element, assumes the extremes of two conditions. On the one hand, he has no compunctions of conscience in appropriating the property of another, nor does his moral nature shrink, perhaps, from plunging the deadly dagger into the back of his unsuspecting victim, while other vicious and ignoble traits are imputed to him; but, on the other hand, he has a heart and much of the sentimental and romantic instinct which invests him with many of the attractions of the bandit.

The most beautiful and distinctive female type of the common people is the China, familiarly known as the China poblana. With many added attractions she may be considered the counterpart of the French grisette. But the China has a rich and luxurious tropical order of beauty that is especially her own, with hands, arms, and feet that could not be excelled for artistic elegance by Praxiteles. She has the warmth of nature and faithful devotion which characterize all Mexican women. Her peculiar costume, now rarely seen, possesses a semi-barbaric charm that interdicts all rivalry; but it will soon be a memory of the past, having given place in great measure to a more modern style.

The common people have, generally, a great dread of having their pictures taken. A sort of superstition haunts them that the process will deprive them of some part of their being, either corporal or spiritual. This dread was realized when the artist took her revenge on a curious crowd who had gathered so closely around us as to almost impede the manipulations of her pencil. I was constantly on the qui vive for some of my former mozos who had left me some years before to go to their families. I was certain on one occasion that I had found one of them, but he had risen from the rank of mozo to a cargador, with all the dignity and equipments of that station. When he entered the house where I was, on an errand, the resemblance to Miguel Rodríguez was so striking that I told him so, and begged him to allow himself to be sketched. But no sooner were the initial marks made upon the paper, than, looking on to examine the work, he became filled with unreasonable but not-to-be-combated terror, saying, perhaps the man he looked like had robbed me, and so, with the inevitable finger motion, and a "No, I cannot permit it!" turned and fled out of the room, down the steps, and up the street like a deer before the hounds.

This class I have allowed to speak for themselves, and surely no history is more reliable and complete than that related by the actors in the events recorded.

They are possessed of a certain amount of piquancy, as expressed in their peculiar dialect and idioms. With this there is united also a strong vein of humor, and they usually see a point as quickly as any people.

In consideration of the fact that they have but little education, their native shrewdness and intelligence are surprising. The most highly educated and enlightened cannot cope with them in the matter of barter and sale and the counting of money. By instinct they know just how, when, and where to strike the weak point of a stranger in any business transaction.

Americans are special objects of interest in this line. They always imagine that all Americans are possessed of boundless wealth.

The love of money is well developed, and the possibility of winning even a tlaco at gambling is sufficient to induce them to lose a whole night's sleep.

These people are made up of that mixed race of natives and whites called mestizos.

Their social life is of a free nature, and consequently but few marriages take place among them. The women are vulgarly called gatas (cats), or garbanceras (bastards); the former are those who usually perform the offices of chambermaids, nurses, and cooks, the latter generally do the marketing.

As the shops where the marketing is done are kept by the common people, when a marchante (customer) appears, the shopkeeper begins to pay her compliments, and say things with double meanings. She usually answers in the same manner, which causes the shopkeeper to laugh. If the servant is at all attractive, and the clerk understands that she is a match for him, and sees that she receives his compliments with pleasure, he takes her basket, keeps on talking to her, and tries to keep her as long as possible. They carry on something like the following dialogue by the clerk saying to her:

" ¿Qué cosa se le ofrece, mi vida?" ("What do you want, my life?")

"No se enoje porque hasta eso sale perdiendo" ("Don't get mad, for you will only be the loser").

"No le importa, anda dispacheme," she replies ("Mind your own business, come wait on me").

"Pues deme la mano y dígame como se llama" ("Well, give me your hand and tell me your name"), he rejoins.

Her reply to this is full of stinging sarcasm, which finds vent in the following way:

"¡Ora sí! que encamisado, tan igualado! Parece que soy su jugete. Anda dispacheme y no esté moliendo que se me hace tarde y la niña me regaña porque me tardo con el mandado" ("Well, I should say you were a naked upstart. One would think I was your plaything. Come, wait on me, and don't bother me, for it is getting late, and the mistress will scold me for being so long doing the erands").

When he sees she is a little angry, he gives her back the basket with the things she has bought. She then throws the money to him on the counter, in an angry manner, for him to take out the cost of what she has bought. When he gives her back the change, he takes her hand, which she pulls away, after he has given it a squeeze. The next day she returns to the same shop or stand, but this time she presents herself a little less reluctantly than before, and without minding at all what is said to her. On the contrary, she leads him on, by throwing little stones at him or giving him a sly pinch.

At the end of a month or two they make an appointment to meet where they may take advantage of the opportunity to treat of their love affairs more freely. The day, hour, and place being appointed, by means of which they can see each other alone (which is the first object of all lovers), they get permission from their employers, and dressing themselves the best they can, hasten to the trysting place.

The first time they look at each other they are somewhat disconcerted, and try to pretend indifference. But she is not so severe in her manner but that he feels authorized in venturing on a caress. From that time he thinks it proper that she should not serve any longer where she has been, although she has been giving him a part of all her wages. In reply she says she "does not want to lose her peace of mind, because men always say the same thing to women, and she does not want him to repent by and by and put her out into the street." But at last she adds, "If

you will not forsake me and will treat me kindly, I am disposed to love you; only you must tell my parents, and, if
they consent, and your intentions are good, you can rely
upon my being your sweetheart."

After this, the man takes the woman by the hand or
puts his arm around her and covering her with his own
serape, which is the general custom, they go to some stand
where things, if not of very good quality, are excessively
cheap, and eat enchiladas and tamales and drink pulque.

Often the honeymoon does not last long; dissension
and strife are apt to ensue, and the old story of domestic
infelicity is repeated. Still, though the woman concludes
her husband does not love her, if he does not use the rod,
they are not so miserable as might appear.

A woman of the common people prefers a man of her
own class, however poor and rough he may be, to one of a
higher station, whatever offers or promises he may make
her. For they still preserve the traditional aversion which
the creoles and native races have always felt for foreigners.

Among the Indians the violation of conjugal faith is
more rare than in any other class of society, not even excepting the middle class, which beyond question in Mexico, as in all other countries, is the most moral and upright.

When legal marriages occur, the parents make every
arrangement when the young people have arrived at an
age at which they are able to bear the responsibilities of
married life. When such a case presents itself, the parents
of the lover go to the house of the sweetheart, and take
with them a chiquihuite (a certain kind of big basket),
containing a turkey, several bottles of native brandy and
other drinks, bread, ears of dried corn, and peppers of different kinds. The first time the parents of the lover go to
ask for the girl's hand, they organize a sort of procession,
composed of some of the relatives and friends of the family
and a band of music, which plays without intermission
from the house from which they start to the dwelling of the
maiden.

Once there, the band and the rest of the procession

are profoundly silent, while the petition is being made.

The first request is generally refused by the parents of the girl, until they consult with the relatives and ascertain the will of her who is sought in marriage. If the result is favorable, they appoint the wedding day; if unfavorable, the answer is reduced simply to returning the basket with its contents.

As soon as the news in the affirmative is received, the family of the bridegroom invite all their friends to the fandango which is given on the day of the wedding, in honor of the newly-married couple.

The bridegroom appears in pantaloons and short jacket of cashmere, white embroidered shirt, red sash, rawhide or deerskin shoes, and a highly decorated, broad-brimmed hat. Followed by his family, padrinos (those who are to give him away), witnesses, and those who have been invited, he proceeds to the house of the bride, where he is overwhelmed with attentions from the family.

The dress of the bride consists of a blue skirt with red sash, and a chemise with a deep yoke and sleeves elaborately embroidered with bright-colored beads, a red silk handkerchief with points crossed in front, and held by a fancy pin. The handkerchief serves to cover the neck and breast, leaving the arms free. She also wears many strings of beads, and silver hoop earrings of extraordinary size. Her hair is worn in two braids, laid back and forth on the back of her head, the ends tied with red ribbons. She wears babuchas, a kind of slipper made either of deerskin trimmed with beads or of gay cloth. The toilet is completed with a white woolen mantle, cut in scallops trimmed with blue, and hanging from the plaited hair.

After they have proceeded to the church and have been married according to the usual religious ceremony, they go to the house of the bride, accompanied by the greater part of the inhabitants of the village where the marriage has taken place, followed by skyrockets, music, and shouts from the boys. In the house there is a large room decorated with wreaths, flowers, and tissue-paper ornaments, with palm-leaf mats and wooden benches running around the room. Here the wedding feast takes place, presided over by the bride and the madrina (the one who gave her away), who sit on the mats at one end of the room, while the bridegroom and his padrino, and other guests, occupy the wooden benches. There they receive the congratulations of relatives and friends. But before the dinner, the bride removes her wedding finery, and puts on a house dress, and grinds all the corn that will be necessary to make the tortillas for the repast.

When the dinner, which generally takes place about six o'clock, is over, the dance begins, accompanied in its motions by songs which, though agreeable, are somewhat melancholy. The older guests remain at the table drinking pulque and recalling their youth, until this cheerful beverage reconciles them to the epoch in which they live. The greater part of the night is spent in this way.

The following day they repair to the house of the bridegroom, where the feast is concluded with another dinner and dance; the only difference being that on this occasion the bride has nothing to do with the preparations.

The two days which are devoted to the solemnization of the wedding being spent, the couple receive the blessing of their parents and retire to their own house to enjoy the honeymoon.

The following is a specimen of a street conversation between a man and woman of the common people.

Says the man: " ¿Pos onde va mi vida, pos de dónde sale tan linda como una rosa? ni siguiera habla?" ("Where are you going, my life? Where do you come from as nice as a rose? Don't you want to speak to me?")

" ¿Pos ande había de ir? ¡Mire qué pregunta!" ("Where am I going? Listen, what a question?"), she replies.

" ¿Pos claro onde va? ¡o ya porque lleva su rebosito nuevo se la hecho de lado!" ("Well, that's all right, but where are you going? Now that you have on your new rebozo, you are beginning to put on airs!"), he retorts. At the same moment he catches her by the rebozo.

" !Oh, suélteme, mire qué aburrición con V. todos los días que lo encuentro me ha d'estar moliendo! ¿Caramba con V.?" ("Oh, let me alone! what a nuisance you are! Every day I see you, you bother me so! Goodness, what can I do with you?") she vehemently replies.

"Pero no se enoje. ¿Me quiere o no me quiere? ¡Dígame y si no me dice no la dejo ir!" ("Don't get mad. Do you love me or not? tell me, and if you don't tell me I shan't let you go"), says he, pacifically.

" ¿Dale otra vez, pos ya no se lo dije el otro día que no me ande molestando?" ("But didn't I tell you the other day not to bother me again?") says she.

" ¿Cuando me lo ha dicho? ¡Mire nada más que embustera!" ("When did you tell me that? See what a storyteller you are!") answers the man.

"¡Bueno, si no me deja, se lo digo al gendarme que ahi viene!" ("Well, if you don't let me go, I'll tell the policeman who is coming there!") she threateningly answers.

"¡Dígaselo, él no tiene que ver con mis negocios!" ("Tell him, then; he has no right to know my business!") says the man, insolently. And when she sees that she can't go, then she says, entreatingly:

" ¿Qué quiere? y déjeme ir que se me hace tarde" ("What do you want? Let me go, now, because it is getting late").

He: " ¿Pos ya se lo dije que si me quiere o no?" ("I have already asked you, do you love me or not?").

" ¿Pos yo lo quisiera pero dicen que es casado, pos para que me quiere? entonces vayase con su mujer!" ("I should like you, but I was told that you are married; if so, what do you want with me? Go on to your wife!") she replies.

"¡Mire! nada más lo que son las gentes de mentirosas. ¿Quién se lo dijo? Si fuera casado, no la quisiera, pos dígame nada más" ("See what storytellers the people are! Who told you? If I was married, I wouldn't love you. Only tell me"), he retorts.

" ¿Bueno, que de veras me quiere?" ("Well, is it really true that you love me?") she now pleasantly replies.

" ¿Pos hasta la paré d'enfrente, cómo no? V. más dulce

que un acitrón y más buena que'l pan caliente. ¡Qual-
quiera sénamora de V. nada más con que se le quite un
poquito el genio de suegra que tiene, entonces si valía la
plata, pero no tenga cuidado que yo se lo quitaré!" ("I
love you about as much as that wall in front of us. Why
not? You're sweeter than preserves or candy, and better
than hot bread. Whoever sees you will love you, only you
must leave off some of that hot temper such as mothers-in-
law have, and then you'll be equal to a silver mine; but
never mind, don't bother yourself, I'll get all that out of
you!")

After this, her hot temper gets the better of her, and,
tossing his hand from her shoulder, and releasing the
rebozo, she says:

"¡Déjeme! ¡déjeme!" ("Get out the way, and let me
alone!"), and, wrapping her rebozo more tightly about
her head, passes rapidly from his sight.

Under ordinary circumstances, the common people
are easily controlled, but if anything occurs suddenly to
rouse their slumbering wrath or animosity, every animate
object had better retire before the advancing frenzied
multitude. Face a stampede of buffaloes—jump into the
raging sea, or risk the relentless cyclone—but always keep
clear of a Mexican mob. Let their anger be aroused at a
bullfight because of the inefficiency of the toreros or the
tameness of the bull, the further one gets from the scene
the better for him. They demolish the ring, tear down its
whole interior, smash the benches and seats into atoms,
and did not the Rurales, or strong police force, take charge
of the bullfighters, they would be in danger of losing their
lives. The mob comes down upon them like a thundering
tornado.

It has been estimated that the number of people who
serve in one capacity or another is about one-fifth of the
common population. That part relating to the household
is in a great measure an inseparable adjunct of it; but
there are also separate services that are performed by
people on the outside, who come daily for the purpose.

The low wages, and the generally poverty-stricken condition of the masses, place the servants in a state of extreme dependence.

An average house in the city has from ten to twenty servants, and I have seen some grand houses where thirty or thirty-five were employed. Each one has his or her separate duties to perform, and there is no clashing and no infringement one upon the other. A larger number of Mexican servants can live on peaceable terms than those of any other nationality. It is a rare occurrence to hear them quarreling, whatever disaffection may exist.

The leading servants of the household may be classified as follows:

El portero—The man who takes care of the door.

El cochero—The driver.

El lacayo—The footman.

El caballerango—The hostler.

El mozo—A general man for errands, etc. (I have given an idea of him in all his glory.)

El cargador—A public carrier.

El camarista—In hotels he is the chambermaid; in private houses he attends the gentleman of the house, brushes clothes, etc.

La recamerera—Female chambermaid, as employed in private houses.

Ama de llaves—Mistress of the keys, literally; the housekeeper.

Cocinera—The cook.

Galopina—The scullion.

Pilmama—In the Mexican idiom, piltoutli niña (mamacargar)—The woman who carries the child out to walk.

Chichi—Mexican idiom, chichihua—Wet nurse.

Molendera—The woman who grinds the corn.

Costurera—Sewing woman.

Planchadora—Ironing woman.

The position of portero is the most responsible one

about the house. Both day and night he is charged with the safety and well-being of its inmates. They are generally excellent and reliable men, and perform their duties with remarkable zeal and fidelity. In large cities he does nothing but guard the door, but in smaller towns the position of portero is often merged in that of mozo, or general man. At the capital one man will have the responsible care of a large building, in which perhaps ten or a dozen families reside. They all look to him for the safety of their rooms or apartments. He lives with his family in some dark little nook under a staircase, or, if the house is so arranged, he may have a comfortable room with a window on the street or patio.

A Mexican lacayo in his picturesque hat and faultless black suit, elaborately trimmed with jingling silver, is indeed a "thing of beauty and a joy forever," but not a single instance have I ever heard of a señorita's eloping with him: the difference in station is never overlooked when it comes to matrimony.

These servants have deep attachments for the family with whom they live. They sometimes serve in one a lifetime, and when no longer able to do so, are succeeded by their children, in the same capacity.

In case of a death in the family where they are employed, they at once don the somber luto (black), and never appear outside the house without it for six months.

This faithful attachment is especially and frequently shown by the pilmama. She will tenderly and patiently nurse each child in rotation, and to the last one her devotion is unimpaired. She also takes charge of baby's clothes, and herself washes the dainty fabrics, rather than intrust them to a lavandera. Children have their own pet name for the pilmama, abbreviating it into nana, "Quiero mi nana" ("I want my nana") being frequently heard. The chichi (wet nurse) does nothing but give sustenance to the babe, and is never permitted to leave the house except under the surveillance of the ama de llaves.

This latter functionary has entire charge of the household linen. She directs the army of servants under her, and is a kind of queen bee in the hive. She holds herself far above the servants, will carry no household packages, and is very tenacious of the dignity attaching to her position. Indeed, it not infrequently happens that she is a relative or connection of the family. She has frequently three or four assistants.

Mexican servants as a whole are tractable, kind, faithful, and humble. They shrink instinctively from harshness or scolding, but yield a willing obedience to kindly given orders. They are accused of being universal thieves, in which accusation I do not concur, although, indeed, the extremely low wages for which they work might seem to warrant, or at least excuse, small peculations. But they have this redeeming trait, that they generally appreciate the trust placed in them, and this sometimes to a remarkable degree. Instances were not uncommon during the days of revolution when porteros, mozos, and other servants voluntarily sacrificed their lives in defense of the life or property of their employers. But they have their peculiarities, acquired and engendered by the various circumstances that have hedged them about, for which all allowance must be made. If due patience and tact be exercised in the outset by foreign housekeepers, they will surely become deeply attached to the entire household, and better servants are not to be found. Especially is this true with regard to American children, to whom they become extremely devoted. But it must be remembered that their customs are overgrown with the moss of centuries, and care must be exercised in disturbing it by foreign methods of labor, or the application of new ideas. They know their own way, and have a repugnance to any interference with their precious "costumbres."

In their various employments their deportment is of the most quiet kind. If the mistress desires their attention, unless near at hand she does not call their names, but merely slaps her hands together, which attracts immediate attention. This clapping is practiced in the street as

well as in the house. Nothing would sooner confuse a servant than calling her name in a loud, harsh key.

On the frontier the mistress is known as señora, but in
interior towns and cities she is always the niña (child), no
matter if she has reached a hundred years.

The hand motion by which a servant is summoned is
the reverse of our beckoning sign—the palm being turned
outward.

The wages of a cook are from $2.00 to $5.00 per
month; coachman, from $10.00 to $30.00; serving
women, $3.00 to $8.00; and so on in like proportion.

With these small sums entire rations are not furnished
them. They are paid a medio and quartillo each day, independent of their wages, to buy coffee and bread in the
morning, and bread and pulque for each dinner and supper; or they are paid 62 ½ cents every eight days, for this
purpose. In some places a medio's worth of soap is given
them each week to have their clothes washed, and the
lower the wages, the less soap they get. The value of this
soap is often collected a month in advance, thus leaving a
glaring deficit in their clean clothes account.

They generally leave the last place in debt, which is
assumed by the new master. If the servant's wages be
$4.00 per month, and she owes $12.00 or $25.00, as the
case may be, she draws only $2.50, leaving $1.50 for her
abono (amount of indebtedness).

A singular method of keeping accounts is that employed by the untutored common people. I saw an Indian
on the line of a certain railway who had engaged to furnish
goats' and cows' milk for the contractors. The cows' milk
he purchased from another party; the account with the
railway and that with the party from whom he bought the
milk were kept on a stick stripped of the bark in alternate
sections. Certain kinds of notches were then cut on either
side, indicating pints or quarts; other notches, straight or
oblique, represented quartillos (3 cents), medios (6 cents),
or reales (12 ½ cents), the payment for the same.

An error occurred in the settlement of the accounts,

which the bookkeeper did not observe, but which was discovered by the Indian, and, though against himself, he would only settle according to the notches on his stick.

Customs may vary in different provinces as to the way of keeping private accounts. At the capital the lives and "costumbres" of the servants are different from those in small towns and interior cities.

The furnishing of the homes of the common people is necessarily meager; sometimes only mats laid upon the dirt floor serve for beds, or a few rudely made bedsteads and chairs, with pictures of the saints and a quantity of home-manufactured toys, constitute the outfit. They are gente ordinario, but their houses are reasonably clean. One corner of the room is generally devoted to an infinite variety of pottery suspended on nails. This is collected from all parts of the country, and is their chief household treasure; even small children can point out the different kinds and tell where each piece was made.

Let one enter when he will, he is sure to be greeted politely, and to have the kindliest hospitality extended to him. I remember one of the houses into which I went where a pretty young woman of twenty years sat crocheting, while the baby slept in his petate cradle and the husband lay sick on his humble cot in the corner. She cordially welcomed me, and when I was seated, he, though feeble and trembling, raised himself upon his elbow, tendering me the hospitality of his pobre casa; then asked his wife to prepare for me a cup of coffee or chocolate, which she did.

I condoled with him on his illness and hoped he would soon be well. To this he replied he hoped so, but as he had consumption, there was little chance for his recovery; but if it were possible, he would like to get well, "in order to serve me the rest of his life!"

I was agreeably surprised to find so many sewing machines, and that the women understand their use quite as well as we do. A machine agent informed me that the women of this class are as prompt to meet their installments as those in any country. But the price of sewing is so very cheap—only one cent a yard—that they must do a great deal to render themselves self-sustaining.

Babies are cared for with great tenderness. They are wrapped as tightly as possible in "swaddling clothes" until about one month old, when the calzoncillos (little breeches) are substituted, for both boys and girls. The cuna (cradle) is a concomitant of every humble dwelling. It is sometimes suspended from the ceiling, but quite as often it hangs under the table. The material of which it is composed is usually palm or maguey, and its quaint little occupant looks quite comfortable, snugly sleeping in the rebozo, while the cradle sways back and forth of its own accord.

These poor women are often the mothers of such beauties as would arouse envy in the breasts of many aristocratic parents.

The evangelistas (letter writers) have a distinct position to themselves. They subserve a valuable purpose to the great army of servants and low-class people, who, through them, carry on a correspondence with their lovers. With a board on his knees, or perhaps sometimes a plain little table, and a big jug of ink, and pen behind the ear, the evangelista is ready to serve his customers. Anxious lovers stand around awaiting his leisure, the desire to transmit their sentiments making his services in high demand. Note paper, variously shaped, is at hand, and for a medio or real, a letter is furnished that will be expressive of grief, jealousy, love, and overweening affection.

Love letter written by "un evangelista."

APRECIABLE SEÑORITA.

Quisiera tener el lenguaje de los ángeles; la dulce inspiración de un poeta; o la elocuencia de un Cicerón, para expresarme en terminos dignos de Vd. Pero por desgracia mi mente la cubre el velo de la ignorancia, y no puedo menos que tomarme la libertad de revelar a Vd. mis aficciones; pues desde el primer día que tuve la dicha de conocer a Vd., la calma ha huido de mi, y dominado por la pasión más violenta, me adverbio a decir a Vd. que la amo, con el amor más puro y verdadero, y que aún me parece con esta declaración que hago a Vd. de mi amor, que no supera el ardor que mi triste y afligido corazón sufre, mientras tanto obtengo la contestación de Vd. quedo impaciente por saber el fallo de vida o de muerte que de Vd. a su apasionado.

Es cuanto le dice a Vd. quien a sus pies besa.

MANUEL GÓMEZ Y SUÁREZ.

[*Translation.*]

ESTEEMED SEÑORITA.

Would that I possessed the language of the angels, the sweet inspiration of a poet, or the eloquence of a Cicero, that I might then express myself in a manner worthy of you. But alas! my intellect, my brains, seem veiled in ignorance, and I cannot resist taking the liberty of revealing my love, my affection. When I first had the happiness of meeting you, my peace of mind fled, and governed solely by the most violent passion for you, I dare tell you *I love you*, with a love most pure, most true, and notwithstanding this declaration of my love you will not even then realize that my sad, afflicted heart suffers until your answer reaches me. I impatiently await your fiat, whether of life or death, to your devoted, passionate one.

Meanwhile I say to you, that I kiss your feet.

MANUEL GÓMEZ Y SUÁREZ.

A character which must be considered in the light of a nuisance, is to be found in both sexes all over the country. Plausible and gifted with all the "*suavidad en el modo*" of their betters, they ply their vocation in the street, as well as in private houses. If in the street, they come upon you unawares. Suddenly brown fingers are thrust under your nose, holding a comb, a toy, jewelry or a piece of dry goods or embroidery. You dare not even look at it, or feign the least knowledge of their presence, for if you should do so, they will haunt and pursue you for squares without ceasing. Enter a store, and be ever so much interested in the purchase of some article or textile fabric, here comes the irrepressible vender and again puts the article in your face, this time with a great reduction in price.

Another class with which strangers are sure to be annoyed, are the women with black shawls drawn tightly about their heads and faces; neat calico dresses, catlike tread, though invariably in a hurry, and with the most benignant expression on their countenances. If in your house, they approach you most humbly, with many kindly inquiries after the health of the family in general, and as to how the night has been passed. While doing this, the shawl goes slightly back, revealing some article of needle-work, a handsome shawl, silk dress, or whatever else they may choose for gulling you. A long history of the article follows, ending by a high price being asked for it. You don't want it, so the price is reduced until perhaps you look a little more inclined; but at last no sale is effected. She goes away apparently much disappointed and almost with tears in her eyes. But be patient! she will come again with softer tread, and with such honeyed words as will surely win their way.

She makes her appearance the second time with a handsome tray in hand, on which rest several kinds of tempting dulces. These she tells you have been sent by Doña So-and-So, also naming the street; that she has heard you are a stranger, and sends these as a token of her regard.

Nothing remains but to accept them with many thanks for her interest, and the hope that she will soon call on you.

The next day the thoughtful woman again enters, with a humility of manner that even Uriah Heep could not excel. She makes all manner of inquiry as to the health of each inmate of the household. She then states that it was a mistake about the regalo she had brought a day or two before (of course you have long since eaten them); that the Doña told her to sell them at a certain house, and she had made the mistake. You ask her the price, that being the only alternative, and it is a startling one. She is paid, and perhaps never again appears in your house, but she has amply paid you off for not buying the first article she offered.

Happily these people do not exist in great numbers, and, though incorrigible wherever found, strangers soon discover their transparent tricks.

The rebozo is the boon of all these women, as they can carry securely concealed any number of articles without being detected by human eyes.

The rebozo also often assists in making the head of the wearer assume a ludicrous shape. Take a rear view, as the women sit cuddled up in groups of several dozen, or even hundreds, on the celebration of some feast, and with the flickering lights of a thousand torches dancing over their tightly drawn headgear, the resemblance to a school of seals, with their heads peeping out of the water, could not be more perfect.

The molendera is a woman who does the grinding on the metate, whether corn for tortillas, coffee, or spices. Should the molendera set up an establishment of her own, and make tortillas for sale, or, as is sometimes the case, go at certain hours each day and make them for families, she then becomes a tortillera.

These tortilleras are a separate and distinct class, and have their own rules and regulations for conducting business. They employ ten or a dozen women, who grind the corn and make the tortillas. When made, the women who sell them in the markets and streets come with their baskets and take them away, paying wholesale rates.

The proprietress of the establishment is called the patrona, and the Queen of Sheba never moved about with more dignity and consequence.

She pays her employees each day a real y medio. I have made it convenient to drop in at the hour for settling up with them. She has a little chair or stool before her, herself unostentatiously occupying the space in front of it on the floor. The real in silver, and six cents in tlacos for each "grinder," are laid in little piles, each one being named for the woman to whom it is to be paid. The patrona sits by and looks on serenely after counting over and over the piles, with satisfaction and self-importance emanating from her, and expressing in unspoken language —"You poor contemptible 'grinders,' you have no position!"

I never went into one of these places without being most cordially invited to be seated. On accepting the invitation, an animated conversation would follow, while eating the delicious hot tortillas, fresh from the smoking comal, and admiring the animated bronze statuettes that ambled and capered about without even the disguise of a fig leaf.

The lavandera is an important outside servant. Owing to the construction of the houses, in part, and to the fact of the water being conveyed to them from the city fountains, washing is rarely done on the premises.

The lavanderas also have their own rules and regulations, and are as rigid in exacting the observance of them by their subordinates and satellites as any other class.

In some cities and towns the lavandera is not also the planchadora. She does not even starch the clothes, but is supplied with soap for the washing. At those places presided over by a patrona, the contract is taken for all, but the custom is to charge by the piece and never by the dozen. But in the smaller towns and cities she will receive a real a dozen for washing alone, having soap furnished.

When she returns them, the planchadora comes, counts, and, on being supplied with starch and coal or wood, again takes them away to finish the job. There is, however, an agreeable offset to all this—the planchadora is also the apuntar; she mends carefully every article requiring it before taking her work home.

At the capital there are laundries inside the houses where lavanderas may go and rent, for a medio a day, a compartment of brick in which the water flows from a fountain.

Springs usually burst from some steep declivity of the neighboring mountains, and not infrequently in the descent to valley and lowland the water circles and winds about through the adjacent trees. In such desirable locations are the spots coveted by the lavanderas. Sometimes for the distance of two miles they may be seen like a bright fringe along the edge of the stream, in costumes which would delight a painter in search of the unconventional.

On these occasions their hair is unbraided and hangs in a superb mass of rippling waves to the end. The only dress is a red woolen petticoat and the chemise, both of which serve only to enhance the classic beauty of form disclosed by the peculiar costume.

Six or seven days of the week, kneeling in graceful attitudes, these laundresses may be seen expending their tireless energy on the ropa (clothes). Armed with the crude washing equipments of the ancient Egyptians—only a stone slab, or at best a wooden tray resembling our bread trays—they make their week's washing whiter than the whitest. However it is accomplished, the fact remains that without boiling, washing soda, washboard, tub or bucket, and even in many cases without soap, this perplexing branch of domestic life is brought to perfection.

The aguador is the most noted of all the classes who serve outside the residence. As there are few houses furnished with pipes, the water supply is transported by this functionary.

His costume is peculiar to himself and well adapted to his vocation. It varies in every province. That worn in the City of Mexico is the most picturesque, and deserves a description. Over a shirt and drawers of common domestic he wears a jacket and trousers of blue cloth or tanned buckskin. The latter are turned up nearly to the knee. With his leathern helmet, broad leather strap across his forehead, called frontera (from which depends the chochocol, or water vessel), leathern apron, and sandals of the same, called huaraches, we might imagine him to be a man in armor, so completely is he enveloped in this substantial equipment.

The piece that covers the back, and on which the chochocol rests, is called respaldadera, or backrest; that which reaches from the waist to the knee, delantal or apron; and that which protects the thigh, the rosadera. All these pieces are fastened by means of thongs to a leather waistcoat, which serves to support and balance the large jar. Both jars are attached to straps which cross on the head over a palmleaf cap with leather visor. It is essential that these vessels correspond in size and perfectly balance. If either be suddenly broken, the aguador at once loses his balance and falls to the ground.

On the opposite side to the rosadera he carries a deerskin pouch called barrega, adorned with figures. This pouch serves for carrying the nickel coins and pitoles, or small red beans with which he keeps an account of the number of trips he makes, being paid at the end of a week or fortnight, according to the number of beans he leaves at a house. He also keeps a corresponding "tally sheet" with beans, and compares notes with his employer when being paid.

The aguador is a person of importance; nobody knows better than he the inner life of the household that he serves. He is often made the messenger between lovers, and when for any reason he may refuse to perform that office, the ingenious lover resorts to artifice, and by means of wax fastens the missive upon the bottom of the chochocol, and the unconscious aguador thus conveys it to the expectant fair one, who informed of the device, is ready to remove the epistle. He often wonders why the young mistress comes out so early in the morning to meet him, and that he so frequently finds her lover standing at the door of his house.

The aguador scarcely ever dines at home. His wife meets him with a basket covered with a napkin at the entrance to some house, and there, together with his children and companions, he dines with good appetite and without annoyance of any kind. Then he goes to the fountain where he is accustomed to draw water, frees himself of his jars, and stretches himself in the shade to take his siesta; or he spends the rest of the day at some pulque shop, playing a game called "rayuela" with his companions, or repeating pleasantries and proverbs to the maids that happen to pass near him, and drinking pulque. But in the midst of this monotony, they also have their days of enjoyment, their days of merriment and diversion. The feast of the Holy Cross arrives, and when day begins to dawn, they burn an endless number of rockets and bombs, which they call salva or salute.

When the sun rises, the sign of the cross has been already placed on the spring of the fountain, or in the center, if the fountain is in a public square. The said crosses are adorned with rosaries or chains of poppies and *cempazuchitl*. On that day the watermen bathe, dress themselves in their holiday clothes and go to dine in community, eating heartily and drinking white and prepared pulque the greater part of the day.

One of the poor waterman's joys is the Saturday of Passion Week, or Sábado de Gloria; but this day is not so animated as the former, for it is confined to strewing flowers on the water of the fountain and burning an image representing their profession.

The superstitions of today among the Mexican lower classes are quite strong and closely adhered to. They are almost numberless, and the most insignificant has its own place, not to be substituted by any other. Evidences of this appear in the performance of the simplest duty. Let them begin to make a fire, and the first movement is to make the sign of the cross in the air before the range; or if about to cook any such articles as tortillas, any of them, as preliminary, make the cross and utter a few words of prayer.

The moon has much to do with these fancies, and many of their individual failings are laid to the account of that luminary.

These are carried with humorous effect into the smallest minutiæ of household labors. In killing fowls, they pull the head off, then make the sign of the cross with the neck on the ground, and laying the chicken on the place, declare it cannot jump about; but I noticed they always held it firmly on the cross.

Many of them keep a light burning both day and night in their houses. In the majority of instances, the light is merely a wax taper placed in a glass half filled with water, with a little oil on the top. Beside the taper a cross is fixed.

On one occasion, I went into a tortilla establishment where were eight or ten women grinding corn, and seeing the light I asked the patrona why she kept this light burning.

"Because," she answered, "I want God and all his saints to keep this house from evil spirits. We have to work very hard all day, and when this light is burning they dare not come near."

"Do you keep it burning always?" said I.

"Yes, always; without it we would be in total darkness." Then, turning to me, she asked:

"Have you not God and saints in your country?"

"Yes; but we believe that God will protect us without the light, and we do not depend on the saints"; which ended the colloquy.

I have been at times much impressed with the seriousness and sentiment so evidently underlying these little superstitious actions. The old tamalera came to our house the evening I left the capital. She released her burden from her back, and then began as usual to chat with me, her extreme age and trembling frame appealing strongly to my sympathies. When I had sung her grito over and over with her, she made the sign of the cross over the olla in which she kept her tamales, then crossed herself, saying:

"In the name of the *Divina Providencia* may I have enough customers to buy these tamales, that I may go early to my home. I am weary of trudging these streets, and *mi pobre casa* is far away." Before leaving, she turned to me, and with tears streaming down her face, placed her hand on my head and said: "Niña, you leave us tonight to go to your home, that is far, far away in another land; may the Divina Providencia take you safely there; may you find your people well, and some day before I die, may you return to us here, and sing again with me this grito!"

On the feast of All Souls, they place a table on the sidewalk containing such articles of food as their dead friends and relatives liked best—even to the pulque. When morning comes, it is, of course, all gone, and the donor is duly happy, because she imagines the dear dead ones have returned and partaken of their favorite food, when in reality, mischievous boys have consumed these precious edibles. On this day the various venders and outside help come for their gifts, just as newsboys come for their contributions on New Year's. These gifts are disguised under the name of calaveras—skulls. Each one asks in his own characteristic fashion, the paper carrier in the following verse:

> Your faithful carrier
> Cheerfully presents himself,
> Encouraged by the hope
> Of obtaining your favor:
> You who are a subscriber,
> Applauded everywhere
> For that sincere loyalty
> With which you are accustomed to pay:
> He only comes to beg you
> To give him his 'Calavera.'

The curandera is another outside household appendage. She is the professional nurse, and as such is faithful, ready, and attentive. In this capacity her services are invaluable. She may also assume the rôle of practicing physician, and with numerous remedies and herbs of every kind, she becomes quite a power in the land. There is a world of witchcraft and superstition in the practice of the curanderas, and the common people stand in great awe of them.

In the rural districts their pharmacy consists of ground glass, beaten shells, white lead, and an infinity of herbs. Their diagnosis embraces calor y frío (heat and cold), and their therapeutics are always directed toward these two conditions. A disease quite common which these women assume to cure is empeche, a condition where undigested food adheres to some part of the stomach. To dislodge the empeche, they give white lead and quicksilver, at frequent intervals, in compound doses. For paralysis, they have been known to give blue and red glass beads, ground up in equal portions, a tablespoonful at a dose. Strange to relate, the patient recovered.

If a child is slow in learning to talk, they recommend a diet of boiled swallows. This is infallible. If he is slow about walking, his legs should be rubbed with dirt. This accounts for the fact that pelado (poor) children acquire the use of their limbs sooner than those of the higher classes

X

Among the Children

One of the many sweet lullabies I have heard the mothers
sing to their children is as follows:

> "Se fueron las Yankis al Guaridame,
>   Y el Yankie más grande
>   Se parece a Pepito.
> *Chorus*:   A la pasadita tra-la-ra-la-ra.

> "Se fueron las Yankis a la Ladrillera,
>   Y el Yankie más grande
>   Se parece a Elena.
> *Chorus*: "Y a la pasadita tra-la-ra-la-ra."

> "The Yankees went to Guaridame,
>   And the biggest Yankee there
>   Looked like Pepito.
> *Chorus*:   To the *pasadita*, tra-la-ra-la-ra.

> "The Yankees went to the Ladrillera
>   And the biggest Yankee there
>   Looked like Elena.
> *Chorus*:   To the *pasadita*, tra-la-ra-la-ra."

The air of this ditty is extremely musical, and though
the words do not suggest anything particularly soothing,
yet, crooned by the low, sweet voice of the mother, it never
fails to produce a quieting and soporific effect upon the
most recalcitrant infant.

This is as popular with the Mexican tots as "Rock-a-
bye baby" or kindred melodies are with ours.

Their nursery tales, too, as well as their ditties, bear
an analogy to our own.

The nana is preparing the children for bed; the little
ones chatter and yawn alternately, and the nurse is hoping

that their drowsiness will spare her this time her nightly task of storytelling. Not so, however. Tucked at last in bed, with the exception of the youngest, whom she holds on her lap, one calls out: "¡Cuentome! ¡cuentome!" ("Tell me a story, tell me a story!") The others quickly chime in— "¡Cuentanos!" ("Tell us a story!")

"Bueno, pero están quietos." ("Very well, then, but you must be quiet"), she answers. Then taking in hers the baby's fingers she begins:

"Niña chiquita y bonita" ("A pretty, sweet little girl"), holding up the little finger.

"El señor de los anillos" ("The gentleman gives the ring"), holding up third finger.

"El tonto y loco" ("Idiotic and crazy"), holding middle finger.

"El lama cazuelas" ("Licks the cook pot"), elevating forefinger.

"Mata los animales" ("Kills the little animals"). This last is accompanied by the very expressive gesture of tapping the thumbnails together.

If this charming recital fails to act as a narcotic to her little hearers, she goes on with:

> Este era un rey que tenía tres hijas,
> Y las metió en unas botijas y
> Catrape el cuento ha acabado.

> Este era nu rey que tenía tres hijas,
> Los vestió de colorado
> Catrape el cuento ha acabado.

This was a king who had three daughters,
And he put them in earthen jugs—
Now my story is ended.

This was a king who had three daughters,
And he dressed them all in red—
Now my story is ended.

And so on to yet more blood-curdling and fascinating

romances till slumber seals her listeners' eyes, and her task ceases.

CONUNDRUMS

" ¿Por dentro colorado y por fuera como salvado?" Answer: El mamey (one of the favorite fruits of the country). Trans.: "*Red* inside and like bran outside? The mamey." Another: "Agua pasa por mi casa. Cate de mi corazón. El que me lo adivinare de le parte el corazón." Answer: "The Aguacate" ("the vegetable butter"). Trans.: "Water passes through my house. Try my heart. Whoever guesses it, his heart will break."

They are not unlike those peculiar "riddles" with which the children of the Southern states were once so familiar, coming from the lips of our black "mammies." One, especially, I remember, suggested by my first quotation: "Throw it up green, it comes down red." Answer: "Watermelon."

That "boys will be boys" all the world over, and the teasing instinct universal among them, is demonstrated in the following dialogue. Says one mischief-loving lad to another:

" ¿Quieres que te cuente el cuento del gallo pelón?" ("Do you wish me to tell you the story of the bald-headed rooster?")

"Sí" ("yes"), answers his companion, eagerly.

" ¿No te digo que sí, que si quieres que te cuente el cuento del gallo pelón?" ("I did not tell you yes; I said, do you wish me to tell you the story of the bald-headed rooster?") says the first boy.

"Sí," again answers the other, growing impatient.

Again the aggravating lad repeats his question, and again his companion signifies his anxiety to hear the interesting tale. And so it goes on till either the storyteller tires of the amusement or the wrath of his disappointed listener brings the unchanging query to an end.

This story reminds one of the abortive attempts to spell Con-stan-ti-no-ple.

XI

Scenes from My Window

The striking characteristics which abound in all parts of Mexico are more plainly exhibited in the capital itself than elsewhere.

The preponderance of the full-blooded Indian is noticeable in the lower classes; high cheekbones, coarse, straight hair, the same sidewise trot, tipping from right to left, and all pigeon-toed.

The poorer classes all wear the serape, which, owing to its brilliant coloring, adds greatly to the effectiveness of a street scene.

Day by day, seated at my window, I watched the various groups that by some strange and happy chance seemed to fall together for my pleasure and entertainment.

The number and variety of articles which are transported by both men and women are certainly noticeable to the most indifferent observer. Young backs are early trained and disciplined, and the boys and girls bear burdens that might stagger a burro.

Clothes are taken home from the laundry in a droll manner. Men carry on their heads baskets containing the smaller articles, while suspended around the sides are stiffly starched, ruffled and fluted skirts, dresses and other articles of feminine apparel. In the rainy season the cargador has his trousers rolled up, so that there is nothing visible of the man but a pair of long, thin, brown legs.

I saw another man toiling along with an American two-horse load of corn husks on his back, held in place by ropes, the whole reaching from about a foot above his head down to his ankles, and almost closing him in, in front.

Venders of charcoal step nimbly along with from twenty to twenty-five bags of this commodity strapped about them, their bodies so begrimed as to render it hard to decide whether they belong to the Aztec or African race.

One obtains a glimpse of rural life in the frequent passing of herds of cattle, all without horns, and in the noisy gobbling of droves of turkeys as they are driven through the city. Halting only when their proprietor finds a purchaser, they strut through the streets of the metropolis as unconcernedly as though on their native hacienda.

Life seems to glide along very pleasantly with these people. As they pass along the street, they hail each other quite unceremoniously, the lack of previous acquaintance forming no bar to a familiar chat. Groups of more than a dozen of these venders, representing as many different commodities, will often congregate together, their forms almost concealed from view beneath their loads. Then, after a general handshaking, each goes his way, crying his wares.

One rainy afternoon I witnessed an amusing quarrel between five Indian women. Each carried a child in her rebozo and held another by the hand, making in all "ten little Indians." They stopped immediately under my window. Their scanty drapery reached a little below the knee, and their shoulders were covered only with their rebozos. Evidently, there was a subject of disagreement between them, which was explained when three men of their own race came across the street and joined them. Then followed angry gestures, bitter intonations, and threatening attitudes, until the passers-by and occupants of the houses eagerly watched the quarrel. The children, quietly indifferent, and as if the affair had no possible interest for them, munched away on their tortillas. The dispute became so violent that I expected as a result to see at least half a dozen dead Indians, but was disappointed.

The man who figured most conspicuously in the scene offered his hand to one of the women. She turned scornfully away, but I noticed, in so doing, she touched the arm of another woman and chuckled in an undertone. He spoke to another. She gave him one thumb only, looking shyly in his face. The next one gave him her whole hand, when he knelt and humbly kissed it, as though it belonged to his patron saint. Then, slipping her hand in his arm, and with her two little Indians, they walked off, leaving the rest of the party to a further discussion of the affair.

Then came a party of three—a huge dog, a grown boy, and an innocent muchacho about one year old. The dog was so loaded down with alfalfa that he could scarcely move. The big boy walked beside him, guiding him with lines. Mounted upon his brother's shoulders, with his feet around his neck, was the little mischief, holding tightly with both hands to a tuft of hair on each side of his big brother's head.

Diagonally across the street is the Teatro Principal. The play "Around the World in Eighty Days" had for some time past occupied the boards. On the outside was an immense painting representing an elephant caparisoned with gold and led by an oriental, while mounted on the elephant, and seated after the fashion of a man, rode a woman dressed in gay colors, and over her a canopy with red draperies. Palms and other tropical trees appeared in the distance.

On the same canvas, and in contrast to this peaceful scene, appears another of quite a blood-curdling nature. A locomotive comes screaming and puffing along. Suddenly myriads of wild Indians, painted red, with feathers on their heads and deadly weapons in their hands, make a furious attack upon it. They ride on the cowcatcher. Dead Indians and horses are piled around, and the headlight throws a ghastly illumination over all!

I witnessed a general review of the infantry troops in the city, a sight which was strictly national in its character, and made a showy and amusing picture.

Mounted upon gayly caparisoned horses, the officers presented a handsome and soldierly appearance, in their uniforms of dark blue, elaborately ornamented with red and gold. The soldiers, neatly attired in blue, piped with red, and wearing pure white caps, were also quite imposing. But the sublime suddenly culminated in the ridiculous, when in the midst of so much glitter, pomp and circumstance—waving of plume, helmet, and sword—not less than fifty burros, meek and unconcerned, entered in the midst of these gallant defenders of their country, and, as if by right of pre-emption, plodded in serpentine lines the whole length of the procession. Some bore mountain loads of golden wheat, straw, others charcoal, and pulque in sheepskins, with other articles too numerous to mention. The soldiers kept up their steady tramp, tramp, tramp; they moved not a muscle, spoke not a word, as the bands played their most exhilarating airs. Now a man, bearing a trunk or wardrobe; an Indian woman, selling fruits, with her children on her back; men with baskets, chairs, shoes, tanned leather, and others selling dulces, joined the procession. At length the acme of a typical Mexican scene was reached when the burros unceremoniously raised their nozzles and brayed loud and long. As far as I could see up the street, the military and their self-constituted escort formed an indistinguishable mass.

I had scarcely recovered my equilibrium from the effects of the procession, when a carriage and horses came flying down the street in wild confusion. The Jehu sat bolt upright, with feet outspread from side to side, as if "down brakes" was in order. His eyes glared wildly from their sockets, as, with clinched teeth, he held desperately to the lines. The animals were evidently uncongenial to each other, one being a young mule, the other an unbroken pony. They reared and plunged violently, while Jehu used every expletive known to the Mexican language. But as this treatment proved unavailing, he jumped down from his lofty seat, and ran beside them, jerking the lines and screaming at them. Still they heeded him not. At this critical moment a sympathetic bystander conceived a fresh and vigorous idea of assistance, and as he ran along, jerked from the shoulders of an uninterested pedestrian (who had not even seen the runaway team) his red blanket, and waving it before the frightened animals, threw them trembling and panting on their haunches. In a twinkling Jehu was on the box, and, laying on the whip, was soon out of sight.

I glanced across the street directly afterward, and saw a boy who had passed several times that day, selling butter, which he carried in a soap box, the cover an odd bit of matting, and the whole suspended from his head in the usual way.

Entering the zaguan, he threw down his cage, and taking the butter out—each pound wrapped in a cornhusk —laid it in rows, and gave his head a scratch, took his money from his pocket, and began to count. Over and over he counted and scratched, evidently apprehensive that his accounts would not balance. The scratching and counting went on for no inconsiderable time, his face still wearing a puzzled expression. At last the solution came in the recollection of some forgotten sale. He rose, a broad grin overspreading his heretofore perplexed face, slapped himself on the hip, laughed, hastily slung his cage on his back, threw his blanket over his shoulder, and the last I saw of him he was vocalizing his occupation: "La man-te-quil-la" ("Butter for sale").

The gritos (calls) of the street venders become each day more interesting to the stranger. Each one is separate and distinct from the other, and each one is an ancestral inheritance. In them, as everything else, the "costumbres" rule, and the appropriation by another vender of one of these gritos would receive a well-merited reprimand. But how indescribable is the long-drawn intonation, with the necessary nasal twang of these indefatigable itinerants! A word with only four syllables stretches out until one may count a hundred.

This is a branch of musical composition that has received but little or no attention from musicians, but by all means some effort should be made to preserve them in their originality, together with exact portraits of the venders as they now appear.

The gritos at the capital possess many interesting features which can be heard in no other city in which I have sojourned; they are wanting elsewhere in that fullness of pathetic and yet humorous melody.

The vocal powers, thus exercised, attain a surprising development, as the voice of an ordinary woman may be heard for squares away. The most noted of all the female gritos is that of the tamalera.

The husky, tremulous voice of a young Indian woman fell upon my ear one morning as I was crossing the threshold of the San Carlos. Around her neck was a strip of manta filled with vegetables. On seeing me, she began importuning me to buy. They were fresh and crisp, but I said to her:

"I am a stranger; I have no home here, and have no use for such things."

"But, niña," she added, imploringly, "I am sick, have no home, and under these vegetables in the rebozo is my sick baby, only two weeks old."

Stooping to peep under the load of vegetables, there I saw the tiny babe, tucked away in the rebozo, and sleeping as soundly under its strange covering as though swinging in its palm-plaited cradle.

The mother asked me to stand godmother to the baby at the Cathedral, one week from that day, but as that was impossible, she seemed reconciled when she found her hand filled with small coins, and bidding me a grateful farewell, she went on her way singing.

These gritos are rather more melodious than those to which our ears are accustomed, such as, "Ole rags 'n' bot-tuls!"

The melodramatic tones of the newsboys at night, when many of the most popular papers are sold, had a more foreign sound than any that came to my ear. The boy who sold *El Monitor Republicano* rolled it round and round his tongue until finally it died away like the hum of an ancient spinning wheel.

Another boy, with an aptitude for languages, sings out, "Las Dos Repúblicas" ("The Two Republics"), translating as he goes along, "Periódico Americano"; while another, not to be outdone, yells out exultantly, "El Tiempo de la mañana ("The *Times* for tomorrow"). Only the word mañana was distinctly articulated, which gave emphasis to his vocation, as the *Times* is printed in the evening and sold for the next day.

An amusing admixture of sounds was wafted to my room one night in the following manner. Two boys were calling at the highest pitch. One was selling cooked chestnuts, and the other the *Times*.

They managed to transpose the adjectives describing their respective wares. "Castañas asadas" ("Cooked chestnuts"), shouted one. "El Tiempo de mañana, con noticias importantes" ("Tomorrow's *Times* with important notices"), screamed the other. They were quite near together by this time, one on the sidewalk, and the other in the street; and when the air was again made vocal, a spirit of mischief had crept into the medley of sounds. The paper boy led off with mock gravity, "¡El Tiempo de mañana asada!" ("Tomorrow's *Times* cooked!")

"¡Castañas de mañana con noticias importantes!" ("Tomorrow's chestnuts with important news!") yelled the chestnut boy, and away they went, laughing and transposing their calls, to the amusement of all within hearing.

XII

WHAT THEY EAT
AND HOW THEY COOK IT

Mexican ladies take great pride in their cookbooks, and watch with deep interest the accuracy with which the ama de llaves carries out the receipts. The cooks, however, frequently have their own books, from which, without further instructions, they execute triumphs of gustatory art.

The first glance at a Mexican kitchen is anything but satisfactory to an American woman. The destiladera (water filter) is primitive in its simplicity. It is made from a porous, volcanic rock peculiar to the country. The water percolates through the pores and drips into a vessel below. Bits of charcoal are generally thrown in, and the water is as cold as ice and sparkling as crystal.

The same leisurely and ease-loving methods that characterize the business life pervade also the home. The most engrossed man of affairs quietly leaves his office with all its cares behind him, and takes to his home only his social endowments. He makes his mid-day meal one of enjoyment and the occasion of a happy mingling with the family circle.

After dinner the siesta follows, and business comes to a lull, until, perhaps, three o'clock in the afternoon.

Unfailing ceremony—a national characteristic—is observed in the serving of every meal. Whether there be three or twenty varieties of dishes, no two are served at once.

The climate seems to demand a rich and highly spiced diet, and, to make it still more luxurious, both fruits and nuts are freely used. But, to judge from the amount of dyspepsia prevailing there, it would seem that even Mexican digestion succumbs to it.

No bread is made in the family, while griddlecakes,

waffles, and muffins are unknown. Pies, tarts, cakes, or pastries have no extensive place in the menu; but their desserts of various kinds, made of eggs, milk, and fruits, are excellent. If, however, they are deficient in homely bread preparations, nature has given them a double compensation in the various delicious fruit beverages, compounded not only in the homes of the wealthy, but also of the humble folk.

In a Mexican home the day begins with the simple desayuno. This consists of a cup of chocolate, coffee, or tea, with bread, and is usually taken in the bedroom, frequently in bed. There is no fixed hour for this repast, which is partaken of according to inclination, no two members of the family being expected to take their desayuno at the same time. To all who enjoy the last drowsy morning nap there is an inexpressible charm in this mode of life.

The cares of the world are at long range, and one respectfully desires them to approach no nearer. No clanging of breakfast bells breaks rudely upon this delicious and intoxicating slumber; no scowling or looks askance from hostess or landlady, for in all probability she, too, is snugly ensconced in the arms of Morpheus.

The servants are up and at their usual labors, but they move about noiselessly as specters; not by the stirring of a leaf molesting the sweet repose of the blissful sleepers.

The most vigorous-minded gringo soon succumbs to this delightful custom. Though his former habit had been to rise with the sun, and eat an enormous breakfast of hash, chops, steak, eggs, hominy, battercakes, hot rolls, and what not, he at once and almost insensibly falls in with the native custom. He will linger longer under the covers, caring less and less for the matutinal cup.

At twelve o'clock the family reunion takes place, when the almuerzo—breakfast—is served. This, however, with its numerous courses, is really the dinner.

Soup is an indispensable part of every Mexican dinner, and is used not only at the mid-day meal, but often, too, at cena (supper).

The soups are of infinite variety and generally excellent. One lady told me she knew how to make one hundred different kinds. I have partaken of as many as twenty in her house. At Señora Calderón's I have seen seven varieties in one week, and all tempting and delicious.

Mexican housekeepers have an endless variety of methods for seasoning and dressing their meats. In a well-appointed household it is no uncommon thing to have the same meats prepared differently several times in a week.

Perhaps it may be somewhat due to the fact of the wretched manner in which the butchers do their work that they must resort to boiling, spicing, and other means to make the roast desirable. But when once prepared, the palate of Epicurus himself would be appeased. Ham, cheese, eggs, spices and the many delightful herbs of the country are formed into a paste, and by means of skewers the entire roast becomes impregnated with the aromatic, spicy flavor.

Their sauces and gravies, however, I do not consider as good as our own.

Every day in the year a Mexican housekeeper can have some kind of delightful salad on her table. The lettuce is whiter and more crisp than we generally see; the cauliflower grows to immense size, and is correspondingly good, while tomatoes, equally fine in color and flavor, gratify at once both eye and taste, supplying at any moment a depleted larder. But while these are all of superior quality, the popular taste prefers them served up in omelettes, with pepper, eggs, and spices. Fortunately, eggs, which fill such an important place in the national dietary, are always excellent and bountiful.

Frijoles, the native beans, are as much a boon to the rich as to the poor. Twice a day they close the meal, and even on ceremonious occasions are not dispensed with. A failure in the bean crop would prove as great a misfortune in Mexico, as a falling off in the potato crop in Ireland.

There is some little art in cooking them, and under no condition are they considered wholesome to be eaten the day on which they are cooked. They are boiled first until tender, and when required, are fried in a quantity of lard with a little chile thrown in.

Housewives have much skill in the preparation of their sweetmeats, and the Mexican preserves and crystallized fruits are certainly superior to our own. They possess the remarkable feature of retaining the original color and flavor of the fruit. The climate is favorable to their preservation, but as they have only the earthenware of the country in which to put them up, it seems strange that they should remain delicious to the last.

The botanical and mineral kingdoms possess untold wealth, not only valuable to the chemist and pharmacist, but also to the housekeeper, who, for a trifling sum paid to an Indian, may supply herself liberally with domestic nostrums.

Tequisquiti, a mineral combining the properties of both soda and ammonia, is a standard remedy for indigestion, gastritis, or other stomach troubles. It is also valuable in the bath.

Tisa, another mineral, resembles prepared chalk, and is not only used as a remedy, but is also the refuge of the housekeeper for brightening her silver, glass, and paint. Mountains of these and kindred minerals are to be found almost anywhere, an ever-ready boon to the housekeeper. These are all supplied and dispensed, for the most insignificant consideration, by the serviceable and ubiquitous Indians.

The maguey that furnishes, in one way or another, food, shelter and rainment for the toiling millions, is also lavish in the bestowal of various medicinal gifts.

Pulque—the national beverage, a prolific and profitable product of the maguey—affords many remedies. For coughs, they drink warm pulque; for indigestion, pulque with a little starch or tequisquiti; and it has been recently discovered that for Bright's disease and diabetes it is a sovereign remedy, while it is a specific for lung trouble, by placing under the bed at night a large vessel filled with pulque from which the patient inhales its healing fumes.

In prrof of its wonderful virtues, a Mexican lady told me that the venders of pulque are always blessed with health, flesh, and strength.

For earache, Mexican mothers resort to the leaf of a plant called Santa María, which is reputed to have a magical effect on the sufferer.

For headache, a rose leaf pasted on the temples, with perhaps the addition of some kind of salve, is said to be a sovereign remedy, and is used by all classes.

For catarrh and colds, rub the breast, forehead, and soles of the feet with hot tallow, in which a little snuff has been stirred. Be careful not to wash the face the next day.

For chills and fever, take a dose of oil, followed by a tea made from *Hojosen* and the camphor tree, to produce perspiration. Then rub the body with a salve made from the *Balsamo tranquillo* or lobelia, and the leaf of the cactus, bitter like quinine. Eucalyptus, which grows luxuriantly in many places, is also used.

For whooping cough, the patient is kept closely in a room without a breath of fresh air for forty days; emetics are frequently given, and pitch is burned at night.

For measles and scarlet fever, tea is made from violets and the *Noche buena* flower; the patient is also quarantined for forty days.

XIII

Summing Up

Previous to the advent of railways, and especially the completion of the Mexican Central, Mexico was a sealed book to the majority of Americans. To take up an abode there at that time, one was as securely bottled, corked and labeled for utter isolation from kindred and friends, as though banished to Kamchatka or the South Sea Islands.

Without railways, telegraphs, and their attendant blessings, Mexico was left to her own internal strife and commotion; the incentives to progress were wanting; while Texas, only across the river, possessing these advantages, has, in an incredibly short period, grown to be one of the foremost states in the Union, basking serenely in the sunlight of an unprecedented prosperity.

Considered geographically and topographically in the great federation of nations, the United States and Mexico should be on better terms, commercially and socially, than any other people. The one is situated mostly within the tropics—in the torrid zone; the other in the temperate; and together they produce all those commodities which are necessary to the comfort and convenience of their respective inhabitants. Their shores are girdled by the same vast water belt, and by nature they were intended to be the full complement of each other. Mexico can produce enough coffee of every grade to supply the world, to say nothing of her sugar, India rubber, indigo, dyewoods, vanilla, as well as numerous other articles of prime export. She has also a large and varied assortment of delicious fruits and an unlimited supply of the precious metals which regulate the commerce of nations.

But Mexico is not a manufacturing country, and perhaps, will never be, while the United States has great need for a wider market for her manufactured goods, which Mexico can purchase of no other country to the same advantage. But as yet our trade is not one-tenth part of what it should be. Lamentable the fact, we have been the very last foreign power to place ourselves on a proper footing with our near neighbors. A deep and subtle influence lies at the foundation. In the fullness of our well-earned greatness and self-esteem, we constitute ourselves teachers and judges of customs, business relations, and social intercourse, under conditions far different from our own. We have made a high standard for ourselves, and if other people do not approximate it, they must be at fault.

But this failure to understand each other is due to several causes. In the first place, we have made no effort to understand them, and, again, unworthy representatives of our country do not hesitate to denounce, publicly upon the street, both the government and the people, and declare in boastful fashion the ability, if not the immediate intention, of the American eagle to swoop down upon them and "wipe 'em out in sixty days." They talk unreservedly and offensively about the prospects of a speedy annexation; of a protectorate, and the gigantic scheme of absorption, all of which cannot fail to engender much ill-feeling and animosity. It recalls afresh to the sensitive Mexican mind the "North American invasion"—the loss of valuable territory, and the general distress that pervaded the country.

Then again we have been full of unjust doubts as to the integrity of our neighbors. The consequence has been that the keen discrimination of our friends across the water has long since gathered to themselves the friendly relations as well as the profitable emoluments of trade which legitimately belong to us.

To compete successfully with the diplomatic methods of the English, French, and Germans requires tact and skillful manipulation. Of the many Americans who gaze from afar with longing eyes on the prospect for business investments, it is safe to say that not one in five thousand has the slightest idea of the nature of the difficulties to be met and overcome in order to realize these prospects. In endeavoring to establish business relations, it must be borne in mind that it is not with one race he has to do, but with various shades, mixtures, and types; with sentiments and prejudices, diverse and in common, all to be met, pandered to, and softened into harmony.

The average American has the impression that, should he locate in Mexico, and exercise his accustomed force and energy, much sooner will he reach the acme of his hopes and the realization of his golden dreams. Delusive thought! It does not require much time to undeceive him. He finds that no push whatever is expected or required; in fact, the less he has the better, for he must learn to bend to the slow—very slow—methods of the Mexican; to accept the *dolce far niente* of the country. Business customs and habits confront him which yield but slowly to modern ideas, while the necessary schooling in the mañana system, and the still more difficult lesson that, Toots-like, time is of "no consequence," must chafe his restless spirit, and dampen his impassioned ardor.

It requires a discriminating eye and a suave, agreeable manner to obtain and hold the trade. So many things must be consulted and considered that in other countries have no relation whatever to business; but without which everything is tame and void of interest to the Mexican. It is necessary to study carefully the language, customs, habits, and sentiments of the people; to familiarize one's self with the business methods, customhouse laws, and the tariff. Usually in the haste to acquire a foothold, the smaller and more important details are lost sight of, but it is only by observing them that success will follow.

The prejudice of Mexicans against Americans is not so strong as the enemies of American interest would have residents of the United States believe. The various concessions, granted Americans both in the past and present, by the state and federal governments of Mexico, are proofs of this fact. But a wider and more extended communica-

tion between the two countries—more travel through
Mexico by Americans and vice versa—would conduce to
a better understanding. Let our people make an effort to
know the "Mexicans in their Homes," and an open hospitality be tendered to them when they visit our country.
No diplomacy could be so effective.

As an American woman I am justly proud of our institutions, of our prowess, strength, and unity of purpose.
We have indeed left behind us in our onward march of
progress every other nation, and are pre-eminently the
"heirs of all the ages." No country nor clime can compare
with ours, and our representative men and women take
rank and precedence wherever they come in contact with
those of other countries. Perhaps it is the consciousness of
our greatness that makes us less adaptable than others.

But our modern progressive institutions cannot thrust
themselves unceremoniously and without caution upon a
country whose civilization dates back more than two
hundred years before our own. We must learn to "apply
our hearts unto wisdom and pass into strange countries,
for good things were created for the good from the beginning."

We must educate ourselves up to the point of believ-
ing that we can attribute the frailties and defects of any
people as much to human nature as to national forces.

Whatever our differences of race, training, and feeling, we can all do something for the happiness and well-
being of those around us, and if other opportunities fail,
there is always room for the bestowal of a helpful and
sympathetic word.

But in no country do fame and friends come to us unless we have earned as well as desired them. Usually, like
success, they come as the hard-bought recompense of persevering effort, and of patient waiting, and at last must
rest with ourselves. We must carry into our common lives
that grand and ennobling sentiment that unless we trust
we will not be trusted.

In brief, if you go to Mexico, do not hope to effect

radical changes, or constitute yourself judge and reformer, but rather be prepared, instead of teaching, to be taught. Go determined to see things in a just light, to make liberal allowances for whatever does not coincide with your own habits and training, and accommodate yourself with becoming grace to what you will there meet.

The much-desired first step toward the establishment of a mutual understanding and an international interest was taken at the New Orleans Exposition of 1884–85, which marked a new era in the history of Mexico, and throughout succeeding time will be turned to, as a beneficent agency, having brought before the public mind in the United States the various resources, the taste, skill, and ingenuity, as well as the musical talent and proficiency of the Mexican people.

Following closely upon this was the Mexican Editorial Excursion to the United States, when the men who wield the instrument "mightier than the sword," were feasted and toasted everywhere. Being thus enabled to see the representative American on his own soil, either with the entourage of high position in political and social life, or at home with his household gods about him, they each and all returned with a better feeling toward our people.

One of these editors, Señor Alberto Bianchi, has published a book with illustrations, descriptive of the journeyings and impressions of the excursionists. Since their return they have interested themselves largely, in their different sections, in the cause of public education, and some have established normal schools.

But the future greatness of Mexico depends more upon the development of her internal resources than upon the introduction of foreign manufactures; more, too, upon her agricultural and domestic industries than on mines, mining, or the now widely scattered factories and mills. An untold wealth lies dormant in her bosom, an uncomputed richness in her veins. The seemingly insignificant agencies which by cultivation have given impetus and strength to our own internal greatness, are today in their infancy in our sister republic.

With a population of ten millions, Mexico cannot, strictly speaking, be called a consuming country, for the reason that the majority of her people are the humble poor who live solely on home product; who neither know nor ask anything beyond manta, tortilla, chile, and cigarette. It is quite manifest, however, that trade with the United States is yearly increasing. There is now a market for hardware of all kinds; agricultural implements, axes, wagons, carriages, harnesses, pianos and organs; also for prints, fine cottons, mill and mining tools and machinery, hosiery, flannels, woolens for ladies' and gentlemen's wear; glassware, lamps and gas fixtures, furniture, leather, hats, trunks and valises, firearms, scientific and surgical instruments, etc.

England and Germany have heretofore controlled the trade in hardware and agricultural implements, while France has maintained the supremacy in fine fabrics. But the superiority of American machinery and manufactured goods has been recognized, and it is now evident that in these lines we are driving other competitors to the wall.

The fact is generally conceded that temporary traveling agents, unless already acquainted with the language, tastes, and habits of the people, can effect no good. A permanent residence is necessary, whereby they are enabled to study the all-important details. Great care should be exercised, in the selection of these agents or commission merchants, that they be of a genial, conciliatory disposition, steady habits, and gentlemanly address, never in a hurry, and give attention to dress and personal appearance.

The enterprising North American commercial traveler, always in a hurry, rushes in upon a quiet Mexican business man, opens his grip, exhibits his samples, and fails to effect a sale. The reason is obvious: he has disgusted the merchant by his too eager and energetic manner. How different with Europeans! They have caught the spirit and habit of the Mexican to a nicety. Not alone in the outside world of business, but in the home life also, are they more in harmony with him. They have learned what we have yet to learn, to make haste slowly. The German or French agent will negotiate through diplomacy, and seek by social courtesy first to enter the good graces of the Mexican merchant. When they come in contact, both are probably well aware what the ultimate aim and object is, but of trade or business not a word is spoken. The agent inquires after the health of the merchant and his family. They smoke, chat of travels, and other kindred topics. The pride of the Mexican is naturally gratified when he finds *one man at least* who knows how to take things slowly and pleasantly and without *brusquerie*. Perhaps half a dozen such interviews occur before a word is spoken about business, but the agent, beyond all doubt, has secured his victim.

The apostolic injunction to "let patience have her perfect work" must here be heeded in the business world no less than in the higher discipline of life.

Good faith in all transactions is a prime necessity; therefore it is essential that goods supplied should be according to samples. Two intelligent Mexican merchants with whom I became acquainted, informed me that their own experience had been unsatisfactory in buying from traveling agents. Goods furnished not only did not correspond with samples in color or texture, but even the prices were different. They also said that in such matters other foreign sellers were careful to send exactly what was ordered, even if it required much time and labor. European importers cater to the popular taste, even to the packing and shipping of goods, making a reduction in bulk and weight by shipping in bales instead of boxes, giving long credit on all bills, and by every available means endeavor to save trouble to their customers. Calculations are also made that the native railroads, in the shape of burros or carts, may readily transport the goods to interior cities.

Americans generally overlook these details, and ship their goods in heavy wooden boxes, in every way objectionable.

Besides, the fastidious taste of the Mexican as to color and texture is lost sight of; they forget his whole nature is antagonistic to dull colors, coarse wool, and unseemly assortment. The French have caught the popular fancy in taste and delicacy. Light and airy fabrics with cunning devices, adding unique effects to the artistic arrangement, catch at once the Mexican eye.

Foreigners from the old country are content to make a very little headway at a time, and to utilize every facility they can command to the very best advantage. If they prosper in business, the young brothers and cousins at home are not forgotten, and as soon as circumstances will permit, they are brought out to act as clerks, and fill other places of confidence, proving invaluable aids to the heads of the establishment and strengthening their position.

An evidence of how other foreigners study to please the Mexicans, even to the details of dress, I observed in traveling with a young Englishman who had lived in the United States for six years. He was then about to join his brother, who had resided for some years in Mexico. Naturally this subject was under discussion between us. He frankly told me that his brother had written to him on no account to wear anything that looked American, and especially to refrain from wearing an American slouch hat, as the Mexicans detested that article heartily. Take warning, my countrymen! If you cannot wear a beaver, then a derby—a stiff, half high, or the genuine wide-brimmed, silver-decked sombrero.

He certainly had obeyed the injunction, for he was a live representative of John Bull, from the apex of his prim-sitting hat, to the tip end of his square English foot. But I was glad to see him thus prepare himself for his future life associations, and candidly told him I should expect to hear of a marvelous success from his sojourn in Mexico.

After my arrival in the capital I found his brother's firm, that of B., S., R., C. & Co., had made for themselves an enviable name as architects, mining engineers, and contractors. I had the satisfaction of seeing with my own eyes that the wise head which had planned his brother's advent into the country had practiced literally what he preached. As an equestrian, the native gorgeousness quite melted into insignificance by comparison; while in whatever society, foreign or native, he was a shining light and noted for the suavity of his manners.

The last I heard of the newly inducted young traveler bent on conquest, he was mounted on a litter going to Oaxaca, a seven days' journey, as a mining engineer.

Mexicans are not generally wholesale merchants. Those who have sufficient means to become such, prefer investing in haciendas, which are a sure source of profit and much less trouble. The smaller retail trade, however, is chiefly controlled by them, and in this field they are both able and successful. They are declared, on competent authority, to be strict, if somewhat slow, in meeting their obligations. But slowness, where everything is slow, need not necessarily be considered detrimental; and it may generally be assumed that if they do not pay, it is because they have not the money—a condition not surprising in the financial depression of the last few years.

Native retailers manage their business most skillfully. With a full estimate of the value of everything they desire to exchange, barter, or sell, they will ask the outside price, at the same time reading critically the character of their customer; if the price demanded will not secure him, most graciously and gracefully they will accept a lower.

To their powers of manipulation may be accredited the fact that in no part of the country have the Jews, to any extent, been able to obtain a foothold in mercantile life. The Mexican is even more suave, more entertaining, and more determined in his mode of selling than the most smooth-tongued representative of the Israelitish race. He can sustain himself comfortably on a smaller profit, and is content to do so, as long as he is assured of holding his customer. The native, however, has not a monopoly of the retail trade. Frequently he has associated with him either a Spaniard, Frenchman, or Italian, and again these are established with success, independently.

The capital is naturally the great emporium, the business of the country being concentrated there. The cities and towns along the Rio Grande may possibly conduct some traffic with the United States, and certainly an immense amount of smuggling is done; but the main supplies come from the capital.

Mexico affords a striking illustration of the extremes of wealth and poverty. A late estimate by one who is well informed gives her only about five hundred thousand people who are wealthy; while the remainder is divided between those with moderately comfortable incomes and the absolutely poor. But among the former there is a large professional and shopkeeping class, who always appear well dressed, and with more or less indications of competency, but whose incomes are meager and uncertain.

Those who have accumulated large fortunes are, after all, at a loss how to find suitable investments. A distinguished Mexican statesman has estimated that an uninvested capital of $50,000,000 exists in the City of Mexico today, a sum large enough to build and equip a railway to some extreme point of the republic.

This is the case in every large city. Immense sums of money are in the hands of the rich in absolute bulk, without any outlet or means of investment.

Stock companies and co-operative plans do not strike, as tangible, the popular fancy. The best thing generally is for this class to build houses and rent them, or lend their money at very high rates.

Banking privileges are not usually resorted to by either the tradespeople or the merchant princes. The "Bank of London, Mexico and South America" has been established for twenty-one years, yet even now the majority of people do not avail themselves of it. Merchants use it for exchange, and also as a means of safety for large sums in silver dollars, this last sometimes for a very short time, perhaps for one day and night, after which their mozos may be seen carrying it back in meal bags. Perhaps a prejudice may attach to mere bits of paper as the representatives of big silver dollars, but checks are not used after our method, nor is banking resorted to except as a means of commercial convenience. For the mechanic or tradesman no facilities whatever exist in the way of savings banks for the deposit of their small earnings. Consequently more or less extravagance is indulged in, or the money is hidden away without profit to themselves or to the country.

Notwithstanding the rainy season, success in agriculture in Mexico depends almost solely on the facilities for irrigation. Every drop of water is skillfully utilized. Often, indeed, the entire body of water is turned from its legitimate course, and employed in irrigating a large and otherwise profitless region. If a river runs near to or through several haciendas, the proprietors unite in constructing a dam across it, with large ditches to convey the water through the fields. They employ a man to take charge of its distribution, and during the farming season he must be on hand both day and night, to turn the water on and off, as may be necessary.

Lands rent for one-third and one-half of the crop. The proprietor furnishes no teams, and the yield of corn is from thirty-five to forty bushels per acre.

A hacienda, it must be understood, is a large plantation, and not a ranch for cattle, although one proprietor may own both. In this case, the farming is kept separate from the cattle raising. A church and store are inseparable adjuncts to the well-kept hacienda. The peons buy the necessaries of life from the store, which of course keeps them always in debt, thus securing their services. Unless the proprietor of some other hacienda pays the debt, they of course cannot leave.

There are two classes of peons, those who are in debt and those who are not. The former are by far the more numerous, and are called calpaneros or gañanes. The names and salaries of the principal employees are as follows:

Administrador, who is paid from $70 to $100 per month.

Mayordomo,	,,	,,	,,	30	,,	60	,,	,,
Ayudante,	,,	,,	,,	15	,,	30	,,	,,
Sobre saliente,	,,	,,	,,	8	,,	25	,,	,,
Capitán,	,,	,,	,,	8	,,	20	,,	,,

Trojero, who has charge of the keys and keeps the accounts of the hacienda; paid from $15 to $30 per month; and a doctor, who is also paid by the month.

The priest is paid for his services as they are rendered. The founder, wheelwright, and carpenters are paid by the job.

The mayordomo and the capitán are allowed horses and certain perquisites from the hacienda.

These capitanes are rare characters in and of themselves. Though in letters he may be the most ignorant, yet in that little narrow skull he can carry more accounts than the most expert bookkeeper. He knows the antecedents of everybody and everything on that place. He is a peon just as they are, but in many ways he shows his power over them.

Every night the raya (an account of the days' doings) is gone through by the mayordomo and capitán, who come to the office of the hacienda to give an account to the administrador of what has been done during the day. The names of the peons are read, and the captain answers: "Cetonale" ("He has worked today"), or "Homo cleno" ("He has not"), as the case may be. The mayordomo has a box full of beans kept for the purpose. Each time the captain answers "Cetonale" or "Homo cleno," a bean is pushed aside. When the calling and answering are finished, the beans in the two piles thus formed are counted, and the result entered in the daybook. The captain retires and the mayordomo takes orders for the next day.

Everything is kept as systematically as in a banking business. The books of the hacienda are under government seal, and any one wishing to purchase the property may satisfy himself by looking at them.

Haciendas have their marketable small products, such as pulque, wood, milk, lumber, charcoal, beans, sheep, goats, and many others known as esquilmos. Hogs are also fattened, but they are little used save to make soap, which is excellent in any part of the country.

The impression prevails that the peon is in such a state of servitude that he can be easily compelled to adopt any methods his employer may see fit to impose upon him; but the fallacy of this is too well known by all who have tried the experiment of farming.

The peon, like the rest of his race, has an instinctive dislike to any innovations, and he clings to his rude methods of agriculture, driving the new-fangled notions to the wall, or stacking them in the fields, while he unceremoniously returns to the ancient forked stick. He hugs the rawhide harness thongs and straps, and the primitive fixtures of his forefathers, and will not yield them up without a determined resistance.

In the hope of compromising matters with these ultra-conservatives, a wide-awake Chicago firm has recently invented and patented a steel plow that is the exact reproduction of the forked stick and makes a furrow much deeper, whereby finer results are obtained.

I visited several haciendas, and on each more or less of our agricultural implements were used. Every agent with whom I conversed spoke hopefully that finally the products of our manufactories would prevail over any and every competition. But with the inherent prejudice of the peon, it is not a source of wonder that even a progressive hacendado hesitates to introduce any new form. On some plantations both the ancient and modern work side by side.

Some Mexican writers have remonstrated against the introduction of labor-saving machinery, fearing it would militate against the interests of that large proportion of the population—the laboring class. But as the undeveloped resources are so immense, it will probably be long before interference in that direction will be felt, for the cry still goes up for more laborers for both mines and haciendas.

One of the principal causes of this want may be attributed to the constant recurrence of feast days, the observance of which occupies at least one-third of the time. It is anything but a pious spirit that induces the laborer to take advantage of these occasions, but rather his innate love of ease and dissipation. These days are to him more holidays than holy days. But it is astonishing how little these people can exist upon. In spite of their small wages being in this way so materially decreased, they manage to live, and not uncomfortably either, on a mere pittance; whole families, sometimes, spending but twelve or even six cents a day.

The difficulty of transportation remains a serious drawback to every enterprise to be carried on in the republic. This is so obvious as to render credible the statement that an over-crop is as detrimental as an insufficient one. When there is a large surplus, much waste must ensue for lack of the means of transportation. If the crop is a short one, the natives must go on foot and carry "corn from Egypt." In any case it is the masses of pobres who suffer, and the need for not only more railways, but also for wagons and roads, is a real one. If only the hoarded wealth of the country were thus applied, Mexico would not long be in the rear of other countries.

Under the present land tenure, the owners almost escape taxation, while the peon, or the man who takes the products to market, must pay enormous taxes, at the gates of the cities, where the tax gatherers are located. A barrel of flour may be taxed a dozen or twenty times before it reaches the market. Every state, city, and municipality through which it passes has its own laws of taxation. Every page of a merchant's ledger or cashbook must have a stamp. Every receipt must have one at the rate of one cent for every $20. Tickets of all sorts—even to the theater—contracts, bills, and a number of other things must have stamps. But the man who owns houses pays no taxes except when they are rented. This, it may be added, is the reason of the high rents.

The lack of water naturally limits and impedes manufacturing, and the scarcity of fuel places a dead incubus upon it. The government has nurtured and given all the aid and encouragement in its power to such enterprises, but it is difficult if not impossible to rise superior to such great natural obstacles. Wood commands from $15 to $18 per cord, which is, of itself, enough to interdict the use of steam. But there is a solution in the future to this question of fuel. There is no wider field for enterprising capitalists than the opening up of the vast coal deposits that exist in the various states. In Durango there are very fine deposits of hard coal. In other places many varieties are to be found; and the states of Oaxaca and Puebla abound in coal of a fine quality. Surely this will prove a great blessing to the country, and a powerful agency of progress. Petroleum also exists in great abundance, but is still undeveloped. Though Mexico is a land of light, still more light is needed.

The culture and manufacture of silk promise success in the future. Mulberry trees flourish in many localities, and the climate is so fine that silkworms require no protection.

There are sections well adapted to the growth of cotton, but it is cultivated only to a limited extent; the principal part of that used being supplied from the United States.

Mining investments for Americans have generally proved a sad experience. But still they venture, working and waiting, hoping against hope. They give up comfortable homes to labor and toil as never before, deprived of every comfort, and at last are forced to leave the scenes of their unfruitful labors ruined in fortune and hopes, and with energies broken and crushed. Some of the most utterly miserable looking men to be seen are these unfortunate American miners. A few have been successful, but they make the exceptions to the rule. Mining laws, however, are said to be excellent, and are quite as favorable to the foreign capitalist as to the native.

In the production of fruits alone Mexico has advantages over other countries. In many places by stretching out the hands one may gather both temperate and tropical varieties. While many have been imported, a large proportion are indigenous and daily tickled the palate of Montezuma. But peaches, apples, and other temperate fruits are in a neglected condition, and consequently lack flavor. For the rest, nature is sufficient for her own free gifts.

The infinite variety and constant succession of fruits, all the year round, offer an attraction to growers as well as to those engaged in canning and preserving. Besides those familiar to home growth, as peaches, pears, lemons, and oranges, or known to us through commerce, as the banana and pineapple, new, strange and delicious fruits meet the eye and invite the taste. At first Americans generally have a distaste to the native fruits of Mexico, but after a time relish them very much.

The maguey (*agave americana*), known to us as the century plant, furnishes everything from a needle and thread to a housetop, as well as a variety of food and drink. Of the latter, several varieties are made, chief among which is pulque, the national beverage. The manufacture of this liquor is as peculiar as it is interesting. Just before flowering time (which occurs much oftener than once in a hundred years) the heart of the plant is extracted and a sap rises to fill the cavity. The tlachiquero, whose business it is to collect this sap two or three times a day, places one end of a gourd syphon in the cavity and the other end to his lips, and, by suction, draws the juice up into the body of the gourd. It is then emptied into a sheep skin which he carries upon his back, and from this put into a vat, also of sheep skin, which, like the other, has the wool turned inward. The odor imparted to the liquid by these skins, as may be imagined, is anything but agreeable. On bringing it to the lips for a draught, the first impulse is to seize the nose, without which precautionary measure it is doubtful if the induction into this beverage would ever be made. It is much pleasanter to the palate, however, than to the olfactories, and its effects upon the system are generally beneficial. It possesses medicinal properties and is considered a specific for Bright's disease. The cultivation of the maguey is quite a source of income, as a single plant yields about one gallon of sap a day, and rarely more than one hundred and twenty-five quarts in all, after which it dies.

The other liquors besides pulque which this plant produces are tequila and mescal. The former, named after the district in which it is principally manufactured, possesses an agreeable flavor, somewhat resembling Scotch whisky. Mescal is made from a liquor obtained by pressing the leaves of the maguey in a mill. Both mescal and tequila are transparent, while pulque has very much the appearance of the milk of the cocoanut.

Tanneries are to be found at many places, but the leather must be of very inferior quality, if one may judge by the rapidity with which shoes break and wear out. There is no greater inconvenience to Americans than the style and quality of shoes. Generally it is not possible for them to wear those made on Mexican lasts. I have seen in the windows of shoe stores, "American shoes made here," but the samples shown were far inferior to our home productions, and did not even resemble them. But for the artistic repairing of old boots and shoes the Mexican cobbler can certainly claim precedence. He sits on his stool on the sidewalk, himself unshod, verifying the ancient proverb, perhaps waiting for the mañana on which to begin his avocation.

More paper factories are needed, and no country offers greater inducements, as the maguey is ever at hand to furnish pulp for the enterprise. France and Belgium have heretofore supplied the market, with a moderate amount from Germany and England. If Americans do not go there to manufacture paper, they should certainly be able to compete with all others in supplying the market with a superior article.

Considerable attention is now paid to the importation and breeding of fine stock of all kinds, and Mexico offers unsurpassed facilities for this purpose, by reason of the equable climate and extensive pasturage. For, while cattle men annually lose thousands in their chosen sites in the United States, in Mexico it is perennial springtime for man and beast.

The meats are excellent in flavor and quality, the mutton being especially delicious. But a difficulty lies, generally, in the butchers, who cut and slash it in so many directions that it is difficult to tell what part of the animal you are eating.

Butter everywhere is a very scarce and inferior commodity. Housewives know nothing of making and caring for this article, which to Americans is a prime necessity. The most primitive means are employed in its manufacture. In some places the milk is put into a sheep or goat skin, then fastened on a mule or burro, usually the latter, and trotted at a rapid rate. Inferior in quality as it is, I have never seen a pound sell for less than from four to six reals. The natives make a cheese from goat's milk that is quite good when one becomes accustomed to it; but no attention is given to cheese making, as we know it, although the facilities are at hand, in the labor, the cattle and feeding, as well as in the tastes of the people, who use it largely in their cuisine. At the capital a pound of American cheese costs 62 ½ cents (five reals). The finest butter and cheese in the world could be produced on the beautiful and abundant alfalfa. Our people should look into these openings for enterprise, particularly as the Mexicans themselves would be constant patrons.

The refining of salt is another much needed industry, for which ample material exists in immense deposits that are in the same condition today as when the conquerors came. A five-cent sack of American table salt costs three reals, while what is generally used is in the crudest state possible, requiring to be washed, dried in the sun and then ground on the metate before it is ready for use.

Bacon and ham are both imported, the United States now furnishing the greater part. The price is never less than five to six reals a pound, even at the capital.

Finer hogs can be produced in no country, and with mountains forever snow-covered, and railways offering inducements to shippers, pork packeries and meat-canning establishments could easily be established and made a paying investment. No improvement can be made on the lard, which is beautifully white and sweet; but the supply in no wise reaches the demand, as shown by the price, which I have never known to be less than from twenty-five to thirty-seven cents, or three reals a pound.

Wheat is one of the best products of the soil, and flouring mills convert it into excellent flour, but either the mills are not numerous enough or the supply of wheat is deficient, as prices are exorbitant—the cheapest I have seen costing three dollars and a half for fifty pounds.

Fond as the Mexicans are of dainties and delicacies, the cracker and wafer, so indispensable in our dietary, are not made in the country, with the exception of one of two factories at the capital from which they are supplied at three reals a pound. Factories of this kind would develop the general taste and doubtless also prove profitable.

By all means let some enterprising spirits establish goose ranches. Strangers are particularly impressed with the unyielding pillows and beds, encountered everywhere in hotels; and with few exceptions they are little different in private houses.

Both climate and soil are favorable to the production of broom corn, and, as the native manufacturers are less skilled in broom making than in almost anything else, I surely think this manufacture would be a desirable enterprise. American brooms, when obtainable, cost one dollar apiece.

I could go on enumerating, the smaller industries which would find a ready demand, and require but little capital. But it is unnecessary. It has only been my aim to show that everything stands waiting for the ready hand

and determined will of some who may desire to begin life in that old country on a moderate scale and grow to affluence.

There is no opening whatever for either American matches or matchmakers; for the matches of the Mexican matchmaker are matchless; a rule that holds good in more ways than one, and may even apply to scenes from the balcony.

I have found an elysium for the Smiths, Browns, and Joneses. By merely crossing the Rio Grande, they will find themselves answering to extremely high-flown names, without legal or legislative intervention, or arousing the suspicion that they left their country for their country's good. Plain William Brown becomes Guillermo Moreno, James Smith flows off euphoniously into Santiago Esmith, while John Jones murmurs in the mellifluous Castilian as Don Juan Jo-nis (Huan Honis).

The very serious question of American families taking up their residence in Mexico is one that demands especial care. We of the United States have such a profusion of comforts, even among the plainer classes, that it is not to be expected of an American woman to settle herself contentedly in her Mexican home with the scanty allowance of furniture and otherwise primitive household arrangements she there encounters. As before stated, hotel life is not proper or customary for families, and there are no boardinghouses; the whole matter must at once resolve itself into the setting up of one's own little household kingdom. Furniture is not only extremely scarce but high-priced, and furnish the house the best one can, with what is to be had, and with a limitless amount of pottery cooking utensils, still there will remain an aching void in the list of supplied necessities. If household goods are brought from home, taxes and customhouse duties will fully quadruple their original cost. No American woman thinks at first that she can exist without a cooking stove, but, to carry one along that has cost twenty dollars at home, it will, when turned over to her, have cost six times its original value. When in its place and man or burro have trotted their score or two of miles with a double handful of wood for cooking purposes, another difficulty is added when the cook tells her: "It will give me disease of the liver," or, "No es costumbre." It is then her disgust reaches a supreme height. If she fails to take pillows and bedding along, it is possible that she may "lie on the floor and cover with the door," or rest on such substitutes for beds as would break the bones of a Samson or Goliath.

This may seem paradoxical, having described the elegant furnishings of some Mexican mansions; but stores exclusively for furniture are not general, with some exceptions at the capital and in the larger interior cities.

The Mexicans have been always accustomed to order their household furnishings direct from Europe or the United States, and strangers generally on going must risk the chances of buying what they can second hand from some one moving away, or have a carpenter manufacture some, on his own plans and specifications. But do not calculate on the time for it to come into your possession. Meanwhile a cot and a few Mexican blankets are blessings in exchange for the soft side of an earthen floor.

You may be able to rent rooms in families, and in gems of precious pottery prepare your meals after your own fashion. Sometimes you will be able to procure comfortably furnished rooms, and have meals sent from a fonda, but you will very rarely find a Mexican family who will furnish them. You may have a room in their house, and be freely invited to a place at their board, but to receive money for anything but the rent would be an infringement upon their established usages and ideas of hospitality.

While the vegetables, meats, and fruits are not so high as in the United States, and are generally better, other necessaries make expenses mount up amazingly.

American men accommodate themselves quite readily in Mexico to the inconveniences of the home life— natural enough, when they have none of the worry—but, with a few exceptions, I have never seen an American woman in the country who was not continually pining to return home.

So far, no educational advantages exist for American children; and this of itself is a source of great perplexity. But the children themselves are extremely adaptable to everything in the country, learning the language with wonderful rapidity, and in their childish communications adopting the customs of Mexican children. Like these, they are universally petted and adored by all classes, from the servants to the highest society. I have seen one American child engage the attention and interest of every Mexican in a railway car.

An American gentleman and his wife who had resided a number of years in Mexico, and had had four children born to them in that country, were returning to Texas. These little ones had completely identified themselves with the country of their nativity and repudiated that of their fathers. Soon after crossing the Rio Grande, they stopped at a ranch house, and seeing some other American children barefooted, they ran excitedly to their mother, exclaiming with mingled scorn and pity, "¡Mira, mama! ¡las gringitas sin zapatitos!" ("Look, mamma! those little gringos without shoes!")

Anglo-Mexican children will never admit that they have American blood in them.

Generally there is but little social interchange between the women of the two countries; but when it takes place, warm friendships are apt to ensue. I wish my countrywomen residing there would make more effort in this direction, that the people of both countries might know and understand each other better; for men, left to themselves, with all their diplomacy, lack the finer tact and instinct of women in uniting and binding together widely separated elements.

Those who intend to become residents will read with interest the late laws relating to foreigners.

There is a law of naturalization lately published

that is important to Americans. Subjoined is a copy of the official notice:

Americans are hereby notified that, in conformity with Article I., Chapter V., of the Law on Foreigners, of June, 1886, foreigners who may have acquired real estate, or have had children born to them within the republic, will be considered by the Mexican Government as Mexican citizens, unless they officially declare their intention to retain their own nationality, and to that effect obtain from the Department for Foreign Affairs a certificate of nationality, on or before December 4, 1886.

Said certificates may be obtained for Americans through the Legation or the Consulate-General of the United States in this city.

Applications for the same must be accompanied by one dollar for the necessary revenue stamps, also by a personal description of the applicant.

LEGATION OF THE UNITED STATES, MEXICO, *August 20*, 1886.

Still another law requires that all foreigners should be matriculated at the Department for Foreign Affairs, that their nationality may be declared and recognized. Foreigners who wish to have a hearing before the courts of the country should not fail to comply with this law, as business interests are not secure without it.

Mexican physicians, as a rule, are highly educated and accomplished men; having not only excellent advantages in the Medical School at the capital, but a large proportion being graduates of celebrated European colleges.

Consumption is not by any means confined to the stranger. It undoubtedly originates among the natives, and usually with fatal results. Another disease in this fine climate, and as much to be dreaded, is catarrh; and a simple cold soon takes this form. No class is exempt from it, and perhaps from this the custom arose of wearing the blanket, shawl, or handkerchief over the nose and mouth. That their fine air, so celebrated and lauded by visitors, should be blamed for every malady that flesh is heir to, seems a contradiction. But in this as in everything else there is a special fitness, for strangers soon find themselves following the same custom. Ask at any time a man or woman of the poorer class why they draw the blanket over the mouth, and you will at once be answered with, "Por el aire" ("On account of the air").

Police regulations are admirable. The men are uniformed, and stationed in the middle of the streets where they cross at right angles; and regardless of wind or weather, each one remains at his post eight hours at a time, blowing his shrill whistle every quarter of an hour, in answer to the call of his co-guardian of the peace. The quiet and order that prevail in all towns and cities attest their efficiency.

The body known as the Rurales constitute in Mexico today the most competent preservers of the public peace existing within her borders. They were once lawless and abandoned men, who led lives of wild adventure, many of them being bandits, fearing nothing.

When General Porfirio Díaz became President, he felt the necessity of providing the rural districts with an efficient mounted police force. The utmost forethought could not have predicted such grand results. Being as they are familiar with every mountain pass and lonely defile, fearless riders, and possessed of extraordinary strength and undaunted courage, they have proved their prowess and valor from first to last. It gives one a feeling of security and satisfaction to see a company of these sturdy horsemen entering a city or town, after a toilsome journey in the wild mountain fastnesses. They wear a gay and picturesque uniform of buckskin, the pantaloons decorated on the outside seams with silver buttons, coat and vest of the same material, a gorgeous red sash, and a red cravat or silk handkerchief around the neck, and sombrero with silver cord and tassels. Behind the gayly-equipped saddle a red blanket is folded and snugly secured, adding an extra charm of color to the invincibles. They come and go as if in haste, the rattling of their accouterments always attracting the attention of strangers.

I am glad to testify to the fact from personal experience that ladies may with safety and propriety travel on any of the lines of railway throughout the country, getting off at any city or town and inspecting it to their satisfaction. Only this suggestion I would make: at the hotels where you stop procure a guide, who knows all the places of interest, and pursue your way quietly, not making undue remarks nor laughing in a loud tone at what may seem ludicrous.

Mexican affairs have been severely criticised by many writers; and objections of every character have been urged. It will be found, however, that there is neither fairness in statements made, nor is there much display of deep study into causes.

Among the chief complaints are: (1) The instability of the Mexican government and the proneness of the people to revolution. (2) Border troubles between Mexico and Texas. (3) Non-progressiveness of the Mexican people. (4) Want of wholesome internal laws conducive to the happiness of all classes.

History shows that the government of Mexico has been unstable; and that the beautiful country has, until within a decade or so, been the scene of oppression and strife, ever since the day when Hernando Cortez first unfurled the Spanish flag, and burned his ships on her shores. But when it is considered that the country was filled with independent peoples, each with its own traditions and customs, living in great cities, and with independent governments, and not nomadic in their character, but holding the soil of their ancestors, it is not surprising that the change from the ancient civilization of the aboriginal races to the modern has been slow, and that governmental disturbances have been frequent. No race that was fixed has been ever suddenly induced to adopt the laws, cus-

toms, and religion of its conquerors; and the tardy progress
of Mexico has been largely due to the restraining influences and prejudices of the original inhabitants, who
slowly discard the habits of their ancestors for the teachings of modern civilization. It takes centuries to work such
a transformation. Then, too, the immutable doctrines of
the Church, with its unvarying teachings and ceremonies,
serve in a measure to influence the people to receive with
caution and by slow degrees anything that would change
their social and political condition. These remarks, of
course, apply particularly to the original races that occupy
Mexico—remnants of the ancient tribes. Mexico has progressed as rapidly as could be expected, when the large
number of her aboriginal inhabitants is compared with
the feebler bands of European strangers that mastered the
government, and engaged in the attempt to indoctrinate
the people with a new religion, new government, and
strange customs.

The English in North America had none of these difficulties, because they met a nomadic people, and there was
no decided attempt to assimilate the Indians with the
Europeans; hence the seeming advance in the United
States and Canadas. There were no fetters on progress,
and the new world kept pace with the old in North America, while Mexico, Central and South America were held
retarded by the almost invincible customs of the aborigines.

With races mixed, revolutions are inevitable for a
time. The situation of the country, and the remarkable dis-
similarities of the people, render a strong central government impossible. Rival parties with interests dissimilar,
headed by bold leaders, are the natural concomitants of
an unstable government; and they multiply and more frequently collide where government is in a transition state,
perfecting itself by slow progression. The internal dissen-
sions that have heretofore distracted Mexico, and her
failure to adopt the standard in progression as fixed by her
neighboring republic, are some of the inevitables; and
there is no remedy save time and perseverance on the part

of reformers who are kindred spirits with the Mexican people. No foreign power need ever expect with ruthless hand to break down Mexican customs, laws, peculiarities and institutions. Such changes as are made must be made slowly. With the American idea of government in Mexico the worst evils would arise. The ultraism of American reforms would defeat all reform.

Mexico has taken no backward step. Since she made her natural secession from the Spanish crown she has progressed, and her institutions have advanced in proportion. From each revolution she has emerged, purified, strengthened, and with government better fitted for a people who in the end will enjoy full liberty under a pure republic. Her revolutions are the fires through which she must pass for refinement. They accomplish in a brief, though desperate, period what it might require ages to perfect by moral suasion.

While the "home rule" has been tumultuous in the extreme, yet it was the only government that was destined by the Allwise to survive; to stand at last, perfected in its own way, a fitting monument to the sore trials and afflictions of a brave people.

The antagonism between the United States and Mexico is unquestionably more largely due to border troubles than to any other cause. The dividing lines between countries have always been scenes of trouble, and, considering the causes that exist for unfriendly feeling, the difficulties that occur on the Rio Grande are not remarkable. On either side of this line the stormy elements break with tumult, the one against the other. The floating, unsettled population drift to both borders, and the magistracy on both sides is feeble.

Let there be a better magistracy on both borders. Let both governments bend their energies to hold in check the wild, disorderly elements that seek their boundaries, hoping to be under no rule. It is only by mutual effort in this direction that these troubles can be suppressed, for it is in these regions that the strong arm of the law should be most heavily laid. In general, too, the chief disturbers of the peace are unworthy of protection.

Let the consulates be filled by discreet and just men. When they can be selected from among those living on the border, speaking each other's language and having some acquaintance with each other's customs, a great advantage is gained.

Neither government should be regarded as intending wrong, violating the laws of nations or treaties, until the case be too plain for dispute. When either republic violates the rights of citizens of the other, let peaceful arbitration heal the breach.

A new era is dawning in Mexico. The advent of railways is opening a wide field; her people are rousing from their slumber. The government is extending her protection over the poor as well as the rich classes, and rapid progress is witnessed on every side. The wealthy and powerful of the Mexican Republic owe it to themselves to let the spirit of freedom and independence find full growth in the bosoms of all, from the toiling peon on the hacienda to the wild, dark Indian in the fastnesses of his mountains.

The administration of President Díaz marks a glorious epoch in Mexican history, and the law recently passed by Congress, making a second term constitutional, gives a still brighter outlook for the future. A few decades with governments like that inaugurated by him and the co-operation of the powerful men in Mexico, and the republic will take rank with the foremost nations.

Far from placing a bar to her progress, it behooves us to extend the right hand of fellowship, and hasten rather than impede a consummation so devoutly to be wished by all lovers of republican institutions. He who would attempt to retard this great work and seek to incite the lawless border element to a breaking up of the existing harmony would be possessed of the remorseless spirit of the piratical Norseman and the inhumanity of the buccaneers, combined with the desperate ambition of the barbarous Huns.

It will only be when Americans have lost their love of freedom and pride of country that they will look with indifference upon such disturbance of our sister republic. This will never be; our wise statesmanship will see to it that the Mexican people be left to perfect their institutions according to those immutable laws that govern from the dawn to the close of a nation's life.